Child
Welfare

Also of interest from the Urban Institute Press:

Reconnecting Disadvantaged Young Men, by Peter Edelman, Harry J. Holzer, and Paul Offner

Juvenile Drug Courts and Teen Substance Abuse, edited by Jeffrey A. Butts and John Roman

Kinship Care: Making the Most of a Valuable Resource, edited by Rob Geen

Timothy Ross

Child Welfare

THE CHALLENGES OF COLLABORATION

THE URBAN INSTITUTE PRESS
WASHINGTON, DC

THE URBAN INSTITUTE PRESS
2100 M Street, N.W.
Washington, D.C. 20037

Library of Congress Cataloging-in-Publication Data

Ross, Timothy, 1964-
    Child welfare : the challenges of collaboration / Timothy Ross.
        p. cm.
  Includes bibliographical references and index.
  ISBN 978-0-87766-756-8 (alk. paper)
1. Child welfare—United States. 2. Abused children—Services for—United States.
3. Foster home care—United States. 4. Social work with teenagers—United States.
I. Title.

  HV741.R67 2008
  362.70973—dc22

                                                              2008047054

Printed in the United States of America

13 12 11 10 09   1 2 3 4 5

THE URBAN INSTITUTE is a nonprofit, nonpartisan policy research and educational organization established in Washington, D.C., in 1968. Its staff investigates the social, economic, and governance problems confronting the nation and evaluates the public and private means to alleviate them. The Institute disseminates its research findings through publications, its web site, the media, seminars, and forums.

Through work that ranges from broad conceptual studies to administrative and technical assistance, Institute researchers contribute to the stock of knowledge available to guide decisionmaking in the public interest.

Conclusions or opinions expressed in Institute publications are those of the authors and do not necessarily reflect the views of officers or trustees of the Institute, advisory groups, or any organizations that provide financial support to the Institute.

Dedicated to Sonia Austrian, John Mollenkopf,
Clarence Stone, and Vernon and Eleanor Ross:
five amazing people whose wisdom, encouragement,
and warmth have shaped the lives of
so many people in my generation.

In memory of Lori Ross Urov, 1966–2003.

Contents

Acknowledgments

This volume came about through the help and assistance of an enormous number of people. Commissioners, middle managers, and frontline staff at a host of government agencies (listed in chapter 1) enabled the researchers to understand better the cross-cutting issues they confronted, the strengths and weaknesses of the data they analyzed, and the history of reform efforts. Many of the people who provided the most crucial information plug away at the day-to-day work of city government, in advocacy groups, or in nonprofit social service organizations. Their willingness to share their experience was crucial to this research.

The people caught up in the child welfare and other systems also played an essential role: children in the child welfare, delinquency, and status offender systems, their families, and their caregivers each provided perspectives and information that influenced the thinking and aims behind this book. The ultimate goal of this book is to improve their experiences with these systems in the hope that they and others in similar situations may find the support they need from government when they need it.

The New York City Administration for Children's Services, the city's child welfare agency, made this book possible. The agency provided access to staff, data, and the financial support for much of the research. John Mattingly and his predecessor commissioners, William Bell and Nicholas Scoppetta, each encouraged outside researchers to critically examine the agency.

As the platform for the research in this book, the staff, directors, and other friends of the Vera Institute played a pivotal role. Those that made special contributions in each chapter are acknowledged individually below. Several people at Vera, especially Michael Jacobson and Neil Weiner, encouraged me to assemble the policy reports that Vera produced into a book. For her encouragement and expert work on contracts and intellectual property, I owe a special thanks to Susan Rai. For teaching me how Vera and government work, I thank Molly Armstrong and Chris Stone. For carrying on the work of the Child Welfare, Health, and Justice Program as I assembled this book while on medical leave, I give my deep thanks to Anne Lifflander, Allon Yaroni, Carla Roa, Sydney McKinney, Tania Farmiga, Sally Trued, Rachel Wetts, and many others. At the Urban Institute Press, I would like to thank Blair Burns Potter, Kathleen Courrier, Scott Forrey, and Fiona Blackshaw.

As this book is a collection of research efforts, a range of people contributed in some way to each chapter. To conserve space, I have listed just the names of people acknowledged on each chapter and omitted their titles and affiliations.

Chapter 1: Joel Miller, Elena Lopez, Lisa McGill, Julie Peterson, Margaret Post, and Chris Sturgis.

Chapter 2: Rob Hope, Francesca Levy, Doreen Miranda, William Bell, Zeinab Chahine, Peter Alexander, Lisa Parrish, Benjamin Charvat, Eric Nicklas, Synia Wong, Tami Suh, Alana Gunn, Michael Farrell, Joanne Jaffe, John Eterno, Tania Hedland, Richard Brown, Charles Hynes, Robert Johnson, Robert Morgenthau, William Murphy, Chris Stone, Molly Armstrong, Heidi Segal, Addie Rasavong, Craig Schwab, Janet Mandelstam, Jill Pope, Robin Campbell, Leah Edmunds, Cybele Merrick, Ajay Khashu, and Dan Currie.

Chapters 3 and 4: Miriam Ehrensaft, Mark Wamsley, Star Kyriakakis, William Bell, Nicholas Scoppetta, Nancy Martin, Erik Nicklas, Benjamin Charvat, Barbara Rubenstein, Synia Wong, Tanya Krupat, Bruce Frederick, Steve Greenstein, Eric Sorenson, Paul Korotkin, Leonard Morgenbesser, Denise Johnston, Ann Jacobs, Martha Raimon, Mary Nerney, Lisa Parrish, and Jennifer Jones Austin.

Chapter 5: Ajay Khashu, Mark Wamsley, Benjamin Charvat, Eileen Sullivan, Russ Immarigeon, and Jill Pope.

Chapter 6: Marni Finkelstein, Mark Wamsley, Dan Currie, William Bell, Lisa Parrish, Jennifer Jones Austin, Pat Brennan, Harry Bryan, Frances Carrero, Benjamin Charvat, Morris Heney, Barbara Rubinstein,

Chris Stone, Molly Armstrong, Eileen Sullivan, Janet Mandelstam, Jill Pope, and Van Luu.

Chapter 7: Sara Mogulescu, Ajay Khashu, Heidi Seigal, Claire Shubik, Eric Weingartner, Tina Chiu, Joseph Lauria, Paul H. Grosvenor, Mary Ellen Fitzmaurice, Lisa Altman, Daniel Turbow, Paula Hepner, Michele DuBowy, Phil Coltoff, Mark Kleiman, Sharon Goldberg, Linda Gibbs, Nancy Hruska, Patricia Brennan, Benjamin Charvat, Mitsy Smith, Pamela Hardy, Joe Dillon, Raymond Napier, Bruce Fisher, Bill Hackethall, Denise Hinds, Harriet Mauer, Paulette LoMonaco, Jim Purcell, Ellen Schall, Francine Perretta, Mary Winter, Meridith Sopher, Kim Dorsey, Molly Armstrong, Dan Currie, Cybele Merrick, David Ries, Jennifer Trone, and Mark Wamsley.

Chapters 8 and 9: Nicholas Scoppetta, Linda Gibbs, Lisa Parrish, Jennifer Jones Austin, Pat Brennan, Harry Bryan, Frances Carrero, Benjamin Charvat, Morris Heney, Barbara Rubinstein, the staff of Project Confirm, Alison Rebeck, Mark Wamsley, Chris Stone, Eileen Sullivan, Molly Armstrong, Janice Mandelstam, and Jill Pope.

I would also like to thank Susan Marki, Gordon Ross, Tom Kamber, Peter Meiland, Michael Ranis, Margaret Nelson, Ellen Simpao, Susan Ranis, Brad Brown, Scott Purdy, Christina Kornilakis, Hank Armstrong, Sue Dupres, Symra Cohn, John Leonard, Maureen Joyce, Mary Catherine Hayes, and many others for their expertise, friendship, and support.

My wonderful family—Anna Kornilakis and children Leah and Martin Ross—gave up many nights and weekends of my company for this volume. Anna's constant encouragement, love, and advice during rough times gave me the strength to finish. Leah and Martin's enthusiasm and smiles remind me daily of how important it is that children and families receive the support they need. No amount of thanks could be enough.

1

Cross-Cutting Issues
in Child Welfare

Many child welfare issues cut across traditional human service agency boundaries. Child welfare agencies often have responsibility for a problem but do not have the authority or capacity to solve the problem without cooperation from other government departments. These types of concerns create frustration for frontline staff and managers not only in child welfare, but also in many other government agencies and nonprofit organizations. These concerns are costly, often absorbing staff time, duplicating services, and using resources inefficiently. Most important, cross-agency issues create injustices and engender distrust among the children, youth, families, and communities that the child welfare system aims to serve. Despite these consequences, other branches of government and the nonprofit sector are often unable, uninterested, or unwilling to work with child protective and foster care staff to solve cross-agency problems.

The book draws on research studies conducted at the Vera Institute of Justice, a 47-year-old nonprofit public policy organization in New York City, to analyze various cross-cutting issues. These studies have several purposes. They describe many topics, primarily those that cut across child welfare to include juvenile and criminal justice agencies. They show how social science research can inform managers and government officials in a child welfare world often driven by anecdotes and high-profile cases instead of empirical data. In many cases, the studies demonstrate how innovations can mitigate or solve cross-agency difficulties and improve the quality of services and justice government provides to those in need. These studies also provide the basis for a discussion of what is needed to solve cross-cutting issues in child welfare and other human services.

This book aims to inform officials, practitioners, funders, advocates, scholars, students, and the general public about cross-cutting problems in child welfare and possible solutions to these problems. This opening chapter lays the groundwork for what follows. It starts by explaining why cross-cutting issues exist and presents a typology of these problems that references many of the chapters to come.[1] The second part of the chapter explains why this type of research is rare, discusses the origins of the research studies that are the basis of the chapters, and summarizes the strengths and weaknesses of the approach used to conduct these studies.

Understanding the Problem: Why Cross-Cutting Problems Exist

Many people who have worked in or encountered child welfare refer to it as "the system" and families who are the subject of child protective investigations as "system involved." This language conjures up visions of an all-encompassing and elaborately engineered machine. A closer look at child welfare agencies and the environment in which they operate suggests fragile webs. These webs have numerous connections within and across each other, but they also have many weak and broken strands, and they need constant re-spinning to maintain their strength. Child welfare agencies, like other specialized human service bureaucracies, are often internally divided and embedded in fragmented, complex organizational structures with multiple stakeholders competing for resources and advantage. The specialization and fragmentation of service delivery creates and magnifies the issues that cut across child welfare and other agencies.

Organizational Factors

Child welfare's primary mission is sometimes narrowly construed as keeping children physically safe, but even this limited definition connects child welfare with many other divisions of government. Children and youth must be safe in different locations—safe at home, safe at school, and safe in their neighborhoods—and responsibility for these locations falls not only on parents, but on many government staff: teachers, school safety agents, police officers, juvenile probation officers, and child welfare workers. In every jurisdiction, government staff from different departments must work with parents and each other to ensure child safety. Expanding the mission to ensuring children's physical, educational, financial, and mental health involves that many more agencies.

Coordinating any two complex systems is a challenge. Government departments are specialized—they focus on one set of services—and they employ large numbers of people. Even in medium-sized counties, child welfare, education, and criminal justice agencies each have dozens of employees focused on their agency's particular mission. In major urban centers, human service agencies have hundreds or even thousands of employees. Because most agencies face an almost limitless demand for help, these departments develop procedures that organize their employees to focus on their core mission. Agency managers usually try to prevent staff from straying into the specialization areas of other agencies because doing so takes away resources from the core mission and risks offending the other agency.

Specialization, however, is hardly the sole origin of cross-agency problems. Competition and culture clashes prevent collaboration between any two agencies, and incorporating additional agencies adds exponentially to the obstacles such efforts encounter. The byproduct of a decentralized government, these challenges often lead to bewildering laws, regulations, policies, and court decisions that further complicate developing cross-cutting solutions.

The executives and managers of government agencies, including those involved in human services, often view other agencies as competitors for scarce resources. They may vie with each other for budget authority, for the attention of elected or appointed officials to their policy positions, or for the lead role in important new initiatives. At the same time, they may jockey to avoid budget cuts, the addition of onerous responsibilities, or "turf" encroachments by other agencies. By their nature, attempts to coordinate activities involve ceding some authority and control to another agency as well as complicating the lines of responsibility—activities that executives often try to avoid. The short tenures of many people who work in child welfare, from senior managers to frontline staff, undermine the development of personal relationships that can mitigate conflict between organizations.

Every bureaucracy, moreover, has its own culture that often differs from and may conflict with those of other departments. Child welfare agencies, for example, are dominated by trained social workers. Social work training emphasizes empathy and resolving conflict through negotiation. In contrast, police departments are paramilitary organizations authorized to resolve conflict with force if necessary. Social workers and police often use different language, have different values, and may come to contrary conclusions when presented with the same facts. Even when the leaders of police and child welfare organizations agree on a course of action, coordinating the staff of two organizations with such dissimilar orientations is a challenge.

Competition among local agencies and conflicting agency cultures are major reasons for cross-cutting issues. Every agency involved in these issues, however, is embedded in a bewildering set of demands created by federalism—the division of responsibilities among federal, state, and local governments which are themselves divided into executive, legislative, and judicial branches. A quick look at the stakeholders involved in child welfare serves as a good example, though a similar description can be created for law enforcement, juvenile justice, education, and most other government departments.

The Role of Federalism

Child welfare authorities have an awesome power—the right to separate children from their parents, in some cases permanently. High levels of government should and are involved in the regulation of this power. Sitting on top of the governmental pyramid is the federal Administration for Children and Families, which is part of the Department of Health and Human Services. Federal officials work to ensure compliance with federal child welfare laws and distribute a significant portion of child welfare funding. For example, the federal government pays for half of all child welfare placement costs, and children in foster care are automatically eligible for Medicaid health insurance.

In most of the country, state government plays a dominant role in child welfare policy. In 40 of 50 states, child welfare is state administered— meaning most child welfare workers are state employees who are hired by and report to state officials. These officials ultimately report to a commissioner appointed by the governor. The other 10 states are state supervised—meaning county or municipal child welfare staff are hired by and report to local agencies whose commissioners are appointed by local elected officials. Even in state-supervised states, however, state officials have the responsibility to hold localities accountable for following state laws and regulations.

Child welfare policy also involves the legislative and judicial branches of the various levels of government. Congress has long played a role in establishing the legal framework and funding of child welfare. Federal laws, including the Child Abuse Prevention and Treatment Act of 1974 (CAPTA) and the Adoption and Safe Families Act of 1997 (ASFA), establish the broad legal parameters of child welfare policy.[2] In the many policy areas without federal mandates, state legislatures influence child welfare practice by passing laws, providing funding, and conducting oversight hearings, as do city councils in many large urban jurisdictions. Family court judges must review and approve significant interventions—such as child removals or mandatory services. In many jurisdictions, advocates have used the courts to advance their causes by suing child welfare agencies over specific practices or failure to abide by laws and regulations. These suits may be filed in state or federal courts. Court decisions have established case law that influences child welfare policy.

The fragmentation of the child welfare field extends beyond government. More than many other child- and youth-serving agencies, child welfare relies heavily on the nonprofit sector. Nonprofit organizations, often including those with religious roots, provide the bulk of preventive services and foster care placements in many jurisdictions. Other nonprofits vigorously advocate for child welfare issues. Public employee unions are also important stakeholders in many areas. While unions, nonprofits, and advocacy groups cannot make policy in the same fashion as government, each can have substantial influence through contract negotiations and lobbying activities.

The diffusion of power in the child welfare field and other human service agencies further complicates coordination. First, keeping up with the different laws, regulations, and court decisions emanating from various levels of government means that child welfare officials rarely have time to deal with issues that may be perceived as outside their core mission. Second, any new initiative usually has winners and losers—and with power so diffuse, those with an interest in the status quo have many options available to them in trying to derail changes they see as detrimental or onerous.

While unrelated to federalism or organizational behavior, a final factor deserves mention. Child welfare agencies are often internally fragmented. Units responsible for child protection, for example, decide whether families are left alone, receive preventive services, or have one or more children placed in foster care. Decisions made by child protective workers ripple through other parts of the agency, affecting budgets, staffing, and workloads, and creating internal divisions among units. In addition, staff inside child welfare agencies often have deep and passionate differences toward the work. Some workers firmly believe that child welfare agencies should work primarily to preserve families through preventive services, while others believe that child welfare should focus primarily on removing children from dangerous situations. These ideological cleavages often exacerbate divisions along race, religion, and class lines among child welfare staff.

In sum, child welfare agencies are shaped by and interact with networks of stakeholders that include departments within each branch of local, state, and national government as well as unions, advocacy groups, and nonprofit organizations. They are rife with internal divisions. The same point applies to the other agencies that work with children and youth, including schools, police, and juvenile justice. Federalism's checks and balances have many advantages: democratic accountability, oversight, forums for debate, flexibility for adapting to local conditions, and other benefits associated with American government. But the fragmentation of service provision and the multiple nodes of influence also contribute to the development of cross-agency issues. As we will see, when such elaborate systems have clients, responsibilities, or problems that overlap, coordination is the exception, not the rule. The typology below provides a more concrete understanding of how these issues develop.

A Typology of Cross-Cutting Issues

The Tunnel Problem, or "Problem Solved!"

A child or youth's entry point into the series of systems that serve this population, not the youth's underlying problems, usually determines how government responds. Each of the many systems that serve youth has fixed services or solutions to offer. Because most agency staff think primarily of the solutions within their system, they usually send youth down one of these "service tunnels." The tunnel may be the most appropriate choice among the agency's options, but it may or may not be an effective course of action. Once a young person starts down a particular tunnel, it is often hard to reverse course and take a different path.

A clinically depressed youth who often skips school and occasionally self-medicates with marijuana, for example, will receive markedly different treatment depending on which tunnel she enters. If the teen receives a referral to the mental health system, she will likely receive some counseling. The school system, however, may demand that the parent file a status offense petition to address the truancy problem (chapter 7 discusses cross-cutting issues in the status offender system). This may result in services that focus on truancy or other educational issues, or merely a warning from a probation officer. Depending on the relationship between the youth and his or her parent(s), a status offense case might lead to a court appearance and placement in foster care. School officials might bypass the status offender system and file an educational neglect petition that triggers a child protective services investigation. If police or school safety officials catch the youth smoking marijuana, she will enter the juvenile justice system. Juvenile justice officials may end up putting the youth on probation, sending her to an alternative program, or ordering her to "placement"—usually a secure facility that is essentially a juvenile prison.

The tunnel problem can lead to perverse and unintended consequences. In one case, police arrested a mother and her early adolescent daughter working together to sell marijuana.[3] Though the daughter might be seen as a child welfare case, the arrest sent the daughter into the juvenile justice tunnel. Juvenile justice officials felt uncomfortable giving the daughter probation because of her unstable home life and recommended that she be sent to placement. The judge concurred and sentenced her to a secure placement for 12 months (the minimum time for placements according to New York State law). In contrast, the mother received a 30-day jail sentence.

In another example, a study of the implications of a new status offender law finds that several New York City schools routinely threaten to file educational neglect charges if a parent does not file a status offender petition (Souweine and Khashu 2001). Yet a study on the educational impact of child welfare placement shows that school attendance rates for status offenders who enter the child welfare system decline (Conger and Rebeck 2001). Another study finds that over half of all status offenders placed with child welfare leave after two months, and 90 percent of those who leave return to their families (Ross, Wamsley, and Khashu 2001). These quick turnarounds mean that youth do not have time to form bonds or mentoring relationships with child care workers. Indeed, child care workers have more of an incentive to invest their time and energy working with other youth, leaving status offenders without appropriate services targeted to their needs. This may be one reason status offenders leave care without permission at far higher rates than youth who enter foster care for other reasons (Finkelstein et al. 2004; Ross et al. 2001). Attempting to resolve a truancy problem may lead youth down a tunnel that exacerbates the issue and creates further obstacles to his or her healthy development.

Any discussion of the services that youth receive would be incomplete without highlighting issues of cultural competency and institutional racism. Youth of color, especially African Americans, are more likely to receive harsher treatment when involved in school discipline proceedings, child welfare cases, or the juvenile justice system.[4] Indeed, widespread disproportionate minority confinement (DMC) led to a federal mandate requiring states to assess the extent of DMC and take steps to address the problem. Tunneling, then, is not only a function of a youth's presenting problem, but is also influenced by conscious and unconscious biases on the part of individuals and institutions.

These examples demonstrate how tunneling can lead to government responses that are either arbitrary or inappropriate. And once youth enter a particular tunnel, the fractured systems that serve youth may cause additional problems for both children and agencies. The constricted flow of information among agencies, including child welfare, often prevents the identification and management of cross-cutting issues.

Information Flow, or "I Didn't Know about the Problem"

Many cross-cutting issues revolve around the difficulties of sharing information across agencies. Agency databases rarely "talk" to each other for bureaucratic, legal, budgetary, and technological reasons, and this lack of communication is reflected in the practices of caseworkers and other staff in different agencies. Many agency managers are eager to solve cross-cutting issues once they identify and understand them. But the fragmentation of policymaking and service delivery means that these issues rarely rise to a managerial level where they can be addressed.

Project Confirm, an effort to bridge the gap between the child welfare and juvenile justice systems discussed in chapters 8 and 9, arose out of a common feeling among New York City Family Court judges, juvenile justice officials, and child welfare staff that the lack of a release resource caused arrested foster kids to be unnecessarily detained in juvenile detention facilities. None of these actors knew the extent of the problem. Initial research showed that foster youth accounted for 2 percent of all youth in New York City but 15 percent of detained youth, even though foster youth were not arrested for more serious delinquency charges than their nonfoster peers (Conger and Ross 2001; Ross and Conger 2002). This information persuaded officials to take action that led to the creation of Project Confirm: a relatively simple intervention that eliminated "the foster care bias" in detention decisions for low-level first-time delinquents.

Information-sharing issues may also complicate efforts by law enforcement and child protective workers to coordinate responses to severe child maltreatment, a challenge discussed in chapter 2. Child protective workers, police, and district attorneys are all trained to share information only when necessary, as much of the work they do involves confidential data that are either protected by law or whose release might compromise investigations, prosecutions, or a third party's safety. In many instances, however, these agencies legitimately need information held by their counterparts, especially when investigating the same situation. For example, child protection investigations may benefit from checks on prior domestic violence convictions, while police investigations may benefit from learning of prior indicated child welfare cases. Without memoranda of understanding or other protocols for information sharing, the missions of law enforcement and child welfare agencies are compromised.

Information-sharing challenges make it difficult for child welfare and corrections agencies to do their jobs as well, as discussed in chapter 4. In many states, parents have the right to visit with their children in foster care even when they are incarcerated. Yet information sharing between child welfare and corrections rarely takes place—resulting in case workers not knowing that parents are incarcerated and often assuming that they are unresponsive to case planning efforts. Children in care may feel abandoned because they have not seen their parents, and parents cut off from their children often experience frustration and anxiety. Advocates, children, and inmates report that the lack of communication can lead to destabilizing behavior.[5]

Diffusion of Responsibility, or "It's Not My Problem"

Information sharing alone rarely ameliorates cross-agency problems. Even when agencies know that they have a common client, tension around appropriate roles and responsibilities—especially in times of high caseloads—often results in a lack of follow-through by frontline staff and their managers. When responsibility is diffuse, kids fall through the cracks.

In Project Confirm, many child welfare caseworkers presumed that once police arrested a foster youth, their responsibilities ended because "the kid belonged to juvenile justice." To solve this problem, Project Confirm routinely faxed a letter to caseworkers and their supervisors from the commissioner of child welfare reiterating caseworkers' responsibility to go to court on delinquency cases. Program planners made numerous presentations to agency staff and foster care providers to educate them on the overlap problem and their responsibility in resolving it.

Status offender systems also encounter diffusion of responsibility problems, examined in chapter 7. Status offenders are youth who have not committed delinquent acts, but their behavior concerns government because of their status as minors. Status offenses include running away from home, not obeying parents, truancy, and drinking alcohol. Child welfare staff may see youth running away from home as a missing persons issue that ought to be handled by the police, while police may view such events, especially repeat runaways from the same home, as a child welfare or juvenile probation issue. The status offender "system" is often an office with relatively little service capacity of its own; thus, it relies on other agencies, including the Family Court, to make decisions for youth and to provide services. Staff in each organization may also look to the parent to take responsibility for the youth's issues as well as city agencies or their contracted service providers.

Similarly, responsibility for the educational performance of foster children is spread among many people, including foster parents, biological parents, group home staff, caseworkers, and teachers. Even when information is shared and each player knows about a youth's status, confusion over roles and responsibilities may result in no one working with a foster youth on educational issues (Finkelstein, Wamsley, and Miranda 2002). After officials have assigned responsibilities, successful implementation requires that frontline employees are trained to carry out their assignments. Many people working with kids in foster care are eager to help after their roles are clarified, but they may be inexperienced in navigating the educational system or intimidated by working with teachers and school officials. To counter this problem, some programs use "train the trainer" sessions and develop materials for caseworkers that explain how best to engage the school system (Armstrong and Mandelstam 2003).

Unloading Cases and Shifting Burdens, or "It's Your Problem Now"

As the examples above show, officials and staff often want to solve cross-agency problems when they have the tools to do so. In some instances, however, agencies, staff, and parents act to rid themselves of troubled youth. Hard data on this phenomenon are rare, but there are enough anecdotes and stories to make this pattern noteworthy.

While planning Project Confirm, program designers heard many stories of foster care staff who called police to have youth in their care arrested—often for minor incidents that biological parents resolve without police interference. Indeed, some frontline staff see calling the police as a way to assert authority or to have responsibility for a kid transferred to juvenile justice.[6] In some cases, these youth may have suffered from mental health problems, but the lack of access to mental health services led to voluntary placements with child welfare. According to the Rochester Youth Study, one in five male delinquents and one in three female delinquents has a diagnosable mental health problem (Huizinga et al. 2000).

The Family Courts in New York City place hundreds of status offenders in traditional congregate care settings filled mostly with youth in foster care (Ross 2001; Ross et al. 2001). Courtroom observations found that if parents demanded placement—in effect, unloading the youth onto the child welfare system—judges almost always acquiesced. Focus groups with parents showed that they usually cared about their children and thought placement was a "boot camp" where their kids would learn discipline, though no such facilities exist in New York.

Given the mismatch between what parents want, what kids need, and what congregate care facilities provide, it is not surprising that child welfare discharges status offenders quickly. Status offenders cycle back into foster care more often than other foster youth as neither parents, nor the status offender system, nor the child welfare system want to take responsibility for these problem cases. In the worst cases, kids bounce between home and placement, and bounce around within the child welfare system—

often having to transfer to new schools with each movement. And, like youth with delinquency records, they may face extraordinary hurdles in their attempts to register in a new school despite regulations that require officials to enroll these children.

Detained youth in New York City are automatically enrolled in an in-facility educational program. Attendance is mandatory. Ironically, students taking courses while in detention receive only half credit for their efforts. Many court-involved youth are already behind educationally, and this policy makes catching up that much harder. Even if delinquent youth manage to register at a school, school policies and administrators may push a youth to drop out (Fine 1991).

Not surprisingly, a review of case files in New York City and other studies finds a strong link between poor school attendance and recidivism. In essence, the education system is unloading problem cases onto the delinquency system. Youth in foster care who have established records of behavioral problems face many of the same challenges, bouncing from placement to placement and school to school.

The examples in this typology show the difficulty of addressing cross-cutting issues. Many professionals in child welfare and other fields have recognized the bureaucratic behavior that creates or amplifies these problems, and some may be familiar with the specific problems mentioned. Given the harm to children, youth, and families as well as the cost and the injustice of cross-agency problems in child welfare, it might be thought that a well-developed research literature describes these issues and some solutions. Such is not the case. The following section discusses why relatively little research on cross-cutting issues exists, describes how the research in this book originated, and discusses the strengths and weaknesses of the approach used.

Studying Cross-Cutting Issues

Researchers face serious challenges in conducting studies of cross-agency issues in child welfare and youth services generally. Research is expensive. Many funders, including government agencies and the legislators that appropriate their budgets, face pressure to fund programs rather than research. Gaining access to child welfare data is and should be challenging—information about abuse, neglect, family health, and relationships is extraordinarily sensitive and legally protected. Many of the same confidentiality protections also apply to data collected by justice system agencies—broadly defined to include police, prosecutors, juvenile justice, corrections, courts, and probation—that are the focus of this book. The quality of child welfare and other administrative data is often poor. Research involving foster children, juvenile delinquents, and incarcerated populations draws extra scrutiny from government agencies and institutional review boards.[7] Research designs that use some form of random assignment of research subjects are rarely approved and difficult to execute in the child welfare and justice fields.

These obstacles make conducting research in any one arena—be it child welfare, juvenile justice, or some other justice field—difficult. Studying cross-agency issues exacerbates these difficulties. Instead of persuading officials in one agency that a study is worthwhile, researchers must persuade two or more sets of officials about the value of the study, develop two or more data-sharing protocols, learn the intricacies of two or more datasets, and gain expertise in additional policy areas. The time this takes adds to the cost of the study, and many skills needed for this work fall outside the bailiwick of researchers and into the domain of lawyers and policy entrepreneurs. For academically based researchers, policy-oriented studies that include areas outside the tradition of the discipline receive few rewards.

Taken together, conducting cross-cutting research on child welfare issues presents challenges that most researchers avoid due to the cost, the aggravation, or the lack of capacity. Funders may also be reluctant to invest in expensive research that has a greater risk of failure. The research presented in this book took place in a setting designed to tackle many of these obstacles.

A Model for Cross-Cutting Research

The New York City Administration for Children's Services (ACS), the city's child welfare agency, paid the Vera Institute of Justice to conduct most of the research presented in this book. New York City created ACS in 1996 in the wake of widely publicized child deaths and widespread concern about the child welfare system's ability to keep the city's children safe. The city split the child welfare agency from a larger agency, the Human Resources Administration, with the hope that a higher profile, a narrower focus, more resources, and direct access to the mayor's office would enable improvements to the long-troubled agency.[8] Since its inception, ACS has received funding to support external research that helps implement and evaluate reforms and informs other issues that the agency encounters. Most of the research in this book is a result of this initiative, though none of it could have been accomplished without the assistance and cooperation of numerous other agencies.

The Vera Institute of Justice (Vera) is a New York City–based non-partisan nonprofit organization that conducts research, plans and operates programs, and offers technical assistance on social justice issues. Established in 1961, Vera serves as an incubator for innovation and a source of new ideas to make government more fair, humane, and efficient. Since its inception, the Institute has launched dozens of demonstration programs and spun off 17 nonprofit organizations. Each nonprofit continues to serve vulnerable populations, such as crime victims, inmates, parolees and probationers, immigrants, court-involved youth, the homeless, and families involved with child welfare. These programs usually arise to fill in gaps in services or to tackle unaddressed problems.

Vera's research applies transparent social science methodologies to public policy issues. The Institute employs researchers from a range of disciplines that have included sociology, public policy, experimental and clinical psychology, political science, criminology, anthropology, and history. The capacity to draw on diverse substantive and methodological expertise for internal peer review helps researchers produce studies that have a reputation for credibility and independence. Vera values its "just the facts" reputation and has a track record of producing reports that present both positive and negative aspects of programs and processes.

The different disciplines and orientations at Vera reduce the barriers to conducting cross-cutting research studies. Researchers have ready access to experts—both researchers and program staff—who know the issues facing justice agencies; the organization, strengths, and weaknesses of administrative data; the details of memoranda of understanding for sharing data; and the people at agencies with the knowledge or authority to "get things done." Lawyers, researchers, and institutional review board members know the issues in conducting research involving child welfare–involved families and incarcerated populations.

Vera's New York City location also helps reduce the barriers to conducting cross-cutting research. The city's budget exceeds that of any other jurisdiction in the country save New York State, California, and the federal government. Combined with the city's many foundations and history of philanthropy, New York City can support research that often exceeds the financial capacity of other jurisdictions. New York's strong progressive tradition, with its emphasis on using government to address social ills and rational public decisionmaking, provides an impetus for research that is not always present in other jurisdictions.

Vera's research model addresses a primary problem in conducting sensitive research that involves multiple vulnerable populations: trust. Trust on the part of clients, frontline staff, and agency managers can help solve numerous problems that might sink a research project otherwise. The Institute's research model builds trust in many ways.

A distinctive element of Vera's approach to research is creating open partnerships with government. Engaging researchers is a leap of faith for government agencies, as evaluators usually need access to nonpublic data, use up valuable staff time, and enter facilities that are often not open to the public. To help gain the trust of government officials, researchers actively solicit the input of government staff and may ask government managers to guide research questions to ensure that studies will be useful to them, not just the research community. The premise is that government officials are more likely to support and act upon research if they understand how conclusions are made and feel they are part of the work the research team undertook. Finding individuals in government who have political capital and a track record of acting on empirical findings further increases trust at all levels.

Vera's research model strives to incorporate four sources of information in each study: administrative data collected by government agencies, conversations with government and nonprofit managers that implement and direct programs, discussions with frontline staff, and interviews with clients or their representatives. Systematically combining multiple data sources produces new knowledge, and taking this approach helps build trust by assuring different stakeholders that their voices have played a role in the research.[9]

Vera is uniquely positioned to conduct research on cross-cutting issues in child welfare and other justice issues. Even with these advantages, however, there are limits to the type and sophistication of the research produced. In addition, the Vera research model has strengths and weaknesses that readers should keep in mind when examining the ensuing chapters.

Strengths and Weaknesses of the Model

The strengths of this approach to research include access, transparency, and practicality. Access includes not only access to administrative data that are not commonly available, but also access to government staff, facilities, and clients. In most cases, Vera researchers have access to staff meetings and other nonpublic events that allow a fuller understanding of agency operations. Transparency refers to the use of replicable social science methods. For example, the findings from the cohort study methods described in chapters 3, 4, and 5 could be duplicated by government researchers or others with access to the same data. Another strength of the model is practicality: by taking an empirical approach, Vera's research aims to draw lessons that government officials can use in carrying out their responsibilities.

The model also contains some weaknesses—weaknesses that are often the flip side of strengths. The price of access is that government agencies usually retain the right to approve reports before they are issued publicly—though often on the condition that approval is not unreasonably withheld. Agencies insist on this right because they need to ensure that no individually identifiable, confidential information is released. In the Institute's experience, the right to approve reports has rarely been used as a way to influence the content of the report. Most government officials know that such efforts will be vigorously resisted and that biased research has less substantive and political value. Still, Vera researchers do not have the unfettered right to publish that university-based researchers enjoy.

Another perceived weakness of the model is the focus on one city. The research is limited to one city because of funding constraints and because all the difficulties of conducting cross-cutting research would be that much more complicated by researching multiple jurisdictions. It takes years to understand how government organizations in one jurisdiction really work, how and why one part of government interacts with another in a particular way, and the strengths and weaknesses of the administrative data that each agency collects. Learning the same information in another jurisdiction or investing in a partnership with another organization further complicates an already complex undertaking.

This drawback is offset by the depth and detail of the research. And, New York is an extraordinarily diverse city. The city's five boroughs are built at different population densities, have demographically distinct populations, and have varying access to resources and opportunities. Borough offices serve client populations larger than most other cities in the country and in many cases have developed distinct organizational cultures.[10] These differences give the research the flavor of multicity studies in some cases, such as the differences in court culture and probation case processing noted in chapters 8 and 9. Most important, the origins of cross-cutting issues cited above are not unique to New York. Other urban child welfare systems exhibit much of the same complexity as New York and are embedded in the same system of service specialization and federalism.

A final critique is that the model produces studies that rarely address broader theoretical understandings of social justice issues. Indeed, there is little discussion of such issues as the socioeconomic structures that contribute to the placement of children in foster care, racial and gender bias, or the social control functions of the criminal justice system in a capitalist society. These are important issues that readers should keep in mind. The technocratic nature of the work, however, often makes the discussion relevant to many areas of public administration. All governments, regardless of their ideology or the demographics of the populations they serve, must deal with coordination and overlap among different bureaucratic units. The research in this volume contributes to our understanding of how these issues play out in numerous ways, whether in American urban jurisdictions, U.S. suburbs and rural areas, or other countries.

Conclusion

Cross-cutting issues in child welfare lead to many problems. These problems have their origins in the organizational structure of providing human services and are made more challenging by the fragmentation of American government and policymaking. Most of these problems can be classified in one or more types that include service tunnels, information flow, diffusion of responsibility, and unloading problem cases. Despite the inefficiencies and injustices that cross-cutting issues often create, the cost and complexity of studying them has limited the research available to guide policymakers. This book presents unique research that informs policymakers about specific cross-cutting issues in child welfare. Despite this sobering introduction, these studies show that in many cases, cross-agency issues can be resolved.

Readers of this volume, especially those not familiar with New York City, are strongly urged to read the appendix to this chapter to have a better sense of the government agencies discussed in the book, their responsibilities, and the data they collect.

Agencies and Data

To make the text more readable, the author aims to avoid the alphabet soup of government acronyms by referring to specific agencies and data sources generically throughout this volume. For example, the term "juvenile justice officials" in the ensuing chapters refers to the staff of the New York City Department of Juvenile Justice, or DJJ. DJJ keeps data on admissions to and discharges from juvenile detention facilities—referred to as "juvenile justice data." Listed below are the primary agencies at the intersection of child welfare and justice and, where appropriate, information about the data sources used in the ensuing chapters. For more information on the data sources, readers are encouraged to contact the author.

The New York City Administration for Children's Services (ACS) is the city's child welfare agency. It is responsible for child protective investigations, preventive services, foster care, adoption services, and other child welfare functions, and it plays a role in the status offender system. ACS also oversees city-supported day care and other children's services not directly connected to traditional child welfare. ACS originated in 1996 as a stand-alone agency reporting to the mayor's office. Before 1996, the city's child welfare agency had several other names: the Child Welfare Administration, Special Services for Children, and the Bureau for Child Welfare.

Child welfare data refers primarily to the **Child Care Review System (CCRS),** a statewide administrative database to which ACS and other local child welfare agencies contribute data. CCRS contains records for foster children who entered care from 1985 to the present, including individual and family demographic data, records of movements a child made while in foster care, reason for discharge, permanency planning goals, and other pertinent information. Child welfare staff also have access to and provided data from the **Welfare Management System (WMS),** which is maintained by the State of New York. It is primarily used to manage services and payments to recipients of public assistance.

The New York City Department of Correction (DOC) operates the city's jail system. People who are sentenced to terms of up to one year are incarcerated in DOC facilities. The agency also provides custody for those who, after arraignment, are remanded without bail or are unable to post bail. DOC maintains a database that includes admission and discharge dates, charges, individual identifiers, and other information. In addition, DOC data include individuals who are detained pending adjudication of their criminal charges but not sentenced.

The New York City Department of Education operates the city's school system, which educates 1 million students at over 1,000 sites with a budget of over $15 billion. In 1998, responsibility for over 4,000 school safety officers moved from education officials to the New York City Police Department. New York City's school safety officers alone constitute the tenth largest police force in the country.

The New York City Family Court hears matters involving children and families. The Family Court's jurisdiction includes custody and visitation, support, concurrent jurisdiction with criminal court for family offenses (domestic violence), persons in need of supervision, delinquency, child protective proceedings (abuse and neglect), foster care approval and review, termination of parental rights, and adoption and guardianship. Family Court does not have jurisdiction over divorce, which is litigated in the New York Supreme Court. Judges of the Family Court are appointed by the mayor to 10-year terms. Court norms, culture, and judicial orientation vary by borough.

The New York City Department of Juvenile Justice (DJJ) operates the city's juvenile detention system. As mentioned above, DJJ maintains a database on entries and exits from detention. The department also contributes data to a larger database maintained by the city, the Comprehensive Justice Information System (CJIS), which contains information on the court processing of juvenile delinquency and status offender cases.

The New York City Police Department (NYPD) employs approximately 40,000 police officers to advance its mission of ensuring public safety. The NYPD has units that focus on youth, child victims, and schools that often interact with other agencies discussed in this book.

The New York City Department of Probation (DOP) provides probation services to both adults and juveniles. DOP also prepares investigations and reports that judges review in juvenile delinquency cases. As discussed in chapter 7, DOP also plays a role in the status offender system.

The New York State Office of Children and Family Services (OCFS) is the state agency with supervisory responsibilities for juvenile justice and child welfare. OCFS is responsible for issuing state regulations pertaining to juvenile justice and child welfare, and for assisting local jurisdictions in implementing those regulations. The agency also supplies funding for preventive services and foster care and operates juvenile placement facilities for juvenile delinquents and youthful offenders.

The New York State Division of Criminal Justice Services (DCJS) coordinates state criminal justice agencies. In addition to many other responsibilities, DCJS collects and analyzes statewide crime data including data on individual arrests and sentences as well as arrest and disposition charges. These data contain flags indicating whether a charge was for an offense related to drugs, prostitution, weapons, a child victim, a violent felony, or motor vehicle crime. Under New York State statute, DCJS is not permitted to provide researchers with sealed records involving juveniles.

The New York State Department of Correctional Services (DOCS) is responsible for managing the confinement of inmates held at all New York State prisons. DOCS data contain information on all prison incarcerations including admissions, discharges, and services provided to inmates, including counseling and substance abuse treatment.

2

Coordinating Law Enforcement and Child Protection in Cases of Severe Child Maltreatment

S evere child abuse is a crime, yet child welfare agencies and police departments traditionally have pursued abuse cases independently.[1] Most allegations of child abuse and neglect do not require police involvement or lead to arrest and prosecution. But in situations involving severe abuse or neglect, failing to quickly coordinate child protective workers, police, and prosecutors can seriously affect a child's welfare and law enforcement's ability to respond. In the worst case, slow responses can result in more abuse. Uncoordinated responses can also lead to multiple interviews by police, child protective workers, and prosecutors, forcing children to recollect painful experiences to strangers again and again. Especially when conducted in environments where children may feel uncomfortable, such as police stations or emergency rooms, multiple interviews can make an already traumatic experience that much more distressing.

Uncoordinated responses may also hamper efforts to arrest and prosecute the perpetrators of child abuse. The arrival of a child protective worker may cause a perpetrator to destroy evidence, influence responses from children, and otherwise hinder law enforcement investigations. Most child protective workers have little or no training in collecting and preserving evidence for criminal cases; their role is to protect children, not to make arrests. If police are not brought in immediately, the evidence of abuse—such as marks and bruises—may disappear. Without a police presence, removing the child from danger is likely to take precedence over enforcing the law.

This chapter examines New York City's effort to coordinate child protection investigations through the Instant Response Team (IRT) initiative. The chapter identifies the hurdles to cross-agency collaboration that these initiatives commonly face, the improvements made to services, and the obstacles other large urban child welfare systems may encounter should they implement a program similar to New York's. The key research questions this chapter seeks to answer include how frequently IRT cases occurred and how that changed over time, the indication rates of IRT cases, the outcomes of IRT cases, and the perceptions of staff that participated in the program.

Understanding the Issue

An example from San Diego, while dated, illustrates some of the difficulties that can occur when child protection and police fail to coordinate their efforts:

> A child was found with teeth marks on her back, [and child protective workers] asked her uncle, the suspect, to submit to photographs of his teeth. . . . he fled the county before law enforcement had the opportunity to question and possibly arrest him. According to the police, [the child protective workers] should have waited to question the uncle until the police were alerted. . . . But, according to [child welfare officials], the workers acted properly [because] they had to determine which family member was involved in order to protect the child's safety. (Smith 1995a, 8)

In this case, the lack of a coordinated response undermined the missions of both the police and child protective workers: the police did not arrest the perpetrator, and child welfare workers could not know when or if the uncle would return to revictimize the child.

Many child welfare administrators recognize the need to respond quickly to severe cases of maltreatment and to coordinate the responses of law enforcement, child protection, and other agencies. For example, Houston, Dallas, and San Antonio divide cases into high and low priority, with high-priority investigations initiated within 24 hours. Chicago has a multiagency team that specializes in investigating head injuries, and Los Angeles has developed an emergency response program that focuses on methamphetamine-related child abuse in families. Philadelphia, Phoenix, and Denver also follow protocols for multiagency coordination.

Changes have also occurred in law enforcement. In the wake of high-profile child abuse incidents and a better understanding of the damage inflicted by abusers, authorities have sought to prosecute perpetrators in criminal courts.[2] Many police departments now house specially trained squads to investigate sexual abuse and child victim crimes. Prosecutors have also become more involved in child welfare cases in some jurisdictions (Smith 1995b). In New York City, for example, the increased involvement of law enforcement produced concrete results: arrests for endangering the welfare of a child in New York City tripled from 303 in 1990 to 1,111 in 1998, even though arrests in general increased by only 29 percent and child abuse and neglect reports remained stable (Vreeland 2000).[3]

Despite these reform efforts, quick responses that coordinate the efforts of child welfare, police, and prosecutors remain the exception, not the norm. The obstacles to coordinating responses to allegations of maltreatment are significant and longstanding. Nationwide, child welfare agencies receive millions of abuse and neglect reports each year, and police departments do not have the resources to accompany child protective workers on every investigation. Efforts at interagency collaboration may be further impeded by bureaucratic turf wars, confusion about roles, and a lack of management attention.[4] Despite the benefits of collaborating, agencies often avoid initiating or joining such efforts.

Creating the Instant Response Team Program

Before IRT's launch, the city's child welfare agency, the police, and the public hospital system attempted to coordinate responses to a limited number of cases in an effort known as the Joint Response program. Formed in the 1980s, this program laid out protocols for interagency collaboration with the goal of coordinating responses to serious cases of physical injury, sexual abuse, and abuse or neglect. The program targeted children under 14 years old. Only physicians could trigger joint responses, and doctors needed the approval of an employee of the State Central Registry, which receives and records all child abuse and neglect reports.

Despite good intentions, the Joint Response program collapsed. The program did not identify any one agency staff person as directly responsible for its operation, and no mechanism held anyone accountable for outcomes. Reports received from sources other than physicians were not eligible for a joint response, severely limiting the program's scope. As a result, no individual agency took ownership of the program.

In 1997, New York's child welfare agency led the planning for a new and more comprehensive effort to coordinate responses to severe allegations of child maltreatment. Program planners identified two primary goals: to minimize the trauma to children and to improve the quality of investigations by collecting evidence in a timely and thorough manner. Over the next year, a task force composed of child welfare officials, police, prosecutors, child advocacy center staff, and hospital staff designed the IRT program and protocol to meet these goals.

Program Description

An IRT case typically begins when the State Central Registry receives a report that a child is being abused or neglected. Anyone can report child maltreatment, though certain professionals, such as doctors, teachers, and social workers, are mandated to report when they suspect a child is being abused or neglected. The State Central Registry routes reports to the child protective services borough office closest to where the family resides. When the allegations meet the criteria for an instant response, the borough office's IRT coordinator contacts the person who reported the abuse for more information and tries to establish the location of and risk to the child or children involved. Only police officers, detectives, and IRT coordinators can initiate an instant response.

The IRT protocol lays out specific criteria for when a case is eligible for an instant response, based on the age of the child and the type of abuse alleged. For children under 11, for example, a case is eligible for an instant response if the abuse includes

> fractures; internal bleeding injuries including subdural hematoma; "shaken baby" syndrome; widespread or serious bruises; lacerations or welts consistent with an injury being inflicted . . . tissue damage caused by serious beatings; burns or scalding; [and] attempted drowning.[5]

While the criteria for physical abuse rely on observable results of maltreatment, there are often less visible signs when sexual abuse occurs. Thus, any report of a sex crime involving a child under 11 qualifies for an instant response.

The protocol divides cases into three types: Type I: fatalities; Type II: felony sex abuse of children under age 18 and severe maltreatment and all sex abuse of children under age 11; and Type III: severe maltreatment of children age 11 to 17 and sexual abuse of children 11 to 17 not covered by type II. Each type of case requires a different response. Type I cases require immediate communication and coordination between child welfare and the appropriate homicide detective squad. Type II cases require an immediate response by a child protective worker and a Special Victims Squad detective. Type III cases require an immediate response by a child protective worker and a patrol officer.

Once the IRT coordinator determines that a case requires an instant response, he or she contacts the police and dispatches a child protective worker.[6] Both the child protective worker and the police aim to initiate the IRT process within two hours of receiving the report. After a "minimal facts only" interview by whoever arrives first, the team members conduct a joint interview and a medical exam if necessary. Whenever possible, the interview and medical exam take place in child-friendly settings—ideally, a child advocacy center (CAC).[7] If an arrest occurs or appears likely, a prosecutor should attend the joint interview as well. If the interview takes place at a CAC, a member of the team—which may include a CAC social worker in addition to the police, a prosecutor, and a child protective worker—conducts the interview in a room equipped with a two-way mirror while the others watch from behind the mirror.

The IRT program is distinguished from many other efforts, including the Joint Response program, by child welfare officials' investment in planning, management, staffing, and training. Though integrated into the child protective borough offices, IRT has a manager who collects and analyzes program data, liaises with police managers, and reports directly to the deputy commissioner for child protection. To handle cases in borough offices, child welfare officials have hired IRT coordinators who report to the program manager. The IRT coordinators screen all allegations to determine whether a report meets the criteria for an instant response. They then arrange for the police and child protective workers to respond, monitor what happens during cases, and record information on response times and other outcomes.

The program also aims to improve information sharing. When the program launched, child welfare, the police, and local prosecutors' offices signed a memorandum of understanding that structured the sharing of information. Copies of the IRT protocol were distributed to the staff of each agency involved. The program manager provides regular updates to the IRT handbook, which contains the protocol as well as contact information for appropriate staff in child welfare, the police, prosecutors' offices, hospitals, and CACs. The program also created two training videotapes that explain its procedures.

To respond quickly to IRT cases, the child welfare agency provides child protective workers with a car service instead of relying on public transportation, the norm in many non-IRT investigations. Depending on the case, a child protective worker may have to make several stops to find the child. Providing a car service is an attempt to enable child protective workers to arrive as quickly as their counterparts in the police department, where operations are already designed for quick response.

The following example of how a case is handled under the IRT protocol offers a stark contrast to the lack of police-child welfare coordination shown in the earlier example.[8]

Jane works at a school in New York City. One Friday, she noticed that Mark, a third-grader, had a chunk of skin missing from his hand and wounds on his head. The child told Jane that his mother had beaten him with a curtain rod and stabbed him in the head with a fork. Jane called the New York State Child Abuse Hotline operated by the State Central Registry, which contacted the city's child welfare agency. Given the severity of the allegations and the possibility that the child might be attacked again, child protective staff initiated an instant response. In less than an hour, officers from the Special Victims Unit and a child protective worker arrived at the child's school.

To minimize the trauma experienced by Mark and his siblings, the police and the child protective worker conducted joint interviews with each child so the children would have to explain what happened to them only once. The interviews indicated that the children were at imminent risk of further abuse, and the child protective worker arranged for them to be transported to the child welfare intake facility. There, a nurse experienced in child abuse cases conducted a physical exam and determined that Mark did not need to go to the hospital for further medical care. Child welfare workers arranged placements for the children in a foster boarding home. Based on the physical evidence and the children's statements, the police arrested the children's mother for child abuse.

Many programs have individual success stories. The research below demonstrates how programs aimed at ameliorating cross-cutting issues between law enforcement and child welfare can be assessed.

Assessing the Instant Response Program

To assess the program, researchers analyzed data collected by the IRT coordinators—the people who select cases for an instant response and coordinate that response—from 1998 to 2002. Researchers matched a portion of these data with records of child abuse reports and investigations from the State Central Registry (SCR) for 2000—the most recent year available for research purposes. The SCR records all allegations of child abuse and neglect in the state and contains details of the subsequent investigation, such as whether allegations were substantiated. To further analyze how IRT cases are reported, researchers studied phone traffic through the IRT hotline, a number designed to give the police a direct link to their local IRT coordinator. Also, researchers conducted 39 interviews with staff from all the agencies involved.

The sections below discuss how IRT members are trained, how IRT cases are reported, and how cases are selected for an instant response. The chapter then focuses on how police, child welfare, and prosecutors coordinate their activities in the field. Finally, it examines the outcomes of IRT cases. The chapter looks at indication rates, how quickly case-workers and police officers respond to IRT cases, the frequency of joint interviews, and how often these interviews take place in child-friendly settings.

Training

In 1998, child welfare and the police conducted joint training sessions for staff assigned to work on the IRT program. The training included videotaped examples of how the program was designed to function, explanations of the IRT protocol, and marketing of the IRT hotline. In-service trainings were held for patrol staff and caseworkers. Since then, the two agencies have trained their staff independently. Training materials for police and prosecutors working on sex crimes include copies of the program's protocol.

While New York City's child welfare agency has an ongoing IRT training program at its caseworker training facility, the Satterwhite Academy, other agencies appear to invest fewer resources in IRT-specific training. New York City police officers who work in the Special Victims Squad (SVS) received training at the program's launch, but the SVS detectives researchers talked to had not received training when interviewed in 2003.

One assistant district attorney felt that more frequent training could improve the program's performance.

The interviews found some role confusion and occasional tension between child protective staff and their counterparts at CACs and hospitals. As is common when two systems overlap with the same client, "ownership" of the client was sometimes an issue. Limits on training time and resources mean that more peripheral participants know less about the program's protocols, which spell out the responsibilities of the many professionals involved in these cases.

Reporting Cases through the IRT Hotline

One innovation designed to coordinate the members of the Instant Response Team is the IRT hotline. The hotline is available exclusively to the police and links them directly to an IRT coordinator. Police can use the hotline to initiate an instant response or to talk with a coordinator if they are unsure about whether a case qualifies for the program. The police still must report to the State Central Registry, but contacting the IRT coordinator first allows child welfare to dispatch a caseworker immediately.

According to phone records from January 2000 to January 2001, 37 percent of hotline calls were placed on weekends. Of calls made on weekdays, 96 percent took place outside of normal ACS working hours, 8 a.m. to 4 p.m.[9] Overall, the police initiated 635 instant responses. Of these, 322 calls went through the IRT hotline, regarding approximately 260 cases, or 41 percent of the cases initiated.[10]

This suggests that the police use the hotline primarily when the regular IRT coordinators are not working: on weekends and after regular working hours. During regular working hours, Special Victims Squad detectives call IRT coordinators directly, eschewing the 800 number. Most supervisors, IRT coordinators, and police staff indicated that the hotline is useful for patrol officers and for detectives unfamiliar with the program. Once police build a relationship with their local IRT coordinator, they use the hotline as a convenient backup during off hours.

Selecting Cases

The program aims to take all reports of severe maltreatment. Still, child welfare and the police face a balancing act in selecting cases for the IRT program. Neither the police nor child welfare has the resources to initiate an instant response in every case of child maltreatment; fortunately, the vast majority of cases do not require one. Yet, both agencies have invested resources in building an instant response capacity that would not be used efficiently if only a small number of cases qualified.

Researchers examined how the number of IRT cases has changed over time and whether the types of cases selected for an instant response match the criteria stated in the program's manual. Researchers also identified how often IRT cases were "indicated"—meaning that child protective workers found sufficient evidence to support at least one allegation of abuse or neglect.

The number of IRT cases has grown in each of the program's five years (figure 2.1). In 2002, 4,064 cases received an instant response, an increase of 160 percent since 1999. As planned, the program added type III cases in 2000. Though type III cases are now the majority of all IRT cases, type I and II cases have also increased over time.[11] During the same five-year period, the total number of maltreatment reports stayed constant at around 55,000, with the police and child welfare initiating cases in the same proportion as in prior years.[12] Citywide, the ratio of cases initiated by the police has remained steady at about 16 percent.

IRT coordinators are selecting cases defined by the IRT protocol. Based on 2000 SCR data for IRT cases, of cases selected for an instant response, 99 percent met the minimum criteria of having at least one allegation of physical abuse, sexual abuse, or neglect, as outlined in the IRT protocol. In addition, IRT cases involved more severe allegations than non-IRT

Figure 2.1. Number of IRT Cases, 1998–2002

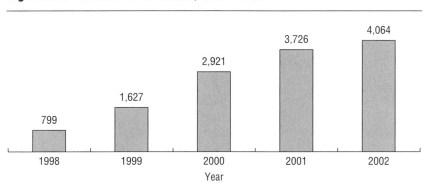

Source: Author's calculations.

cases, and more of these allegations were substantiated. While both IRT cases and non-IRT cases averaged 3 allegations per case, an average of 1.4 allegations were substantiated in IRT cases, compared with 0.9 in non-IRT cases. Overall, 52 percent of IRT cases were indicated, compared with 35 percent of all other New York City cases—well above the national indication rate in maltreatment cases, 29 percent.[13]

Although IRT coordinators select cases that meet the program's criteria, selection is as much art as science. Allegations of child maltreatment come from various sources and differ in quality and amount of information provided.[14] Cases called in by mandated reporters generally have higher indication rates than cases reported from other sources. Even so, less than half of all non-IRT cases reported by mandated reporters are indicated.[15]

In practice, IRT coordinators have substantial discretion in selecting cases, and they exercise that discretion in different ways. Some coordinators said that they took a "better safe than sorry" approach and initiated instant responses whenever they felt it might be warranted. Others said that they called for an instant response only when they felt it was absolutely necessary. Because many reports meet the minimum criteria for an instant response, how IRT coordinators exercise their discretion plays a large role in determining the number of cases the program handles.

Internal Coordination

Insufficient organization and instability *within* (as opposed to between) individual organizations may hinder attempts at interagency coordination (Wolff 1998). A collaborative effort is only as strong as its weakest partner.

Overall, child welfare staff—IRT coordinators, supervisors, and child protective workers—worked well together. Despite some initial difficulties, particularly in adjusting to a new chain of command, the program kept internal conflict to a minimum. Child protective workers and IRT coordinators almost universally reported good relationships with each other. Only one caseworker and one IRT coordinator in the group of 14 discussed any complications with working together, and the issues they described arose in the early days of the program and have since subsided.

There is occasional friction between IRT coordinators and child protective supervisors. By designating cases for instant response, IRT coordinators are forcing supervisors to immediately assign a child protective worker. Supervisors have no say in determining whether a case should be deemed an instant response. Yet child protective workers on IRT cases report to these supervisors, not the IRT coordinator. These cross-jurisdictional demands can create conflict. Yet most supervisors and managers were able to balance these sometimes conflicting demands. Only one person in this group felt strongly that the challenges of coordination outweighed its benefits.

Responding to Cases

Nearly every person researchers interviewed reported that the IRT program vastly improved coordination among the agencies. Special Victims Squad detectives reported that the program led to more information sharing, better case processing, and improved relations. IRT coordinators and their contacts in the police department developed solid working relationships and a high level of phone contact. "I think the IRT program is one of the best things we've ever done," reported one detective, expressing a common level of enthusiasm.

All five assistant district attorneys believed that agency coordination improved prosecutions, and most said that the IRT program strengthened the partnership between law enforcement and child protection. "Pre-IRT, no one was coordinated with each other," said one. "Everyone was just doing their own job and not even thinking about how it might be affecting children. Post-IRT, everyone understands why they should be working together."

This widespread support exists despite the obstacles that staff must overcome to implement the IRT protocol. For the program to be effective, frontline staff must address the complications inherent in coordinating fieldwork and balancing workload pressures. The sections below examine how child welfare workers and the police respond to IRT cases, the various pathways that IRT cases may take after contact is made with a child, the challenges in arranging joint interviews, and the outcomes of IRT cases.

Timing

Researchers examined response times by looking at data collected by the program and by discussing the subject in interviews.

All IRT coordinators keep a weekly log of response times, which they uniformly define as the time that elapses from when the borough office receives a report to when the caseworker leaves the borough office, not when the caseworker makes contact with the child. The response data are divided into ranges: less than an hour, one to two hours, and more than two hours.[16] The log data show that between August 2001 and July 2002, half of all caseworkers responding to IRT cases left the office less than an hour after a case's initiation, and almost 90 percent left within two hours—although times varied widely depending on in which of New York City's five boroughs the case occurred (table 2.1). Since the first year of the program, caseworkers citywide have decreased the amount of time it takes them to leave the office. In 1998, it took more than two hours to depart in 26 percent of cases. By 2002, it took that long in only 8 percent of cases (figure 2.2).

A number of factors hinder even faster departures. The city's child welfare agency has markedly lowered the caseloads of child protective workers in the six years since the program started, but during busy periods a worker may not be immediately available. At other times, an IRT unit may be "capped," meaning the unit has exceeded the number of cases it is authorized to respond to per month. If a unit is capped when a new case arrives, the IRT coordinator must find another unit to handle the case. Though the vast majority of caseworkers respond quickly to IRT cases, a small number account for a disproportionate percentage of slow responses.

Once caseworkers leave the office, they must navigate obstacles over which they have little control. The car service may come late, and traffic may cause delays. In contrast, the police have their own cars and can clear traffic with sirens. Once in the field, caseworkers need to find the

Table 2.1. ACS Response Times by Borough, August 1, 2001, to July 31, 2002 (percent)

Borough	Less than 1 hour	1–2 hours	More than 2 hours
Bronx	38.2	54.8	7.0
Brooklyn	20.9	66.7	12.4
Manhattan	80.2	18.8	0.9
Queens	71.3	8.4	20.3
Staten Island	85.9	10.7	3.4

Source: Author's calculations.

Note: Response time refers to the time elapsed between the receipt of the report that triggered the instant response and the time the caseworker left the field office.

Figure 2.2. ACS Response Time by Year, 1998–2002

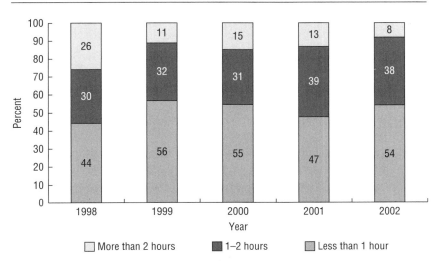

Source: Author's calculations.

Note: Response time refers to the time elapsed between the receipt of the report that triggered the instant response and the time the caseworker left the field office.

child or children who are the subject of the allegations. By contract, the car service waits one hour for the caseworker at any one location. If the caseworker stays at a location for more than an hour, he or she must request another car through the service. In some cases, this can cause serious delays: workers report that finding a child may involve as many as six different stops, including school; the child's home; the homes of the child's extended family, friends, and neighbors; and other locations.

The police, too, face challenges in responding to IRT cases. In two boroughs, child protective workers in type II cases frequently go to the scene alone and bring the child to a CAC or other facility for a joint interview with an SVS detective. Both child welfare staff and the police reported that workload pressures could make detectives and patrol officers reluctant to accompany child protective workers on IRT cases. To balance these competing interests, police officers may ask child protective staff to start investigations alone and let them know if they are needed. One police officer reported that for him, the typical IRT case involved going to the interview site—usually a hospital—after child welfare workers had transported the child. Both officers and child protective workers reported making good-faith efforts to work together, but noted that when their counterparts did not arrive when they did, time constraints made it necessary to proceed without them.

At the Scene

Police and caseworkers reported few problems coordinating their work when they were at the scene together. Both parties perceived the other as additional help and appreciated their presence. When asked who decides who will conduct a joint interview, child protective workers and the police both responded that whoever has the best rapport with the child conducts the interview. Mentions of conflict over this issue, which other research in the field highlights, were notably absent (see Moran-Ellis and Fielding 1996). Police and child protective workers knew their roles, did not argue over "turf," and avoided other common frontline problems associated with collaboration.

Prosecutors, police, and child protective staff all agreed that the speed of the response by child protective workers and the availability of the police play key roles in determining what happens in the field, including whether joint interviews occur, the number of interviews that take place, and the follow-up required by all parties. Reliant on a car service instead of a fleet of radio- and siren-equipped patrol cars, child protective workers face a bigger challenge than the police. Detectives and district attorneys reported that when they arrived on the scene first they waited for child protection, but the pressure of other work meant they could not afford to wait too long. In some situations, the facts of a case may force police to investigate immediately. If the police believe that an interview needs to be conducted right away to collect evidence, then they will not wait for child protective workers to arrive. If child protective workers find children that need urgent medical attention, then they will not wait for the police to arrive.

Police officers who reported experiencing delays still expressed support for the IRT program. When asked what he does if child protective workers have not arrived at the scene, one detective remarked, "We try to wait. If [the case] is with the IRT unit there are not too many problems. If they're capped and it goes to the normal unit, you can forget about it. You might as well do the case yourself." For many reasons, the typical pace of frontline police work is usually faster than that of child protection. The additional resources devoted to IRT cases increase the capacity of child protective workers to respond quickly in critical situations.

Minimizing Trauma during Interviews and Exams

The IRT program seeks to minimize trauma for children involved in investigations of abuse or neglect in two ways: by reducing the number of interviews and medical examinations and, whenever possible, by conducting joint interviews and medical exams in child-friendly settings, such as CACs and specialized hospital-based centers.

Before IRT, no agency collected data on the number of exams or interviews conducted. Since the program's inception, however, cases involving multiple exams and interviews have declined. Among children needing a medical exam in 1998, 19 percent received more than one exam, and 10 percent were examined three or more times. Four years later, in 2002, almost every child experienced only one exam (96 percent), and no child underwent more than two exams.

Similar progress has occurred in the number of interviews children undergo in the initial investigation. In 1998, 14 percent of children involved in IRT cases were interviewed three or more times. By 2002, almost no cases involved more than two interviews. This change is not because of the addition of marginal cases; the absolute number of cases with two or more interviews has declined.

It is not possible to know how many interviews and exams took place before the IRT program began, but the sizable number of cases with multiple interviews and exams that occurred during the first year—when key managers focused attention on the issue—suggests that there were more of these cases before the program existed. Child welfare staff, police, and prosecutors who worked on child abuse cases before IRT believe that the program streamlined case processing. One detective commented that child welfare used to refer criminal cases of child abuse to the district attorney's office, which then referred the case to the police for investigation a week or two after the initial allegation. This meant that at least two interviews were conducted (one by child protection, another by the detective), and that marks, bruises, and other evidence of child abuse had often disappeared. This detective now rarely receives a case from the district attorney; most start either as IRT cases or become IRT cases after an initial investigation.

Joint Interviews

The IRT program seeks to conduct joint interviews whenever further investigation of a case is warranted. Child advocates have long argued for more joint interviews and investigations, and a five-city study of cases of sexual abuse and serious physical abuse concludes that "joint investigations result in good outcomes for both children and practitioners" (Tjaden and Anhalt 1994, iv).

The overall rate of joint interviews in IRT cases has stayed near 55 percent over the five years of the program, twice the 27 percent rate found in the Tjaden and Anhalt study cited above. This rate includes all cases, even those that did not need medical exams. Cases that receive the higher levels of attention, type I and II cases, had higher rates of joint interviewing in 2002 (81 and 61 percent, respectively) than type III cases (44 percent).

In cases with more legal activity, joint interviews took place more often. The rate of joint interviews significantly increased ($p < .001$) within each type when child protection or the police removed a child, the Family Court was involved, or when the Family Court granted remand. For example, police and child protective workers conducted joint interviews in 71 percent of type II cases that involved removals, compared with 57 percent of type II cases that did not involve removals.

To further understand the factors associated with joint interviews, researchers used the program's data to conduct a multivariate analysis. This analysis identified five factors that contribute to the likelihood of a joint interview occurring: the type of case, where the interview occurred, arrival sequence, and the borough in which the case took place ($p < .001$). Joint interviews occurred more often in CACs, police stations, and hospitals, and least often at the child's home. The multivariate analysis also had an interesting finding on response times: joint interviews took place more often when child protection and the police arrived at about the same time (within the same response time category). If either the police or child protection arrived before the other, the likelihood of a joint interview declined in about equal amounts.

Joint interviews do not occur in every case for many reasons. Differing response times or lack of staff can make coordination difficult. Having the police and child protective workers on the scene at the same time is a necessary but not sufficient condition for a joint interview. When emergency rooms are experiencing high volume, child protection or police may not be able to wait for doctors to finish their exam so they can conduct a joint interview. Four of the five assistant district attorneys assigned to child abuse or special victims prosecution that researchers interviewed regularly attend joint interviews, but the fifth cited understaffing in the prosecutor's office for not having attended a joint interview.

Interview and Exam Locations

The IRT program aims to have interviews and exams conducted in child-friendly settings such as child advocacy centers or specialized hospital centers. The type of case can affect where interviews take place. About 20 percent of type II cases hold interviews in CACs, compared with just 4 percent of type III cases. The majority of type III case interviews take place in a child's home, compared with a third of type II cases. Less than 10 percent of cases have interviews in child welfare offices or schools.[17]

Three of every four medical exams take place in hospital emergency rooms, with the remainder occurring in CACs, pediatric centers, and at private doctors' offices. Given the urgency of IRT cases, this is not surprising.

Many barriers prevent more widespread use of child advocacy centers. There were no CACs in some areas, including Queens. Most CACs do not have doctors on 24-hour call, and child welfare staff reported that others turned away cases because of inadequate staffing. Also, some CACs only accept certain types of cases. The primary obstacle, however, seems to be that most child advocacy centers operate only during normal business hours. While many IRT cases are initiated during the day, by the time caseworkers and police locate the children and decide that exams or interviews should take place at a CAC, the facilities are often closed. Cases initiated after hours or on weekends cannot use most CACs.

Occasionally, confusion and conflict occur between CAC or hospital social workers and child protective workers because responsibilities are not clearly delineated. Hospital, CAC, and child protective workers all voiced concerns about these issues. Two of the seven CAC and hospital representatives researchers interviewed reported that they felt better qualified to interview children than child protective workers. Several child protective workers and IRT coordinators voiced concerns that child welfare representatives were not included in joint interviews at CACs and were usually relegated to an observation role. Said one IRT coordinator, "It stifles the caseworker; it doesn't allow them to develop their skills as interviewers."

Case Outcomes

In combining child welfare and police investigations, the IRT program seeks to remove perpetrators from the home, rather than children, while maintaining child welfare's goals of ensuring child safety and preserving families. Those who advocate for a greater role for law enforcement point out that before the program was established, reports of abuse and neglect often resulted in the removal of children, while the alleged perpetrators remained at home. From this point of view, the lack of a police presence risked further trauma to already abused and neglected children.

The trends in IRT cases show a decline in the removal of children and an increase in arrests (figure 2.3). The proportion of cases in which only the perpetrator was removed (defined as arrest made, but the child not removed) rose from 10 percent in 1998 to 16 percent in 2002. The percentage of IRT cases in which only a child was removed fell from 15 to 7 percent during the same period. Cases that resulted in the removal of both the child and the perpetrator also fell. Overall, cases involving child removals fell sharply from 34 percent in 1998 to 15 percent in 2002, while arrests declined from 29 percent in 1998 to 24 percent in 2002.

These trends in removals are consistent with the program's goals. In most IRT cases, no one is removed from the home. But in IRT cases

Figure 2.3. Removal Trends in IRT Cases, 1998–2002 (percent)

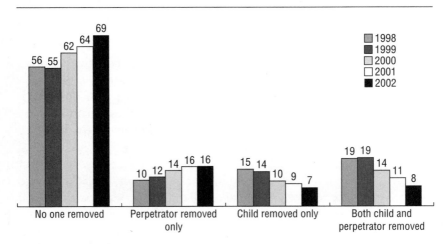

Source: Derived from Instant Response Team program data.

Note: Perpetrator removals are defined as an arrest made (N = 11,750).

resulting in the removal of either the child or the alleged perpetrator, children were removed more often than alleged perpetrators in 1998 (57 percent of such cases). By 2002, alleged perpetrators were removed more often than children (68 percent of such cases). Among those cases where no removal took place in 2000, SCR data show that two-thirds were unfounded. The remainder involved cases with substantiated allegations that did not result in removals.[18]

Discussion

Child welfare and law enforcement implemented a program to coordinate responses to severe child maltreatment reports successfully. On key indicators, the program changed how children involved in these cases are treated. As with most efforts, the program might build on its success.

Child welfare officials planned to have the IRT program respond to every allegation of *severe* maltreatment. Indeed, the program expanded to more than 4,000 cases from 1998 to 2002, a period when the caseloads of child protective workers declined. IRT may contribute to the capacity of child protective workers to handle cases. Child protective workers on IRT cases save travel time that can be used to handle other cases. In addition, increasing the size of the program brings economies of scale. The human resources that child welfare devoted to the program—a program manager and the IRT coordinators—have remained constant despite the increase in caseloads.

The continued growth in the number of IRT cases increases demands on the police and prosecutors. While researchers found strong support for the program among frontline staff at these agencies, workers at each agency cited workload pressure as a primary concern. Police often see their job as making arrests and developing cases. With only a quarter of all IRT cases resulting in arrests, some officers may fear that responding to IRT cases makes them look unproductive. In some boroughs, heavy workloads appear to be the primary reason that frontline police and prosecutor staff have developed work patterns that deviate from the IRT protocol.

Many people researchers interviewed recommended that the program receive more resources. Adding more staff at each of the three agencies, providing additional funding for CACs, and arranging more comprehensive access to car services would likely improve the program. Budgetary constraints, however, make this development unlikely.

While IRT is a joint program, the child welfare agency has the most at stake. It has committed the most resources and has the management and data resources best suited to address issues associated with growth. The ideas below might improve the program's efficiency, allowing IRT to better target cases that are most likely to require police involvement. In addition, introducing some data-driven accountability mechanisms for individual caseworkers and IRT coordinators might further improve the performance of frontline staff.

There is no established limit on the number of cases that the IRT program can handle, and for good reason: all cases of severe maltreatment can benefit from an instant response. To manage how its coordinators use their discretion in selecting cases, child welfare implemented a cap system to restrict the number of cases each unit handles. This system has not produced the desired results. Well-intentioned staff have found ways to work around the cap system, but these improvisations reduce the program's timeliness as coordinators scramble to find uncapped units.

As part of this study, the IRT program revised its data collection instrument. The revised instrument allows managers to disseminate aggregate, coordinator-level reports on the results of IRT cases, lets coordinators see patterns in the cases they select, and allows managers to identify and work with coordinators who may be selecting inappropriate cases. Regular borough-level meetings with managers to review the borough's data would create opportunities for increased learning. Child protective managers might set up these meetings using the New York City Police Department's widely heralded CompStat model and could include a police and prosecutor representatives.[19]

The coordinator-level information also could be used in regular meetings of the IRT coordinators to review case studies of decisions that each IRT coordinator made. These meetings might involve examining the data IRT coordinators received from the State Central Registry and other information that coordinators used to decide about initiating an instant response. By working as a group, the coordinators could share successful techniques for weeding out unfounded cases and develop best practices to inform their work.

Finally, managers could use data available in the redesigned IRT database to reward caseworkers with consistently strong performance and work with the few weak performers to identify and solve problems. Making response times a component of caseworker evaluation would further emphasize the need to handle IRT cases with the utmost urgency. Improving coordinators' abilities to spot the most serious cases would reinforce the fact that IRT cases are special events that demand immediate attention.

IRT cases are already divided into three types, with the primary operational difference being the rank of the police respondent. A more radical reform might keep the current types but split IRT cases into two categories. One category could involve the most serious allegations that warrant an immediate police response. This category might be reserved for cases involving allegations of severe maltreatment where the child's location is known and there is imminent danger to the child. Police would be expected to arrive within two hours, as would ACS caseworkers. A second category might include cases involving allegations of severe maltreatment where the location of the child is unknown or where the child does not appear to be in imminent danger. In these cases, caseworkers would be dispatched immediately by car service, but police would be called in only after an initial investigation by the caseworker. Police could meet caseworkers at CACs or other locations once doctors had completed necessary medical exams. If caseworkers needed a police officer or SVS detective at the scene, they could request one through the IRT coordinator or the 911 system. This approach would allow a quicker response than the existing "rapid response" standard (a visit within 24 hours) and might use the police more efficiently.

Improvements in response time and case selection would give child welfare managers leverage in efforts to increase training of police and prosecutors. More regular training that included combined classes of child protective workers, police, and prosecutors would lead to a better understanding of the program. CAC and hospital social workers might also benefit from these sessions. Outreach to these groups could smooth the process of conducting joint interviews, and training could clarify roles and emphasize the need for child welfare caseworkers and medical social workers to share knowledge.

Conclusion

Child welfare agencies, the police, and prosecutors have much to gain by coordinating child protective investigations. The IRT program demonstrates that fast, coordinated responses can improve information sharing and case processing as well as increase the effectiveness of law enforcement. The vulnerable children involved in these cases are the biggest and most important winners: reduced trauma and a process that allows more children to stay home are major improvements.

The IRT program is a model for how local jurisdictions can handle reports of severe child maltreatment. But localities interested in creating a version of the program cannot simply replicate the program's protocol. This study and past research show the value of planning and management resources. IRT succeeded in large part because of the investment in solving issues of accountability, role definition, information sharing, management, and case processing procedures—issues that were not sufficiently addressed in past efforts in New York City and elsewhere.

Other studies show that collaborative efforts often require ongoing attention. Collaborative routines can deteriorate over time as excitement about new programs fades and the environments in which they operate change. These tendencies are countered, however, by the benefits of a well-functioning collaboration. IRT has created a new way of handling reports of severe child maltreatment—a method that advances the mission of each agency involved. The web of interagency relationships and strong support of frontline staff has created a reserve of goodwill that each agency can draw upon to sustain its enhanced ability to serve children in need.

3

Does the Criminal Justice System Force Children into Foster Care?

I n the 1980s and 1990s, survey after survey showed that crime topped the list of citizen concerns in the United States (Jacobson 2005). In response to high crime rates and popular concern, big cities across the country hired more police officers. Police departments instituted new forms of policing modeled on the "broken windows theory" of crime that called for aggressive enforcement of minor offenses.[1] Many departments developed data-driven management initiatives that used geographic information systems to hold local police commanders accountable for crime in their jurisdictions. New York City pioneered this new approach, hiring thousands of new officers in the early 1990s, developing the widely replicated CompStat process in 1994, and increasing arrests of panhandlers, squeegee men, and other low-level offenders (Silverman 1999). Crime declined drastically across the nation and especially in New York City.

While child advocates lauded the decline in crime, the increase in female incarceration raised concerns that aggressive enforcement might be driving more children into foster care. Law enforcement focused on areas with the highest crime rates, which also happened to be minority neighborhoods with high unemployment, substance abuse issues, and poverty rates—all factors correlated with foster care placement rates (Derezotes, Poertner, and Testa 2004). Could aggressive policing have pushed kids into foster care by incarcerating their mothers—even for minor infractions? Were mothers in these hard-hit neighborhoods facing a double punishment, incarceration and the removal of their children? And for city budget mandarins, did the increased emphasis on enforcing and prosecuting minor infractions impose a double cost by requiring increased criminal justice and foster care expenditures?[2]

This chapter presents the first large-scale study of the criminal histories of the mothers of children in foster care. It identifies the frequency of criminal justice involvement by mothers with children in foster care, the types of offenses, and the sequence of those offenses relative to foster care placement. Almost 66 percent of the mothers had no criminal history whatsoever, and only 3 percent of the total had convictions for violent felonies. Instead, among mothers with criminal histories, those histories were rarely the cause of the removal of children, but at times appeared to be a consequence of removal.

Understanding the Issue

From 1990 to 2000, the annual rate of growth of incarcerated women averaged 8.1 percent, higher than the 6.2 percent average increase of incarcerated men. While the number of incarcerated men grew 77 percent during that period, the number of incarcerated women increased 110 percent (Bureau of Justice Statistics 2003). The rise in female incarceration has particular implications for children since an estimated 66 to 80 percent of incarcerated women are the primary caretakers of their minor children before arrest (Beatty 1997; Beckerman 1994; Johnston 1995; Snell 1994). Thus, an apparent consequence of the increasing rate of incarceration among women is a rising number of children who are separated from their primary caregivers.

The incarceration of an abusive or neglectful parent may bring relief in some cases, but scholars generally agree that a parent's incarceration usually has far more adverse than positive effects on children (Hagan and Dinovitzer 1999; Hairston 1991). A parent's absence alters a family's structure and dynamics. In addition, a parent's incarceration usually brings more economic hardship for family members who are left to care for children (Hagan and Dinovitzer 1999). Since arrest and incarceration disproportionately affect minority and disadvantaged communities, those communities may face increased challenges in caring for the children of prisoners.

The rates of conviction and incarceration among women also have implications for child welfare agencies. Removing a primary caretaker raises the possibility that children may be placed outside the home, sometimes in foster care. This risk is increased if the primary caretaker is a single parent (Smith, Elstein, and ABA Center 1994). Most child welfare systems do not collect data on the involvement of mothers in the criminal justice system, and they typically do not have programs designed to address the special needs of children separated from their mothers in such situations. Police departments may have policies regarding the minor children of people who are arrested, but police officers do not always inquire about an arrested person's children, and their interpretations of existing policies may vary.[3]

Incarceration of a mother can complicate the child welfare agency's family reunification policies. Although continued contact between parent and child is usually a necessary component of family reunification, arranging and supervising visits with incarcerated parents takes time and resources, and it requires cooperation between child welfare and corrections agencies (see chapter 4). Finally, the absence of parental involvement can ultimately result in the termination of parental rights (Genty 1995). The 1997 Adoption and Safe Families Act requires child welfare agencies to file a termination petition if a child has been in foster care for 15 of the most recent 22 months, unless the agency can document a compelling reason that termination would not be in the child's best interest.[4]

Little research has been conducted on the association between mothers' criminal history and children's placement into foster care. Basic questions about the issue are unaddressed: What proportion of foster children has mothers who were ever convicted or incarcerated? What proportion of foster children has mothers who are incarcerated while they are in care? Does a mother's conviction or incarceration tend to precede or follow a child's placement in foster care? Do children's outcomes in the foster care system—their length of stay, the frequency of their placement changes, and their level of institutional care—tend to vary as a function of their mothers' criminal histories? Finally, does a mother's incarceration make it more likely that her child will be adopted?

To provide some answers to these questions, researchers matched identifiers of foster children's biological mothers from child welfare records with criminal history records collected by state and local criminal justice agencies. Using this data match, the researchers identified the rate of conviction and incarceration among mothers of foster children, described the events leading to conviction and incarceration, and tracked the timing of parental convictions/incarceration and children's entry into foster care. The match also provided descriptive data on the relationship between mothers' criminal history and children's experiences in foster care, including their level of care, absences without leave, and chances of being adopted.

Research Methods

This chapter presents a study of two entry cohorts of biological mothers of foster children drawn from the New York City's child welfare administrative data. An entry cohort is defined as all the children who first entered New York City foster care during a particular period—in this case, a year. The first entry cohort consisted of all mothers whose children entered foster care in calendar year 1991; the second, those who entered care in fiscal year 1997.[5] Crime rates, police staffing, and crime prevention strategies varied between these two periods, as did child welfare policies and characteristics of the children entering foster care. Having two cohorts allowed the researchers to compare the criminal histories of the mothers at two times to see if policy-related differences strongly affected criminal justice characteristics.

In theory, the child welfare administrative data contain information that identifies all foster children and the relatives living with them at the time they enter the child welfare system. Although the database contains information on some fathers, in most cases the father's name is unlisted; most children in New York City foster care come from female-headed, single-parent families, and, for many reasons, mothers may not want to divulge the name of a father to child welfare workers. This lack of information prevented researchers from incorporating fathers into the analysis—an unintended and unfortunate weakness in this approach. The administrative data also include data about children's movements within the foster care system, such as transfers from one placement to another, legal activities such as hearings and dispositions related to Article 10 abuse/neglect petitions, and a host of additional information. The data are linked with another database that contains the maternal Social Security numbers needed to match foster care data with records maintained by state criminal justice agencies.[6]

1991 Cohort

The 1991 cohort included 13,579 children. Child welfare administrative data were available for the mothers of 11,349 of these children. The cohort contained 8,897 parents, including 7,657 biological mothers. The mothers in the cohort had a median age of 31 years, and the children had a median age of 5 years. Figure 3.1 displays the age distribution for children on the date that they first entered care. Fueled by widespread crack cocaine use and policies that often led to immediate placement following positive maternal or neonatal drug tests, close to half the children were less than 1 year old. Early adolescents age 11 to 15 made up another large group.

The children who entered care in 1991 stayed in foster care for an average of 1,056 days (or 2.9 years) before their first discharge.[7] Most children lived in foster boarding homes (54 percent) with the remainder evenly split between living with a relative in kinship care (24 percent) and congregate care—group care staffed by professional child care workers (21 percent). Children initially placed in foster boarding homes were slightly younger than those placed in kinship care. As expected, teenagers made up the bulk of children initially placed in congregate care.

Figure 3.1. Child Age Distribution

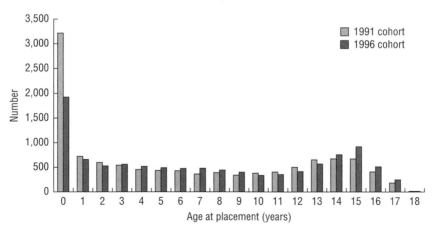

Source: Child Care Review Service.

1996 Cohort

For the 1996 cohort, researchers used New York City's fiscal year dates (July 1, 1996, to June 30, 1997), which allowed them to incorporate the most recent WMS records available at the time this research started. The fiscal year 1996 entry cohort included 12,269 children, with available mother information on 10,565 children. A total of 7,128 biological mothers were matched with children in the entry cohort. The mothers had a median age of 34 years; the median age for the children was 7 years. The age distribution of children in the 1996 cohort was similar to that found for the 1991 cohort for children over the age of 1, as seen in figure 3.1. Reflecting in part reductions in crack cocaine use and a policy change that barred automatic removal based on a positive drug test alone, the 1996 cohort included substantially fewer infants.

The findings on the children's foster care variables are similar to those described for the 1991 cohort. Table 3.1 shows the age, ethnicity, religion, and marital status of mothers in the 1991 and 1996 cohorts. Both religion and marital status were unknown or missing for many mothers and were not included in later analyses.

Design and Procedure

Matching child welfare and state criminal justice data.[8] The child welfare data used in the matching process included the biological mothers' name, age, date of birth, marital status, and, in most cases, Social Security number. Using a standard algorithm developed over the course of numerous prior matching projects, state criminal justice staff matched these data with individual arrest and sentencing histories. The algorithm used various combinations of Social Security number, name, gender, and dates of birth to match criminal history data on the mothers. Once matched, the state criminal history data includes criminal history variables as well as a New York State Identification Number (NYSID) for each person in the sample with an adult arrest history. Because NYSIDs are assigned and then matched based on fingerprints obtained each time an individual is arrested, they provide a high degree of reliability.

The state criminal history data include arrest charges, Uniform Crime Reporting charge categories, and flags indicating whether the charge was for an offense related to drugs, prostitution, weapons, child victimization, violent felony, or motor vehicles. State staff matched the cohorts with

Table 3.1. Characteristics of Mothers for the 1991 and 1996 Cohorts

	1991 cohort (N = 7,657)	1996 cohort (N = 7,128)
Mother's median age[a]	31 (SD = 8.39)	34 (SD = 8.57)
Child's median age[a]	5 (SD = 5.84)	7 (SD = 5.64)
Percent male	50.2 (n = 5,697)	50.8 (n = 3,621)
Ethnicity (%)		
White	5.0	3.3
Black	55.2	43.9
Hispanic	20.1	19.0
Asian	0.5	0.5
Other/unknown[b]	19.3	33.4
Religion (%)		
Catholic	13	9
Jewish	1	0
Protestant	19	11
Other	2	3
Unknown/none	65	77
Marital status (%)		
Married	5	15
Single	46	71
Separated/divorced	1	3
Widowed	0	1
Missing	48	10

a. Median age is shown because the age distribution was not normally distributed.

b. The special panel that oversaw New York City's child welfare system from 1996 to 2000 cited missing race and religion data as a problem. In a separate study, Vera found that overwhelmed data entry staff often entered only basic information needed to open cases and track movements in the early 1990s.

their records of arrest charges, disposition charges, and sentencing information for each person's entire adult history (since age 18). Researchers for this chapter reduced the dataset to information associated with the top charge for each event because state data sometimes returned information that included multiple charges for a single arrest event. This ensured compatibility with data provided by the city's department of corrections that was also based on the top charge. The state data include only those arrests that resulted in convictions.

The matched files and NYSID data obtained from the state were then sent to city corrections staff to obtain data on detention. City corrections data include information on admissions and releases from jail. Unlike state data, city corrections data incorporate information on individuals detained but not sentenced and have more accurate dates of admission and release for those who have their sentences commuted or secure work releases. None of the data included juvenile cases, which are sealed under state law.

Measurement

Researchers extracted from the child welfare administrative data the date of the child's placement, the level of care of that placement (kinship, foster boarding home, or congregate care), and the length of time spent in foster care before any discharge. They also aggregated the number of transfers to new placements and the number of times a child went absent from foster care without permission (commonly referred to as AWOL [absent without leave] events; see chapter 6 for more information on the limits of these data). As expected, for both the 1991 and 1996 cohorts, a child's age correlated positively with a shorter length of stay in foster care, a higher level of care (i.e., older children were more likely to be placed in congregate care), and the likelihood of being AWOL at some point in their foster care stay.

Maternal Arrest and Conviction

Classifying arrest history into meaningful groups is difficult. Dividing the sample into mothers who had *ever* been arrested and convicted versus mothers who had *never* been arrested and convicted meant grouping together mothers convicted many years ago with those who were convicted more recently. The researchers reasoned that, compared with more distant arrest events, recent convictions are more likely to affect children's well-being.

Arrest and conviction data were available through December 1998 and included a maximum of 18 months following June 1997, which was the last possible date of entry into foster care for children in the 1996 cohort (fiscal year July 1, 1996, to June 30, 1997). Researchers selected an 18-month window before and after each child's date of admission into care because they wished to examine the rate of maternal arrest in a comparable time frame before and after children entered foster care.

Maternal Incarceration

Most convictions do not result in incarceration in jail or prison, but incarceration carries implications that are more drastic. Though state criminal justice records contain data on *any* history of sentencing, including time served before sentence and incarceration, researchers used both state and local data to measure maternal incarceration. The state operates the prison system, while cities and counties are in charge of jails in New York and most other states.[9] Thus, the state has the highest quality data on prison sentences, while local jurisdictions usually have the highest quality data on jail sentences. The local data also contain information on detention spells without sentencing (such as pre-trial detention) that the state does not record. An important difference in these data is that the state records have incarceration data based on *sentencing,* whereas the New York City records contain data on *actual time served.* To reconcile these differences in the two data sources, researchers assumed that the incarceration began on the date the individual was disposed (state criminal justice data do not include the sentence date) and assumed that each person served the minimum sentence.

The local data contained information for each cohort on jail and detention records for up to three years before and three years after the target date—the date of the child's placement into foster care. As detention and jail time are limited to a maximum of 12 and 15 months, respectively, allowing three years before or after the child's placement should capture the possible effects of local sentences and detention time on child outcome.

Results

Lifetime Conviction Rates and Arrest Charges

Most birth mothers of children in foster care have no contact with the criminal justice system. Among those that do have contact, the involvement may be brief and take place many years before the placement of the child. Given the social and economic marginalization of this group, this point needs emphasis. This research is not intended to further demonize a population that already faces enormous obstacles in raising their children and leading productive lives.

Just over a third of mothers with children in foster care have at least one arrest that led to a conviction. Thirty-nine percent of the mothers in the 1991 cohort were arrested and convicted, as were 35 percent of mothers in the 1996 cohort. In each cohort, arrested and convicted mothers had a median of two arrests and convictions in their adult lifetime, but an average of five such events—suggesting that relatively few women accounted for a large share of the total. In the 1991 cohort, mothers who were ever arrested and convicted were younger (30 versus 32.2 years) and had younger children (4.9 versus 7.1 years).[10] The average age at first conviction was 25.9 years in the 1991 cohort and 25.8 in the 1996 cohort.

Table 3.2 shows the number and percent of mothers in the 1991 and 1996 cohorts who were arrested and convicted for misdemeanors and felony offenses since the age of 18. Misdemeanor offenses made up most of the convictions, though about half those with a record had at least one felony conviction. Mothers with a felony conviction had more arrests that led to a conviction than those with only misdemeanors.

Table 3.3 breaks down convictions for each type of charge for the 1991 and 1996 cohorts. These results suggest that drug, prostitution,

Table 3.2. Mothers' Aggregate Arrest Statistics, 1991 and 1996 Cohorts

	1991		1996	
Cohort	Number	Percent	Number	Percent
Entire sample	7,657	100.0	7,128	100.0
Ever convicted	3,004	39.2	2,483	34.8
Only misdemeanor charges	1,192	15.6	1,091	15.3
At least one felony charge	1,408	18.4	991	13.9
Unknown charge/no disposition	403	5.3	401	5.6
Convicted subsample	3,004		2,483	
Total convictions	16,461		11,598	
Total misdemeanors	10,957		7,612	
Total felonies	5,504		3,986	
Total convictions for misdemeanor-only group	5,832	35.4	4,365	37.6
Total convictions for at least one felony group	10,155	61.7	6,755	58.2
Unknown arrest charge or no disposition info group	474	2.9	478	4.1

Table 3.3. Total Convictions for Mothers by Type of Charge, 1991 and 1996 Cohorts

Cohort	1991		1996	
	Number	Percent	Number	Percent
Mothers in sample	7,657	100.0	7,128	100.0
Ever convicted	3,004		2,483	
Total convictions	16,461		11,598	
Violent felony	1,320	8.0	980	8.4
Firearm offense	146	0.9	146	1.3
Child victim	400	2.4	471	4.1
Drug offense	5,365	32.5	4,096	35.3
Weapons	703	4.3	550	4.7
DWI	40	0.2	22	0.2
Prostitution	4,392	26.7	2,753	23.7
Larceny/theft	3,286	20.0	2,001	17.3

and theft or larceny charges account for the greatest proportion of arrest charges.

Temporal Changes of Conviction Rates

Researchers examined how the number of arrests leading to convictions changed over time, with a special focus on the year before and after child placement. If maternal contact with the criminal justice system contributes to a child's placement into foster care, it stands to reason that the most powerful effects occur when contact with the two systems takes place at about the same time. Figures 3.2 and 3.3 illustrate the annual number of misdemeanor and felony arrests for the 1991 and 1996 cohorts. Many contacts with the criminal justice system took place many years before placement. However, the number of convictions rises steadily in the years before placement, peaks in the year of placement, and remains high in the years following placement. The patterns for both cohorts are similar, but the 1991 cohort provides a clearer indication of this pattern over the seven years following placement. Findings for the 1996 cohort are less definitive.

Figure 3.2. 1991 Cohort Felony and Misdemeanor Arrests, 1980–98

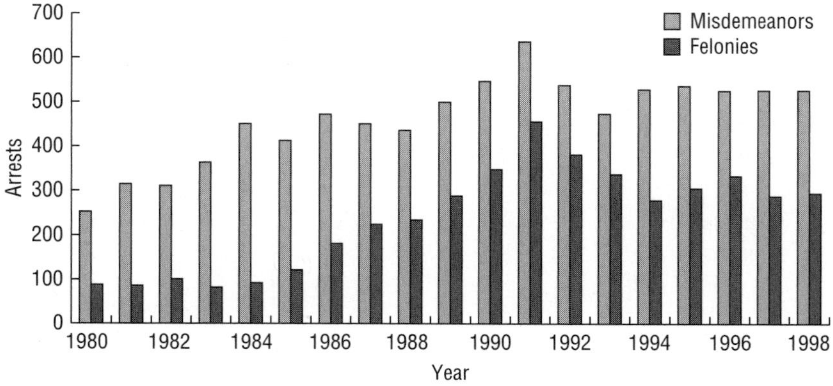

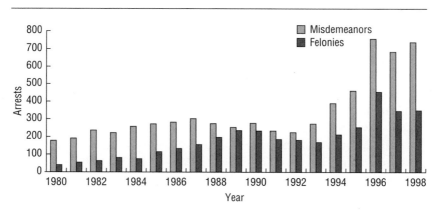

Source: Researchers' calculations based on data obtained from New York State criminal justice staff and New York City child welfare and corrections staff.

Figure 3.3. 1996 Cohort Felony and Misdemeanor Arrests, 1980–98

Source: Researchers' calculations based on data obtained from New York State criminal justice staff and New York City child welfare and corrections staff.

Researchers paid special attention to patterns in the rate of the most common convictions—for drugs, prostitution, and theft or larceny—to see if the rate of maternal conviction for these charges changes around the time of foster care placement. They plotted the number of convictions in both cohorts for these three categories from 1980 to 1998. This analysis is based only on the top charge recorded for these convictions. If a given conviction included multiple charges, the data used for this analysis would only record the most serious of those charges. Figure 3.4 shows the rates for the 1991 cohort and suggests that the rate of drug conviction charges increases over time and remains high, especially following the year when the child was placed, whereas the rate of prostitution convictions decreases in the years after the child is placed into care. Theft or larceny convictions rise along with drug charges, peaking during the year the child enters care, but decline after that year. One explanation for the increase in drug convictions is that it reflects a worsening spiral of substance abuse and involvement in the drug trade that began before the child's placement and continues in the years after the removal.

For the 1996 cohort, figure 3.5 presents slightly different trends from those observed in 1991. While prostitution convictions decline over time, reaching their lowest levels during the year the child enters care, they also rise sharply after that point. Theft or larceny convictions also

Figure 3.4. 1991 Cohort Drug, Prostitution, and Theft Convictions, 1980–98

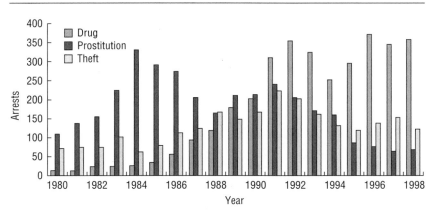

Source: Researchers' calculations based on data obtained from New York State criminal justice staff and New York City child welfare and corrections staff.

Figure 3.5. 1996 Cohort Drug, Prostitution, and Theft Convictions, 1980–98

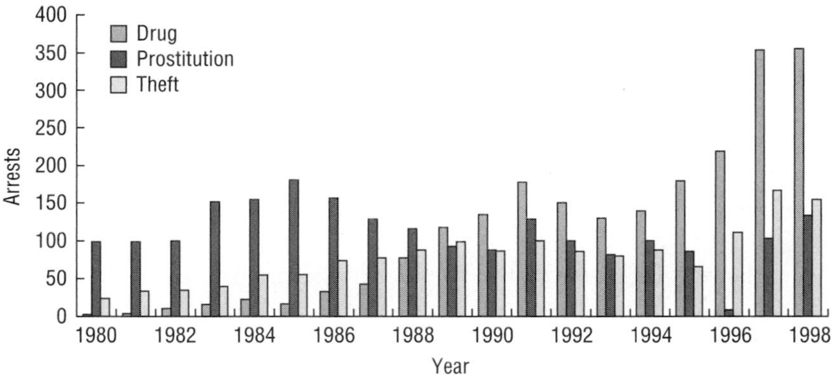

Source: Researchers' calculations based on data obtained from New York State criminal justice staff and New York City child welfare and corrections staff.

rise after the 1996 entry year. Only drug convictions demonstrate a similar pattern to that of 1991, showing a slight rise in the early 1990s and then, around 1996, a sharp rise that continues in the following years.

Rates and Types of Maternal Convictions around the Time of Child Placement

Researchers focused their attention on the convictions of mothers that occurred in the 18 months before and 18 months after their children's placement in foster care. Far fewer mothers were convicted in this shorter period than were ever convicted—1,194 mothers (15.6 percent of the 1991 cohort) and 1,279 mothers (17.9 percent of the 1996 cohort). The most common types of convictions remained the same for this period: drug offenses, prostitution, and theft or larceny.

Figures 3.6 and 3.7 show the percentage of mothers that fall into each arrest category during the 18 months before and after child placement. *The vast majority of mothers were not arrested on charges that led to a conviction during the period before and after placement* (84 percent of the 1991 cohort and 82 percent of the 1996 cohort). Roughly 1 in every 14 mothers (7 percent of the 1991 cohort) and 1 in every 10 (10 percent of the 1996 cohort) were convicted for at least one misdemeanor but no felony. Fewer mothers

Figure 3.6. Convictions among 1991 Cohort by Type

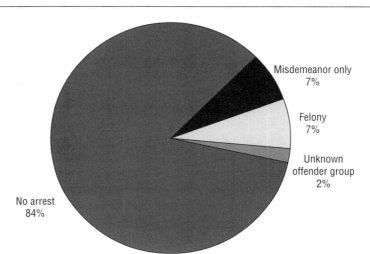

Source: Researchers' calculations based on data obtained from New York State criminal justice staff and New York City child welfare and corrections staff.

Figure 3.7. Convictions among 1996 Cohort by Type

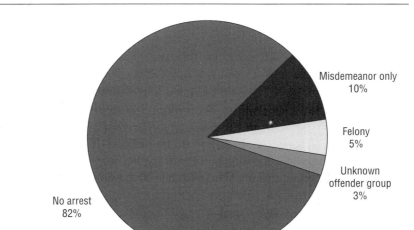

Source: Researchers' calculations based on data obtained from New York State criminal justice staff and New York City child welfare and corrections staff.

had felony convictions during the period surrounding placement (7 percent of the 1991 cohort and 5 percent of the 1996 cohort). A small proportion was convicted for an unknown charge (2 percent of the 1991 cohort and 3 percent of the 1996 cohort). For both cohorts, misdemeanor convictions outnumbered felony convictions.

Incarceration Rate of Mothers

While the arrest and conviction data in this study show the degree of criminal activity among mothers of foster children, researchers also examined events that led to incarceration. For both cohorts, researchers classified mothers according to the type of incarcerations they experienced: no conviction and no incarceration, arrest and conviction but no incarceration, detention with no sentence, jail sentence, and prison sentence. When more than one sentence occurred, researchers grouped according to the most severe sentence. For instance, mothers who served jail time for one offense, but who had been sentenced to prison for another offense, were included in the prison sentence group.[11]

For the 1991 cohort, 22 percent of the mothers experienced incarceration, but most of these sentences were for jail, not prison. As shown in figure 3.8, 61 percent of mothers (4,564 of 7,567) were never convicted, and 17 percent were convicted but never sentenced to jail or prison. About

Figure 3.8. Number of Mothers per Sentence Category, 1991 Cohort ($n = 7,657$)

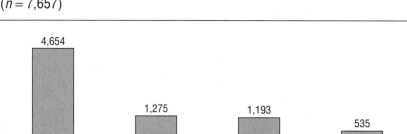

Source: Researchers' calculations based on data obtained from New York State criminal justice staff and New York City child welfare and corrections staff.

16 percent were sentenced to jail but never to prison, and 7 percent were sentenced to prison. The percentages of children in care with a biological mother in each category are similar. The figures for the 1996 cohort are similar to the 1991 cohort, though slightly smaller—likely because the cohort had five fewer years at risk for incarceration. Twenty-two percent were sentenced to incarceration during their adult lifetime, and jail accounted for the majority of the sentences. Overall, 65 percent of mothers were never convicted and 13 percent were convicted but never incarcerated; 13 percent were sentenced to jail, and 5 percent were sentenced to prison. Additionally, 3 percent were detained without being sentenced in the three years before or after their child was placed in care (figure 3.9).

Child Placement and Maternal Arrest

These data cannot test whether a mother's conviction *led* to a child's placement into foster care. Researchers can, however, estimate how closely linked the two events are chronologically and make reasoned assessments that a mother's conviction may have contributed to child placement. Researchers examined the sequencing of the convictions of mothers that occurred in the 18 months before and 18 months after the children's placement. They were especially interested in convictions that occurred closest to the date of placement.

Figure 3.9. Number of Mothers per Sentence Category, 1996 Cohort ($n = 7,127$)

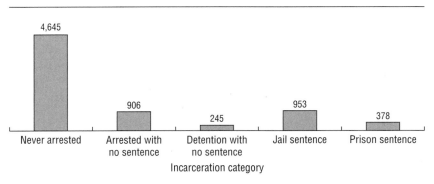

Source: Researchers' calculations based on data obtained from New York State criminal justice staff and New York City child welfare and corrections staff.

Examining convictions that took place near the time of placement shows that mothers were arrested more often *after, rather than before,* their children were placed in care (though some mothers were arrested both before and after the placement). Figure 3.10 shows that of the mothers in the 1991 cohort who were *ever* arrested and convicted, 58 percent were arrested at least once on a misdemeanor charge in the 18 months before the children's placement, and 70 percent were convicted at least once in the 18 months after the placement. Figure 3.11 shows the same pattern for the 1996 cohort. For both cohorts, mothers who were arrested for misdemeanor offenses accounted for the greatest increase in the conviction rate.

Maternal Conviction around the Time of Child Placement

Within the 18-month time frame, the mother's last arrest charges before the children's placement into foster care were most likely for drug offenses, theft or larceny, and prostitution. In the 1996 cohort, a common charge was "crimes against a child" (15 percent), which occurred as often as theft or larceny, whereas this pattern was not pronounced for the 1991 cohort. As discussed in chapter 2 of this volume, the police made deliberate efforts to arrest parents in more child abuse cases starting in 1996.

Figure 3.10. Maternal Arrest Rates by Offender Group, 1991 Cohort

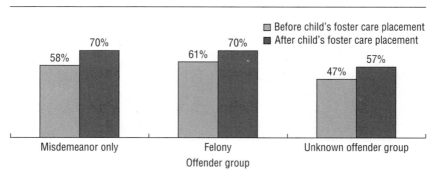

Source: Researchers' calculations based on data obtained from New York State criminal justice staff and New York City child welfare and corrections staff.

Note: Some mothers were arrested both before and after the placement.

Figure 3.11. Maternal Arrest Rates by Offender Group, 1996 Cohort

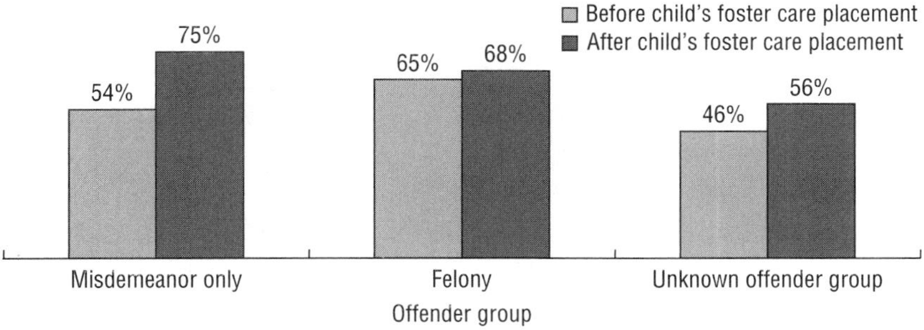

Bar chart with legend:
- Before child's foster care placement
- After child's foster care placement

Misdemeanor only: 54%, 75%
Felony: 65%, 68%
Unknown offender group: 46%, 56%

Offender group

Source: Researchers' calculations based on data obtained from New York State criminal justice staff and New York City child welfare and corrections staff.

Note: Some mothers were arrested both before and after the placement.

Less than 3 percent of the children in each cohort have a pattern that suggests a strong connection between a recent conviction and child placement. Of the arrests leading to conviction that occur on the same day as children were placed into foster care (18 arrests in 1991 and 44 arrests in 1996), over two-thirds were for offenses with a child victim. Of convictions within five days before or after placement, the number increases but remains a very small fraction of the overall number of children placed in care: 36 arrests in 1991 and 78 arrests in 1996. Convictions for child-victim crimes remain the most frequent, with drug-related offenses and violent felonies also present. These results suggest that few children in foster care have a mother arrested in the days immediately preceding their placement. While drug, prostitution, and larceny are most likely the last crimes committed by mothers before their children enter care, the handful of arrests with the strongest likelihood of contributing directly to a child's entrance into foster care are for more serious and often violent offenses, which may have been directed at the children themselves.

Examining the conviction that took place closest to the child's placement shows a similar pattern. Only 4 percent of the 1991 cohort (501 children) had a mother whose closest arrest leading to conviction occurred within one year before the placement.[12] The comparable figure for the 1996 cohort is 7 percent (695 children) (figures 3.12 and 3.13).[13] For both

Figure 3.12. Children in 1991 Cohort with Mothers Arrested before Foster Care Placement, by Arrest Closest to Child's Entry into Care (*n* = 1,498)

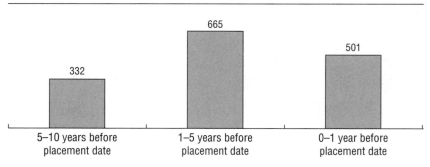

Source: Researchers' calculations based on data obtained from New York State criminal justice staff and New York City child welfare and corrections staff.

cohorts, the arrests that occurred within the *year* before placement were especially likely to occur within the *month* before placement (figures 3.14 and 3.15). In the 1991 cohort, 148 children (or 1 percent of the sample) had a mother whose closest arrest leading to conviction occurred within the month before placement. The number for 1996 is 319 children, or 3 percent of the sample.

Figure 3.13. Children in 1996 Cohort with Mothers Arrested before Foster Care Placement, by Arrest Closest to Child's Entry into Care (*n* = 1,004)

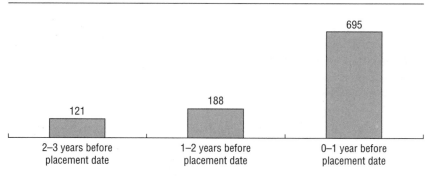

Source: Researchers' calculations based on data obtained from New York State criminal justice staff and New York City child welfare and corrections staff.

Figure 3.14. Children in 1991 Cohort with Mothers Arrested in the Year before Foster Care Placement, by Arrest Closest to Child's Entry into Care (*n* = 501)

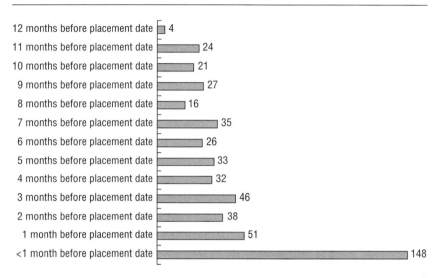

Source: Researchers' calculations based on data obtained from New York State criminal justice staff and New York City child welfare and corrections staff.

Maternal Incarceration around the Time of Placement

It stands to reason that a child with an incarcerated or recently incarcerated mother may be at greater risk of foster care placement than a child whose mother is not in jail or prison—even when the child is in the care of a family member or friend. The incarceration patterns in the data, however, mirror the patterns seen in convictions. In both cohorts, more mothers were incarcerated in the years *after* a child was placed in foster care (figures 3.16–3.19). In the 1991 cohort, 18 percent of all birth mothers were incarcerated after placement, compared with 11 percent before. In the 1996 cohort, 14 percent of mothers were incarcerated after their children's placement, compared with 10 percent before.

These figures may be misleading, as an incarceration event may have ended many years before child placement or taken place after a child left care. The data allowed comparisons between the dates of the mother's incarceration and the dates of the child's foster care placement to deter-

text continues on page 68

Figure 3.15. Children in 1996 Cohort with Mothers Arrested in the Year before Foster Care Placement, by Arrest Closest to Child's Entry into Care (*n* = 695)

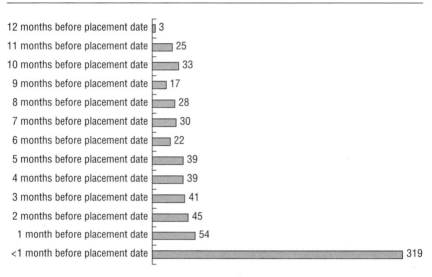

Source: Researchers' calculations based on data obtained from New York State criminal justice staff and New York City child welfare and corrections staff.

Figure 3.16. Children in 1991 Cohort with Mothers Incarcerated during Child's Foster Care Placement, by Arrest Closest to Child's Entry into Care (*n* = 475)

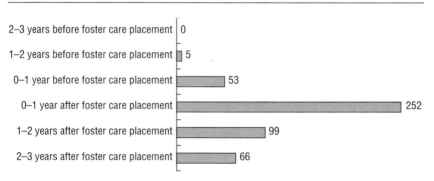

Source: Researchers' calculations based on data obtained from New York State criminal justice staff and New York City child welfare and corrections staff.

Figure 3.17. Children in 1996 Cohort with Mothers Incarcerated during Child's Foster Care Placement, by Arrest Closest to Child's Entry into Care (*n* = 666)

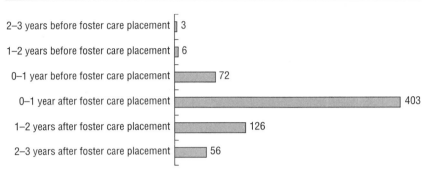

Source: Researchers' calculations based on data obtained from New York State criminal justice staff and New York City child welfare and corrections staff.

Figure 3.18. Children in 1991 Cohort with Mothers Who Were Not Incarcerated during Child's Foster Care Placement, by Arrest Closest to Child's Entry into Care (*n* = 688)

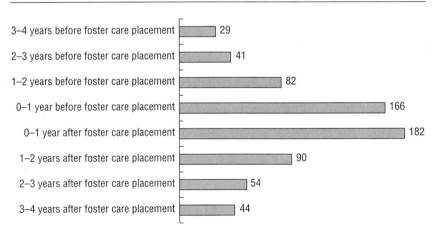

Source: Researchers' calculations based on data obtained from New York State criminal justice staff and New York City child welfare and corrections staff.

Figure 3.19. Children in 1996 Cohort with Mothers Who Were Not Incarcerated during Child's Foster Care Placement, by Arrest Closest to Child's Entry into Care (*n* = 581)

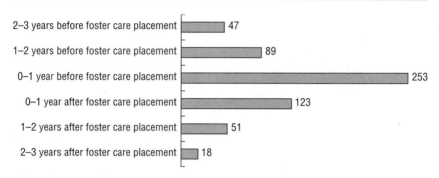

Source: Researchers' calculations based on data obtained from New York State criminal justice staff and New York City child welfare and corrections staff.

mine if these two events overlapped. Considering the incarceration event closest to the child's entry into foster care—no matter how many years before or after the placement the event occurred—the incarceration of 10 percent of mothers in the 1991 cohort and 12 percent of mothers in the 1996 cohort overlapped with their children's stay in foster care.[14]

For both cohorts, most of the mothers' incarceration that overlapped with the children's foster care placement occurred within the year after placement. The incarcerations that did not overlap were about equally likely to begin in the year before and the year after placement for the 1991 cohort, and much more likely to begin within the year before for the 1996 cohort.

These incarceration data do not take into account the length of the incarceration. Even a day of incarceration that overlaps with placement puts a mother into the "overlap" category. Because the overlap of incarceration and placement raises several additional issues, the next chapter is devoted to this topic.

Discussion

This study matched the New York City child welfare and criminal justice records of women with children in foster care to determine the proportion of these mothers that was convicted or incarcerated and analyze the sequence of maternal arrest, incarceration, and children's entry into foster care. What can stakeholders—policymakers, police and child welfare managers, frontline staff, children and families—make of these results?

This chapter started by asking whether the criminal justice system drove children into foster care. According to the data, this is rarely the case. While maternal involvement with the criminal justice system may have important implications for stakeholders, most birth mothers of foster children are never involved in the criminal justice system. Among mothers who have involvement with the criminal justice system, much of that activity takes place well before placement and appears to have little to do with involvement in child welfare. Most contacts with law enforcement are for low-level offenses; only rarely are the mothers arrested on violent charges, and even more rarely are the arrests related to charges of crimes against a child. Based on these data, aggressive law enforcement is not driving a large portion of children into foster care.

Still, for a significant minority of birth mothers and their children entering care, maternal involvement in the criminal justice is part of their experience. The results for this group also do not point to aggressive policing as a driver of placement because much of the criminal justice involvement among mothers takes place after placement occurs. If aggressive policing were driving kids into care by leading to convictions of their mothers, one would expect contacts with law enforcement to occur before, not after, placement.

Instead, the offenses and their sequencing suggest a different pattern. The most common offenses—drug possession, petty larceny, and prostitution—are correlated with substance abuse problems.[15] Substance abuse is often implicated in child abuse and neglect.[16] Putting these facts and the data presented above together suggests that substance abuse issues are likely for many women involved with the criminal justice and child welfare systems at the same time. That criminal justice involvement occurs more often after child removal suggests that the child's or children's presence may act as a brake on maternal substance use and its often-associated criminal activity. Removal may be part of a downward spiral for the mother that accelerates once her children are in foster care.

Child protective workers are already mandated to explore substance abuse issues when investigating families. The interpretation presented above, however, implies that successful treatment may have benefits even beyond keeping children with their families and avoiding child welfare costs—both human and financial. Successful treatment may also reduce criminal activity and the large costs associated with criminal justice system involvement. Treatment may serve as both a family preservation and crime prevention tool.

Conclusion

This chapter focused on the overlap of child removal and criminal justice involvement with an eye toward identifying the relationship between the two. However, many more questions and issues that are part of the intersection of criminal justice and child welfare were not answered here. More information is needed on the intersection of paternal criminal justice involvement and child removal and the effect of a parental criminal history on child welfare outcomes. There are also issues related to the coordination of corrections and child welfare, both of which have rehabilitative missions. The next chapter looks at one critical component of this latter area: visitation.

4

Hard Data on Hard Times

An Empirical Analysis of Maternal Incarceration, Foster Care, and Visitation

Chapter 3 presents a study that focuses on how often the biological mothers of foster children are involved in the criminal justice system. That research finds that most birth mothers of children in care have no contact with criminal justice or corrections. Among the few mothers that have criminal histories, most convictions are for low-level offenses and occur years before child removals take place. When maternal incarceration overlaps with foster care placement, however, it places additional demands on families, child welfare agencies and correctional institutions. This chapter uses the dataset described in chapter 3 to examine the impact of this phenomenon on mother-child visitation.

For visits to take place, several cross-agency issues must be resolved. Child welfare agencies need to identify children who have parents in jail or prison. After determining that maintaining contact is in the best interest of the child, a caseworker must arrange to have a child visit the proper corrections facility. The security of corrections facilities makes this a challenge in the best of circumstances—lockdowns, limited visiting hours, efforts to prevent contraband from entering corrections facilities, and other barriers make visiting time consuming and often frustrating. As people unrelated to the incarcerated person, caseworkers may have an especially difficult time navigating the corrections system unless child welfare and corrections agencies work together.

Visitation, Incarceration, and Family Preservation

The impact of mass incarceration on children generally and foster children in particular has drawn increased attention in the past decade owing to two significant changes in the child welfare landscape.[1] First, the rise in female incarceration that first started in the 1980s resulted in more mothers spending time in jail or prison (Sabol, Minton, and Harrison 2007). In addition, the federal Adoption and Safe Families Act (ASFA), passed and implemented in the late 1990s, creates several deadlines that speed up termination of parental rights proceedings and place a premium on continuing parent-child contact.

Social service regulations and policies in many states and jurisdictions, including New York, require that child welfare agencies make reasonable efforts to facilitate visits between foster children and their incarcerated parents.[2] Several concerns and potential benefits underlie this policy. Many believe that regular visits between parents and their children in foster care aid a child's development and are a necessary—though sometimes insufficient—step for family reunification.[3] This is no less true for incarcerated parents, though additional hurdles to family preservation may exist.[4] Without visitation, the government imposes a double punishment on convicted parents: in addition to a loss of liberty, lack of contact may further strain parent-child relationships. In the worst case, lengthy separation without visits leads to the permanent dissolution of the family.

The importance of visitation is often codified in other child welfare laws. New York State Social Service Law s384b, for example, states that

> a child is "abandoned" by his parent if such parent evinces an intent to forgo his or her parental rights and obligations as manifested by his or her failure to visit the child and communicate with the child or agency, although able to do so and not prevented or discouraged from doing so by the agency. *In the absence of evidence to the contrary, such ability to visit and communicate shall be presumed* [emphasis added].

Thus, if a child welfare caseworker cannot locate a parent because of incarceration, or if an incarcerated parent cannot locate a son or daughter in the child welfare system, the child welfare agency may ask the Family Court for an abandonment finding. If a child is declared technically abandoned, his or her permanency planning goal may change to adoption. Once a child enters the adoption track, arranging visits and parental contact may become even more difficult. Caseworkers in adoption units specialize in adoption procedures and may be less familiar with visitation regulations and less experienced with arranging visits and promoting contact with biological parents. Thus, not only is visitation necessary to maintain family connections, but lack of visitation can have significant legal implications.

ASFA mandates the initiation of termination of parental rights (TPR) proceedings if a child spends a total of 15 of any 22 months in foster care. Lawmakers passed the bill to prevent "foster care drift": placement of children in foster care for years at a time without acting on a plan to find the children permanent families (either their biological families or adoptive families). Caseworkers can petition the court to retain parental right if they believe that a TPR is not in the child's best interest, but such a determination must be made case by case and approved by a Family Court judge. The level of contact and visitation is one criteria that may be used to approve extensions of the "15 of 22" rule. As with the six-month abandonment rule, this ASFA rule may have a decisive impact on incarcerated parents and their children if visitation is not arranged.

The welfare of the child and the family are paramount concerns, but other interests also support the requirement that foster children have contact with their parents. Without effective visitation policies within a family preservation framework, more children may enter the adoption track. This places additional pressure on the adoption divisions of child welfare agencies. Some of these children will not be adopted, which may lead to long term spells in foster care. For children who reside in group care facilities in particular, lengthy spells are very expensive.

Efforts to arrange visitation to incarcerated parents, however, must overcome many obstacles. Caseworkers must first learn of a parent's incarceration. Parents with children in foster care may be reluctant to inform child welfare agencies of their incarceration. Even when children learn of a parent's incarceration, shame, fear, or embarrassment may prevent them from sharing this knowledge with their caseworker.

Once caseworkers learn of parental incarcerations, they must navigate the corrections system. As secure facilities, jails and prisons have elaborate and time-consuming procedures regarding visits to prisoners. Corrections officials must receive prior notification of a visit to ensure the parent's presence in the visiting room, and caseworkers need to prepare children for what they will experience when entering a jail or prison. Finally, caseworkers need to schedule transportation, and either a caseworker or other staff member must accompany foster children during these visits.

In sum, arranging visits is not a task easily undertaken by individual caseworkers.

In light of the importance of visitation and the complicated logistics of arranging visitation to correctional facilities, child welfare and correctional officials in New York City started a van service to the city's jail in June 2000 as part of the agency's Children of Incarcerated Parents Initiative. These weekly trips seek to reduce the barriers to visiting the city jail and to create a more family-like atmosphere in an otherwise institutional setting. The program identified a substantial number of incarcerated mothers with children in foster care, but project staff needed hard data to estimate the likely number of children eligible to visit New York City's jail, as well as information pertaining to both the foster care placements and maternal criminal history of children with incarcerated parents.[5]

Relations between advocates for inmates and child welfare agencies have often been strained. Advocates point to heart-wrenching examples of incarcerated women who desperately want to maintain contact with their children in foster care but have not been able to navigate the child welfare system while behind bars. Child welfare agencies may question the benefit to children of maintaining contact with mothers convicted of crimes. Advocates respond that many mothers are victims of poverty, domestic violence, or other circumstances over which they have little control but that do not make them love their children any less than other parents and that do not make them incompetent caretakers. Given the disproportionate incarceration of people of color and the overrepresentation of African American children in the child welfare system, issues of race and class amplify an already-explosive issue.

The lack of available empirical research regarding the size of the incarcerated parent population with children in care often leads to inconclusive debates. This chapter is one of the first efforts to estimate how many children in foster care may be entitled to visits with their incarcerated parents.

Research Design

A parent's incarceration does not place an automatic responsibility on child welfare workers to arrange a visit. Incarceration may be short, lasting less than a week. Lengthy incarcerations that occur during a child's placement, however, are likely to profoundly affect children, caseworker efforts to facilitate visitation, and possible terminations of parental rights. Learning of an incarceration, locating the incarcerated mother, and facilitating visits to prisons and jails usually consume large amounts of time, and child welfare agencies cannot be expected to arrange visits to parents incarcerated for only a few days.

Based on conversation with child welfare and corrections staff, the researchers of this chapter decided that child welfare *visitation operations* are most affected when

1. the contact with the criminal justice system involves an incarceration spell.
2. the incarceration spell overlaps with a child's foster care placement.
3. the overlap lasts at least 30 consecutive days—in many jurisdictions, visitation policy requires a minimum of one visit between a parent and child each month.

The researchers selected these criteria for many reasons. Though maternal criminal activity is usually a concern for child welfare agencies, when a child is out of care, receiving preventive services, or on trial discharge to the parent, it is not a visitation issue. The effect of maternal criminal activity that does not involve incarceration is likely to be limited to the degree of supervision during visits, while incarceration creates several additional barriers to visitation that are not easily overcome. Though shorter incarceration spells are still reason for concern, child welfare officials often have a much clearer obligation to facilitate visitation when incarceration spells last at least 30 days. Though child welfare agencies, in theory, must meet their statutory obligations regardless of cost, another reason to examine this group is that these cases are likely to use a large amount of resources as caseworkers must arrange transportation and accompany children in care to correctional facilities that may be hours away.

The researchers considered including a fourth factor: limiting the study group to only those children involved in cases without terminations of parental rights. Child welfare agencies do not have an obligation to facilitate visitation following TPRs—though many feel that post-TPR visits should be allowed and are beneficial. The researchers decided against using this factor because including it may have had the perverse effect of underestimating the number of children with incarcerated mothers entitled to visits: TPRs may occur because a parent abandons a child or because incarceration and incarceration-related issues prevented contact. Further, the data describe a time before ASFA, when TPRs in many jurisdictions often occurred years after placement—and were less likely to happen in the three year follow-up period examined here than they are today. In sum, teasing out the causal relationships between TPRs and incarceration is a complicated process beyond the scope of this chapter. However, the researchers found significant adoption-related activity among the study group and report these data to place the findings in context.

Matching Foster Care and Criminal Justice Data

To recap the construction of the dataset described in chapter 3, this research examines children who entered foster care in New York City's fiscal year 1997 (July 1, 1996–June 30, 1997). Researchers identified the mothers of these children, then asked state and local criminal justice agencies to match these names with the criminal history databases that they maintain. This data match allowed researchers to identify all convictions and incarceration spells in New York City's jails and New York State's prisons that involved biological mothers of the children who entered New York City foster care in fiscal year 1997. Researchers also identified incarceration spells that involved detention without sentence, which usually occur when charges are dropped or the defendant is acquitted. They collected detailed information concerning arrest charges, location of incarceration, and length of incarceration stay and/or sentence. Child welfare data contained detailed records on each child's length of stay, reentry into foster care, transfers while in placements, demographic characteristics, and other information.

The researchers used the results of this data match to identify *children* in the 1997 cohort who fit the visitation criteria outlined above. It is important to understand that the authors used children, not mothers or families, as their unit of analysis. Mothers may have multiple children, including some children who never enter care and others who enter care at different times, thus complicating the analysis. Further, though placement assignments privilege putting sibling groups (brothers and sisters) together in the same home, multiple placements in the same home are not always available. As a matter of logistics, visitation services involving these families are often initiated by child welfare caseworkers for individual children.

Results

The researchers obtained information on the mothers of 8,586 of the 10,022 children (86 percent) who first entered foster care during fiscal year 1997. Child welfare data did not contain information on the mothers of the remaining 1,436 children, primarily because the mother did not take care of the child at the time of removal. Because the researchers were unable to obtain the criminal justice histories of all mothers, the percentages listed below, rather than the raw numbers, are better indicators of the prevalence of certain types of criminal histories. If the caretakers of children with unavailable information on the mother have the same distribution of criminal histories as the rest of the cohort, the raw counts reported below would increase by 17 percent. The researchers adjust for this factor in their final estimate.

Of the 8,586 children where information existed, 2,874 (33 percent) had mothers with criminal records (figure 4.1). Among children whose mothers had criminal histories, 1,629 children, or 19 percent of the entire cohort, had mothers who experienced incarceration. For 973 children, or 11 percent, the incarceration overlapped with a foster care spell. The mothers of 502 children (6 percent) had incarceration spells that overlapped with placement for a *total* of 30 days or more. In cases involving

Figure 4.1. Foster Children by Biological Mother Incarceration Overlap Category

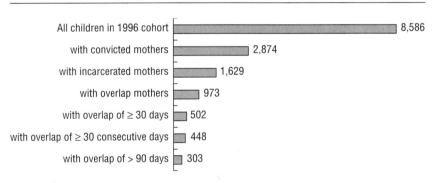

Source: Researchers' calculations based on data obtained from New York State criminal justice staff and New York City child welfare and corrections staff.

448 children (5.2 percent), the overlap lasted 30 or more *consecutive* days. The researchers defined the children with these mothers as the study group.

From 1996 to 1999, an average of 9,700 children each year entered foster care for the first time in New York City. Generalizing from the results presented above, just over 5 percent of these children, or 504 children in each entry cohort, have caregivers with 30-day overlap incarceration spells *at some point* during the first three years of their foster care stay. The number of children entering foster care declined dramatically in the ensuing years, dropping to approximately 4,800 in 2005 before rising to 6,300 in 2006. If the results above held for the years 2001–06, an average of 345 children in each New York City entry cohort would have mothers who experienced 30-day overlaps.[6]

The estimate of 5 percent of children may be conservative in some ways, liberal in others. In an examination of the 1991 entry cohort in chapter 3, researchers found that the average first foster care spell for a child with an incarcerated mother is 3.9 years. Since the criminal justice data for the fiscal 1997 cohort extend only through July 1999, the researchers capture only those overlaps that occur in the first two to three years of each child's stay in foster care. Also, the average length of stay of 3.9 years refers only to the first spell in foster care. Though relatively few children reenter foster care, those discharged from care may reenter at a future date, during which a substantial incarceration overlap may occur.

Still, children stay in foster care for shorter periods now than in the 1990s, and ASFA regulations have led to quicker TPRs. Both these factors may reduce the estimate. For example, if ASFA led to a TPR filed after 12 months due to factors unrelated to criminal justice, then maternal incarcerations that overlapped with foster care two years after placement would not necessitate arranging for visitation.

Many children in the study group experienced changes in permanency planning that limited the chances of family reunification. Because electronic permanency planning data at this time may not have been input in every case, these numbers should be interpreted cautiously. Caseworkers assigned an initial permanency planning goal of adoption to only 2 of the 448 children in the study group, as family reunification is the standard goal in most cases for the first year. By July 1, 1999, 57 percent of the group had their permanency planning goal changed to adoption, and an additional 3 percent had it changed to independent living. Forty-three percent were approved by the local service district to be freed for adoption, with almost two-thirds of these actions taking place after the incarceration overlap.[7] Two percent of the study group had parental rights terminated but were not completely freed for adoption (there is short period between the termination and formally freeing the child for adoption). Among the 10 percent of the study group (47 children) completely freed for adoption, three-quarters were completely freed after the incarceration overlap, and over half of these were freed due to technical abandonment. Because only 12 percent of the children had guardianship transferred from their biological parents to the commissioner of social services, these data suggest that visits were mandated for most of the study group.

Arranging visits for this population imposes a substantial burden on child welfare and corrections. To put the numbers in perspective, if an average caseworker has a caseload of 25 children at any one time, and likely many more than that over the course of a year, most caseworkers should anticipate that they will need to arrange visits to a correctional facility for one or more of the children for whom they have responsibility each year.

To aid child welfare agencies in their efforts to manage this issue and to add to the knowledge base regarding incarcerated parents of foster children, the chapter authors explored the chronology of placement, arrest, and incarceration, as well as the offenses that led to substantial overlaps between placement and maternal incarceration.

Chronology of Placement, Arrest, Conviction, and Incarceration

As discussed in chapter 3, many observers fear that more punitive law enforcement sanctions may have increased foster care placements. This concern arises from the possibility that increased enforcement and punishment for minor crimes has resulted in more incarcerated mothers. Because some of these mothers will not be able to arrange for the care of their children, foster care placements will escalate as a direct result of more aggressive policing.

Data on the mothers of the study group children strongly suggest the opposite is true. Instead of criminal activity leading to placement, placement may produce increases in maternal criminal activity that lead to incarceration. If children entered foster care because of maternal incarceration, then arrest and incarceration should occur before placement. For 9 in 10 children in the study group, the mother's incarceration that overlapped for 30 days or more started *after* placement. It is possible that though an incarceration spell started after placement, the arrest that led to the jail or prison sentence occurred before placement. Again, the data refute this scenario: 85 percent of the arrests that led to 30-day overlaps occurred after placement, not before.

Examining the entire criminal history of the study group mothers further supports this conclusion. Figure 4.2 shows the number of convictions for mothers of the study group by fiscal year for the three most common crimes—drug-related offenses, prostitution, and theft—as well as other felonies and misdemeanors. Though these data should be interpreted carefully because individual mothers may have multiple convictions, the pattern in the graph is clear: convictions increase radically in fiscal years 1997, 1998, and 1999—the period following the child's placement. Because each mother experienced a significant incarceration spell at some point between 1997 and 1999 that curtailed offenses during that period, the increase in conviction activity is that much more striking.

Virtually all the 30-day overlaps involved incarcerations in jail, not prison. The city jail generally holds people awaiting trial or serving sentences of 15 months or less. The length of the overlaps split evenly between those that lasted one to three months and those that lasted between three months and a year.[8] Only 6 percent of the study group, or 27 children, had mothers with overlaps longer than a year.

That the majority of overlaps take place in jail instead of prison makes addressing many visitation issues related to maternal incarceration easier. In many large urban areas, prisons are located outside the metropolitan area. Many take hours to reach by car, and public transportation is limited. In addition, corrections officials frequently move people in prison to different facilities in different parts of their states to deal with crowding, security, or other issues. The jail population, in contrast, has few of these issues.

Nature of the Convictions

The nature of the criminal activity engaged in by the 30-day overlap mothers has important implications for policy. If mothers go to jail or prison for violent offenses or crimes against children, then permanent separation of the mother and child may be a matter of child safety. The social service laws allow visitation plans to be altered if visits are not in the child's best interest, though it usually takes a court order to do so. If violence is involved, efforts to encourage visitation should receive

Figure 4.2. Criminal Histories of 30-Day Overlap Mothers, 1981–99

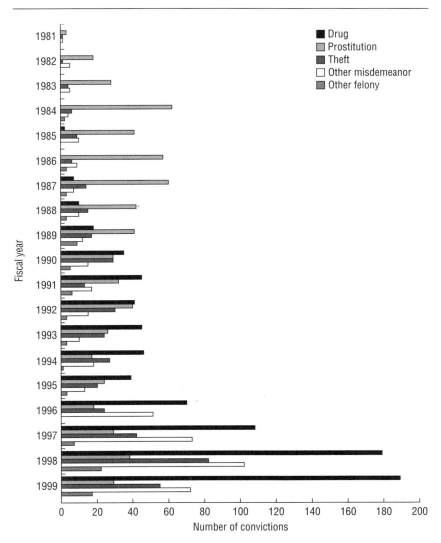

Source: Researchers' calculations based on data obtained from New York State criminal justice staff and New York City child welfare and corrections staff.

additional scrutiny to ensure that visitation is in the best interests of the child.

Violent crimes, however, are uncommon among the mothers studied, and high-level violent felonies are rare. Only 15 percent of 30-day overlap charges involved convictions for crimes against persons (figure 4.3). Even in this group, 30 percent of the top charges fell below the felony level, and another 37 percent involved the lowest level felonies.[9] Only 5 percent of study group mothers started their incarceration because of a high-level violent felony conviction, and just 2 percent of the top disposition charges involved endangering the welfare of a child.

Instead, over half the top disposition charges that led to 30-day overlaps involved drug-related offenses. Another 13 percent involved property crimes—offenses often connected with drug use. The remaining disposition charges vary. Among drug-related crimes, three-quarters involved sales, with the remainder for possession. Over half of all drug charges involved B felony sales, a category that composed one-third of all top disposition charges. The elevated proportion of high-level felonies among the drug offenses is probably related to New York State's strict sentencing laws. The Rockefeller drug laws, as they are commonly called, require mandatory minimum sentences based on the weight of the specific drug involved in the transaction, and they generally eliminate mitigating factors from consideration in sentencing.

Figure 4.3. Top Disposition Charges for 30-Day Overlap Mothers

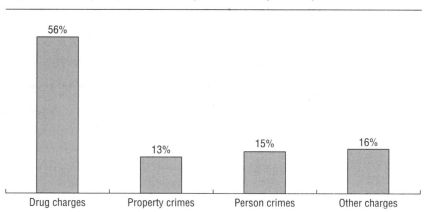

Source: Researchers' calculations based on data obtained from New York State criminal justice staff and New York City child welfare and corrections staff.

The researchers also examined the criminal histories of study group mothers before their overlap incarcerations. Again, the level of drug and drug-related activity is striking. Eighty-three percent of the study group had mothers with prior convictions; of those with convictions, 81 percent had prior drug convictions. In addition, 17 percent of study group mothers had prior convictions for prostitution and 22 percent for property crimes.

The chronology of criminal involvement depicted in figure 4.2 also shows a strong connection between child placement and drug use. Between fiscal years 1996 and 1999, the number of drug convictions rose 170 percent, theft convictions rose 129 percent, and prostitution convictions rose 61 percent. The number of misdemeanors outside these categories doubled between fiscal years 1996 and 1998. Though none of the mothers in the study group committed nondrug felonies in fiscal year 1996, this group committed 22 felonies in 1998—more than the previous nine years combined. Indeed, the study group mothers averaged 2.3 convictions each from fiscal year 1997 to fiscal year 1999. The overall pattern of rising convictions is remarkable not only because the study group mothers spent some of this time incarcerated, but also because crime, arrest, and convictions declined in New York City during this period.

Discussion

These results show a need for efforts to facilitate visitation for foster children with incarcerated mothers. Though maternal incarceration spells that overlap foster care placement are unusual for foster children, they are prevalent enough to raise concerns for all stakeholders. The implications of the study's findings, however, go beyond the impact of incarceration on visitation.

The data paint a disturbing portrait of how the mothers of foster children become incarcerated, and they suggest ways that both incarceration and placement—or at least length of stay—might be reduced. Like the mothers of a substantial number (though a minority) of other foster children, the mothers of many study group children had prior encounters with law enforcement that involved minor offenses. For the mothers of study group children, however, the removal of their children appears to be a critical event in a downward spiral. Being responsible for a child often puts a brake on a parent's destructive behavior, including drug use and illegal activities. Once that brake is removed, destructive behavior accelerates. For a substantial number of mothers, arrest and incarceration may follow.

As evidenced by the proliferation of drug courts and mandatory treatment policies, policy experts and the public increasingly agree that incarceration is an ineffective treatment for substance abuse problems. Indeed, the elevated number of convictions among mothers of the study group even after periods of incarceration suggests that being behind bars did little to prevent future criminal activity. Convictions rose dramatically despite the intervention of the criminal justice system.

The stakes involved in turning around the lives of these women are high. Alternative treatments that could reverse the downward spiral afflicting the mothers of study group children would lead to substantially better outcomes for families and children, fewer crime victims, fewer foster children, shorter lengths of stay for those that do enter care, and cost savings for taxpayers. Given the burdens imposed on society in the absence of effective services, even a marginally effective alternative would be a cost-effective undertaking.

This research suggests at least two barriers will need to be overcome. As part of this study, researchers talked with advocates and corrections staff who work with incarcerated mothers around the United States. According to some advocates, many local district attorneys collect little or no information on the families of incarcerated women during adjudication and sentencing. Court officials rarely know that a mother has a child in foster care, and maternal status is not a factor in sentencing. Other advocates claim that transfers of incarcerated women to new jails or prisons are not routinely reported to either families or child welfare. This often leads to communication breakdowns that may prevent contact and visitation between mothers and their children in foster care. In both cases, the lack of information makes it difficult to identify situations suitable for intervention.

Another challenge to consider is the availability of quality treatment programs that have the flexibility to keep families together. Child welfare–involved mothers who realize they need treatment and have some mechanism to pay for it often encounter long waiting lists. Some treatment programs require clients to cut off contact with the outside world for a period—and complying with that requirement when a child is in foster care may be held against a mother in future planning for her child. Inpatient programs may last several months, and those that have limited capacity to arrange visits with children in foster care again place the mother at risk of losing her children permanently. Given the high rates of poverty among parents with children in foster care and the under-provision of treatment alternatives in many inner-city communities, cost and quality are that much greater barriers for the mothers of study group children. In the absence of easily accessible substance abuse treatment, it seems likely that these mothers will continue to have an elevated level of substance abuse–driven criminality, at least until they commit a crime that results in a long-term prison sentence.

The barriers are formidable but not insurmountable. In the past few years, many child welfare agencies have tackled this problem. While a full discussion of these efforts is beyond the scope of this chapter, several models are available. In New York, child welfare and corrections officials started the Children of Incarcerated Parents program, or CHIP. CHIP trains caseworkers on the rights of children with incarcerated parents and the responsibilities of the caseworkers, consults on specific cases, and operates a visitation program that runs a weekly bus to the women's jail for mother-child visits.

New York's courts and corrections system have engaged in several innovative projects related to drug treatment, including drug courts and the Drug Treatment Alternatives Program that allows prosecutors to recommend treatment sentences instead of incarceration. A nonprofit that normally works with women in prison has developed a partnership with child welfare officials. The local court–appointed special advocates (CASA) group is considering making a CASA available in every case of a child in Family Court with an incarcerated parent. Others envision a special facility that will house mothers with substance abuse problems and their children while providing drug treatment services on site.

Because many of these programs offer the possibility of improving outcomes *and* saving substantial incarceration and child welfare dollars, and in some cases are backed by a judge's order, payment and access problems may be manageable issues.

Conclusion

The involvement of biological parents of foster children in the criminal justice system raises many issues. Some observers may want to emphasize that this involvement validates decisions to remove children from the home. Others may assert that criminal involvement in itself makes a parent unfit to assume responsibility for a child. This research suggests that in some circumstances, these conclusions are valid. None of the results or discussion presented here should be interpreted as a recommendation that child safety should be sacrificed to reunify families. Child welfare officials remain responsible for ensuring that children are safe.

While some incarcerated mothers may never be able to resume their parenting responsibilities, others will have the capacity and the desire. In either case, the child welfare system is still obligated to make reasonable efforts to reunify the family. The efforts to arrange visits to corrections facilities and maintain parental contact for these children, as difficult as that may be, are an important and necessary step in meeting this requirement. To do so will require that child welfare and corrections agencies coordinate their efforts much more than they do currently.

This study is a first step to identifying the size and scope of the issue, but there is much more to do. To make more progress, a more comprehensive process for identifying and serving these dual-involved families needs to be established. Future research will need to focus on the characteristics of the families caught up in the child welfare and criminal justice systems and how this dual involvement might be prevented.

5

A Cohort Analysis
of Early Adolescents
in Foster Care

Children who enter foster care for the first time as early adolescents face burdens that younger children and their nonfoster peers do not, including the trauma or conditions that led to their placement in foster care and their adjustment to life in care. Early adolescents also may enter care through avenues other than abuse or neglect—as part of a status offender case, as a result of juvenile delinquency, or through a voluntary placement. This chapter uses cohort analysis to examine the experiences of these children, discusses how these experiences vary by their reason for entering care, and explores the implications of these experiences for different youth-serving systems. Unlike many other chapters, the study presented here is exploratory rather than focused on a specific cross-agency issue. The central research question is how do the experiences of this vulnerable group of children vary by the way they enter foster care?

Even in the best of circumstances, early adolescence is an awkward and volatile time in the lives of young people. Many mental illnesses and behavioral disorders manifest themselves in early adolescence, and the increased physical size of these youth makes them more difficult to control (Broering and Irwin 1987; Mechanic 1983). Contact with delinquent peers and poor school performance may become more apparent during this time (Hawkins and Catalano 1993; Wasserman and Miller 1998; Wasserman et al. 1996).

The research below is the only large-scale cohort study the researchers know of that breaks down the foster care experience by the reason an early adolescent enters the foster care system. The data demonstrate that young people who enter foster care through avenues other than abuse or neglect have different trajectories through the system. Unlike abuse or neglect cases, early adolescents entering foster care through other mechanisms are much more likely to be placed in congregate care facilities, have different lengths of stay, and reenter care after discharge at different rates. These differences have implications for the design of foster care placements.

How Early Adolescents Enter Foster Care

Most young children enter foster care on abuse or neglect petitions filed by child welfare agencies in the Family Court. In the entry cohort examined, over 90 percent of the children who entered foster care at age 10 or younger entered via abuse/neglect petitions. These petitions are triggered when a neighbor, relative, or mandated reporter (such as a teacher, doctor, or social worker) calls the State Central Registry to report abuse or neglect. If an investigation substantiates the report, child welfare lawyers may petition the Family Court to allow child welfare officials to take action in the case. A Family Court judge may place the family under supervision, order preventive services, or place some of or all the family's children in foster care. A Family Court judge must periodically review the placement to make sure that reasonable efforts are being made to meet statutory requirements concerning permanency (for example, return to family, adoption, or independent living). Federal and state laws mandate how often these reviews take place, with a general trend over the past 10 years toward more frequent reviews.

Early adolescents, in contrast, have additional pathways to foster care that are infrequently traveled by younger children: voluntary agreements, status offenses, and the juvenile delinquency system. Historically, child welfare researchers have paid less attention to youth who enter foster care for reasons other than abuse and neglect. As this chapter will show, however, the reason an early adolescent enters care influences the legal requirements surrounding the placement, the time a youth stays in care, and other important measures.

Voluntary Agreements

In most states, a parent or legal guardian may voluntarily transfer custody of a child to a child welfare agency, pending the approval of a judge.[1] Parents may place a child in care for many reasons. They may conclude that poverty, mental or physical health issues, substance abuse, or other problems have diminished their capacity to care for their children. Abandonment or the death of parents can also lead to voluntary agreements to place children into foster care. In some cases, children may have developmental or physical disabilities that families can no longer handle physically, financially, or emotionally. Disobedience and other behavior problems are also common causes for voluntary placements of children.[2] Child welfare officials usually must return a voluntarily placed child within 30 days of a parent or legal guardian's request.[3]

Status Offenders or Persons in Need of Supervision

Many early adolescents enter the foster care system through the status offender system.[4] Status offender laws vary by state. New York State Family Court Act §712(a) creates a special class of youth called "persons in need of supervision" (PINS). At the time of this research, this law defined PINS as "a person less than 16 years of age who is truant, incorrigible, ungovernable or habitually disobedient and beyond the lawful control of a parent."[5] Generically, these cases are referred to as "status offenders" because the actions of the youth are not criminal or delinquent but of concern to the court due to the youth's status as a juvenile. Though the police, school officials, or neighbors may initiate PINS proceedings, parents usually start the process by filling out PINS intake forms with the department of probation. In New York City, status offenders are eligible for various diversion programs that attempt to address the problems faced by the family and the child. Diversion from the Family Court also keeps youth out of foster care.

Status offenders enter foster care through two mechanisms. A Family Court judge that finds a youth "guilty" of a status offense may place the youth in foster care. Alternatively, judges may remand a youth to foster care while the status offense case is decided.

Juvenile Delinquents

In some states, delinquency may result in placement in foster care facilities. Juvenile delinquents are usually young people who are charged with an act that would be considered a crime if committed by an adult. Family court judges hear juvenile delinquency cases. When a judge determines that a youth is delinquent, he or she may order placement. Usually, juvenile delinquents are placed in facilities that operate under the direct supervision of a state agency—the functional equivalent of juvenile prisons. In New York, before a judge can place a child in a state facility, probation officers must conduct an "exploration of placement" to see if less restrictive facilities will serve the youth. In a small number of cases, this exploration results in placement in foster care.

In sum, youth who enter foster care for the first time as early adolescents may do so through many different pathways. In some ways they form a distinct group, as they share age and developmental traits. In other ways, they are fragmented by their different experiences. There are few, if any, large-scale empirical studies of the experience of this population in foster care. To learn more, researchers conducted the study described below.

Research Methods

This study is a cohort analysis. A cohort is a group that experiences an intervention, in this case entry into foster care, at about the same time and tracks members of the group over time (Norval 1977). Cohort data better reflect the length of time a typical child spends in care as opposed to point-in-time data, which contain a greater percentage of children with longer lengths of stay (Goerge, Wulczyn, and Fanshel 1994). Cohort analysis also follows children who are experiencing the same policies and institutional system.

The study sample consists of all 11- to 15-year-olds who entered New York City foster care for the first time in 1994 and were tracked through May 1, 1999. Using the 1994 entry group allowed the researchers to identify patterns in outcomes over a period that covered most of the children's foster care experience but was not too distorted by the great spike in New York City's foster care census that took place in the late 1980s and early 1990s (Wulczyn, Brunner, and Goerge 1999).

The researchers limited the upper end of the age spectrum to 15 years old because New York State delinquency and status offense statutes applied only to children below age 16 at the time. This age range also matches the theoretical division between young children who enter foster care primarily because of abuse or neglect and early adolescents that enter foster care mainly for other reasons. Though the start of adolescence varies, this age range identifies a reasonably distinct group.

The data for the study come from electronic files maintained by New York City's child welfare agency.[6] The researchers used these data to obtain the following information on children in care: age, gender, and race; reasons for entry into care; changes in status (for example, entries into and exits from care, transfers to new placements, and absences from care); permanency goals (for example, return to parents, adoption, independent living); and reasons for discharge.

To examine the experiences of the cohort in the juvenile justice system, the researchers used entries into the juvenile detention facilities operated by the New York City Department of Juvenile Justice. These data contain information about all youth who entered juvenile detention facilities in New York City from January 1, 1994, through September 1, 1999. The database also shows when a young person went from detention to juvenile placement facilities operated by the state. Researchers matched records from the child welfare data and the juvenile detention data to identify children involved in both systems. For detained foster children, the researchers checked to see if they went to state facilities.

The researchers first identified all children who entered foster care for the first time in 1994. They then eliminated children not in the 11–15 age group and youth who were in the child welfare database but had gone straight to juvenile delinquency placements and not foster care.[7] To determine how a member of the cohort entered care, the researchers used docket numbers and other legal activities recorded in the child welfare data. A weakness of the study is that the data did not allow researchers to identify a reason for entry for every child (table 5.1). The researchers asked the child welfare agency's Quality Improvement Unit to examine a sample of 50 uncategorized cases. They found that 26 percent entered care because of a status offender petition, but they were unable to identify a reason for entry for the remaining cases. The researchers did not redistribute the children in the "no legal activity" category into a specific reason for entry but kept them together with the "unable to determine" group as "uncategorized." The outcomes of the uncategorized group did not consistently mirror those of any other group and in some instances differed from all other groups.

Table 5.1. Reasons for Entry into Foster Care by Age Group

	Entries Age 11–15		All Other Entries		Age 11–15
	Number	Percent	Number	Percent	share (%)
Abuse/neglect					
Abuse	45	2	214	3	17
Neglect	387	19	3,931	63	9
Undifferentiated	144	7	705	11	17
Subtotal	576	29	4,850	78	11
Status offense	666	33	44	1	94
Juvenile delinquency	14	1	1	0	93
Voluntary placement	482	24	647	10	43
Uncategorized					
No legal activity	162	8	360	6	31
Unable to determine	119	6	321	5	27
Subtotal	281	14	681	11	29

Source: Child Care Review Service.

Results

Like other children in New York foster care system, early adolescents who entered foster care in 1994 were predominantly black and Hispanic. Over half were girls, and they were on the older side of the age range—that is, 14 and 15 years old (table 5.2).[8] The early adolescent group had proportionally more girls and more Hispanics than the younger children in the 1994 entering cohort. Because most foster children first enter care when they are 5 years old or younger, the average age of those under 10 is just 2.6 years.

Foster Care Experiences

Length of Stay

Length of stay was calculated in two ways. The first counted all time during which the child legally remained in care (table 5.3). This is the standard method. The second method excluded time spent on trial discharge

Table 5.2. Demographic Characteristics of 1994 Entry Cohort

Characteristic	0–10-Year-Olds		11–15-Year-Olds	
	Number	Percent	Number	Percent
Gender				
Male	3,004	53	935	46
Female	2,762	48	1,084	54
Race				
Black	3,077	54	919	46
Hispanic	1,146	2	497	25
White	194	3	100	5
Other	77	1	42	2
Unknown	1,230	22	445	22
Age				
11			238	12
12			300	15
13			378	19
14			529	26
15			574	29
Average age	2.6		13.4	

Source: Child Care Review Service.

or absent without leave. This latter method is useful for examining how long children physically reside in foster care and for determining cost— foster parents and congregate care providers are not paid once a child goes on trial discharge or if a child is AWOL for longer than three days.

To determine average and median length of stay, the researchers first calculated the number of days in care for youth discharged after the first spell. For those youth who never left care or who were in care on a subsequent spell, researchers counted the number of days from the date of entry to May 1, 1999, the last date for which they had data. This adjustment applied to 15 percent of the study group. Thus, these figures necessarily undercount the actual length of stay because some youth had not completed their stays in care. The median length of stay is not affected by this problem.[9]

Both methods for calculating length of stay show a sharp divergence by reason for entry. Children in care through abuse/neglect petitions

Table 5.3. Adolescents' Length of Stay in Foster Care Including AWOL and Trial Discharges

		1st Spell			2nd Spell				3rd Spell			
	Number	Number still in care	Mean days in care	Median days in care	Number	Number still in care	Mean days in care	Median days in care	Number	Number still in care	Mean days in care	Median days in care
Abuse/neglect	576	165	902	832	87	38	703	761	11	3	239	167
Status offense	666	36	284	62	175	20	371	183	33	3	212	88
Juvenile delinquency	14	2	575	105	2	—	353	353	1	1	823	823
Voluntary placement	482	109	750	520	81	14	362	126	23	2	241	105
Uncategorized	281	19	313	17	47	12	530	336	9	2	312	312
Total	2,019	331	578	203	392	84	462	262	77	11	244	142

Source: Child Care Review Service.

have the longest median length of stay (25 months) followed by children who enter care on voluntary agreements (15 months). The first spell length of stay for status offenders, just 50 days, departs radically from others in the sample (table 5.4).

Excluding the AWOL and trial discharge time from the calculation reduces the cohort's average length of stay during the first spell by about a month and a half, and the median by about a month. It does not change the relative ranking of reason for entry groups, although some groups experienced more considerable drops in their length of stay than others. Voluntarily placed children exhibited the sharpest reduction in length of stay when taking AWOLs and trial discharges into account, losing more than two months from both their mean and median.

Stability of Foster Care Placements

The stability of foster care placements reflects the number of placement changes children experience while in care, as well as the number of times they leave those placements through AWOLs and admissions to juvenile detention facilities.

Number of Unique Placements

The term "unique placements" refers not to placement types but to placement settings—that is, a child in two different group homes would occupy two different placements. To measure stability, the researchers distinguished between children with one or two placements and those with three or more on the other. Child welfare systems often place children in transitional facilities as workers seek the most appropriate placement. New York does not have a central transitional facility, but the child welfare agency operates diagnostic reception centers, emergency foster boarding homes, and other temporary placements that serve a similar purpose. Since temporary placements are intended to increase the likelihood of ultimately stable ones, the researchers considered that one or two placements indicates a high level of placement stability.[10]

Over half of the study group experienced only one placement, and three-quarters experienced one or two placements during their first spell. Of the children who entered care through abuse/neglect petitions—a group with relatively long stays in care—65 percent had one or two placements, compared with 77 percent of status offenders, who have

Table 5.4. Adolescents' Length of Stay in Foster Care Excluding AWOL and Trial Discharge Time

		1st Spell				2nd Spell				3rd Spell		
	Number	Number still in care	Mean days in care	Median days in care	Number	Number still in care	Mean days in care	Median days in care	Number	Number still in care	Mean days in care	Median days in care
Abuse/neglect	576	165	846	742	87	38	620	544	11	3	233	167
Status offense	666	36	248	50	175	20	300	145	33	3	172	78
Juvenile delinquency	14	2	540	105	2	—	353	353	1	1	822	822
Voluntary placement	482	109	683	455	81	14	297	104	23	2	167	67
Uncategorized	281	19	288	15	47	12	483	329	9	2	268	236
Total	2,019	331	530	174	392	84	393	208	77	11	199	92

Source: Child Care Review Service.

much shorter stays in care. Seventy percent of voluntarily placed youth had one or two placements (figure 5.1).

Even considering all spells in foster care, almost two-thirds of the study group still had only one or two placements over their foster care stays (figure 5.2). The gap between the reason for entry groups narrows primarily because status offenders are more likely than the other groups to have multiple spells in care and, thus, more placements when all spells are included in the analysis.

Absent without Leave (AWOL)

Forty percent of the study group (812 children) left care without permission, or were absent without leave at some point during their cumulative time in foster care. As discussed in chapter 6, incidences of AWOL are usually undercounted in child welfare administrative databases. In total, the group went AWOL 1,745 times (table 5.5). A small number of children accounted for most AWOLs: only 10 percent of the cohort (205 children) accounted for 59 percent of its AWOLs (1,025 incidents).

Figure 5.1. Number of Unique Placements for First Foster Care Spell by Reason for Entry (*n* = 2,019)

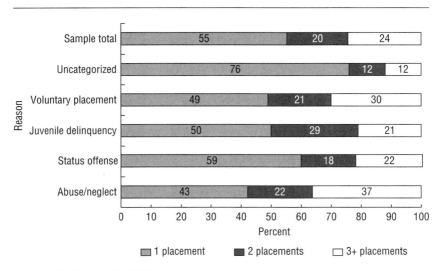

Source: Child Care Review Service.

Figure 5.2. Number of Unique Placements for All Foster Care Spells by Reason for Entry (*n* = 2,019)

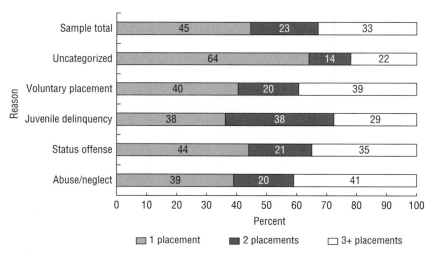

Source: Child Care Review Service.

Table 5.5 also shows that children who enter care via status offense petitions and voluntary agreements are disproportionately involved in AWOL events. Forty-eight percent of status offender entrants and 49 percent of voluntarily placed children left care without permission at least once during their stay. To account for the different lengths of time these children spend in care, researchers created an AWOL rate by dividing the

Table 5.5. Children with AWOL Activity by Reason for Entry

	Children	Total AWOLs	Children with at least one AWOL	% of total children
Abuse/neglect	576	357	169	29
Status offense	666	695	321	48
Juvenile delinquency	14	10	3	21
Voluntary placement	482	504	235	49
Uncategorized	281	179	84	30
Total	2,019	1,745	812	40

Source: Child Care Review Service.

number of AWOLs for each reason for entry group by the number of "care days" and multiplying by 1,000. Table 5.6 shows that for each 1,000 days of care, 1.4 AWOL events occurred. Status offenders, however, had a rate of 3.1 AWOLs per 1,000 care days, compared with 1.4 for voluntary children and 0.7 for abuse/neglect entrants.

Most AWOLs occur near the time of placement; half occurred within the first year. More specifically, 29 percent occurred within the first 90 days, and 17 percent occurred in the first 30 days.

Juvenile Detention

The involvement of foster children with the juvenile justice system is a longstanding concern of child welfare agencies (see Bilchik 1995 and chapters 8 and 9 in this volume). Entering detention following an arrest can result in a loss of placement, educational disruption, loss of employment, and possibly greater risk for future criminal activity. In addition, detention can be brutal; at the very least, the loss of liberty is sobering.

The proportions of the sample that entered juvenile detention while in foster care do not vary much by reason for entry. However, since these children spend varying lengths of time in care, the researchers created a detention rate by dividing the number of detained youth in each group by the average number of "care days" for that group, and multiplying by 1,000 (table 5.7). For each 1,000 days of care, .14 individuals were detained. Status offender entrants stand apart from the others with a rate of .27 detentions per 1,000 care days, a rate twice that of voluntary placements and more than three times that experienced by youth who enter foster care due to abuse/neglect.

Permanency

Permanency refers to a child residing in a permanent home. Establishing permanency, whether a return to biological family or adoption, is considered one of the most important outcomes for foster care by all involved in the child welfare system. To examine permanency among early adolescents, the researchers looked at children's destinations when they leave care and the number and nature of their re-entries into care.

Table 5.6. Frequency of AWOL Events in Years Following Foster Care Placement

	Years Following Placement						Total care days	AWOLs per 1,000 care days
	1	2	3	4	5+	Total		
Abuse/neglect	149	50	59	71	28	357	534,744	0.7
Status offense	431	146	61	39	18	695	225,774	3.1
Juvenile delinquency	0	0	2	7	1	10	9,100	1.1
Voluntary placement	183	122	76	72	51	504	360,536	1.4
Uncategorized	99	28	20	24	8	179	106,499	1.7
Total	862	346	218	213	106	1,745	1,236,653	1.4

Source: Child Care Review Service.

Table 5.7. Early Adolescents Admitted to Juvenile Detention Facilities

	11–15-year-olds	Admitted While in Care		Total care days	Detentions per 1,000 care days
		N	%		
Abuse/neglect	576	45	8	534,744	0.08
Status offense	666	62	9	225,774	0.27
Juvenile delinquency	14	1	7	9,100	0.11
Voluntary placement	482	50	10	360,536	0.14
Uncategorized	281	9	3	106,499	0.08
Total	2,019	167		1,236,653	0.14

Source: Child Care Review Service.

Destination of Last Discharge

As figure 5.3 shows, 82 percent of the study group were discharged from care at the end of the study period, which ranged from four to five years depending on the time of year the youth entered foster care in 1994. The likelihood of discharge varied by reason for entry, ranging from 92 percent for status offender entrants to just 68 percent for abuse/neglect entrants.[11]

Table 5.8 shows the destinations of the most recent discharge from foster care that a youth experienced by reason for entry. If a child had only one spell in care, the table reflects the destination of that discharge; if the child had two or more spells, only the destination of the last discharge is reflected. For the entire cohort, by far the most common discharge destination is a return to a parent or relative (71 percent of those discharged), followed by AWOLs and administrative discharges (18 percent of those discharged).[12] From two-thirds to three-quarters of those discharged from every group were discharged to parents or relatives, and AWOL and administrative discharges were the second most common destination for each group.

More children probably returned home than these numbers suggest. While no data exist on where the youth discharged to AWOL go, anecdotal information and some research studies suggest that many "run away" to their homes, to kin, or to a friend's residence (see chapter 6 of this volume; Biehal and Wade 1999; and Courtney and Wong 1996). This phenomenon may be especially prevalent for status offender entrants and children voluntarily placed. In such cases, when children AWOL to home, parents are not violating court orders by accepting them into their residence. Abuse/neglect placements, in contrast, require

Figure 5.3. Proportion of Reason for Entry Groups Discharged from Foster Care

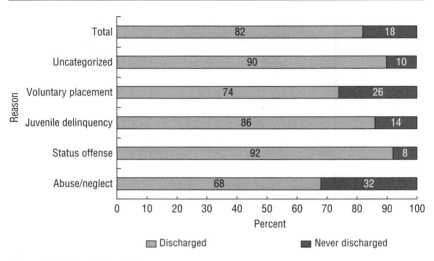

Source: Child Care Review Service.
Note: Study group size is 2,091; number discharged is 1,628.

child welfare approval before a child may legally visit home. Hence, parents or relatives face a legal risk for accepting an AWOL abuse/neglect entrant into their home.

Only 1 percent of the study group left care because of an adoption, and only 3 percent aged out or were emancipated. Of the 69 emancipated children in the study group, only one entered care at age 11 or 12; the rest entered at older ages. The number and percentage of youth aging out of foster care, however, is bound to increase: youth not discharged by 1999 are almost certain to age out. This will alter the outcomes for the group substantially, likely by raising the proportion of youth who age out to a quarter of the cohort. Most of these youth entered care because of abuse or neglect.

Reentry into Foster Care

Approximately one in five youth in the study group reentered care at least once (table 5.9). Status offender entrants, who have shorter lengths

text continues on page 105

Table 5.8. Destination of Last Discharge from Foster Care by Reason for Entry

	Parent/Relative		Adopted		Institution		AWOL & Admin		Aged Out		Other		Total
	n	%	n	%	n	%	n	%	n	%	n	%	
Abuse/neglect	299	76	9	2	16	4	42	11	25	6	1	0	392
Status offense	442	72	0	0	34	6	119	19	14	2	5	1	614
Juvenile delinquency	8	67	0	0	0	0	4	33	0	0	0	0	12
Voluntary placement	229	64	9	3	26	7	68	19	22	6	2	0	356
Uncategorized	172	68	2	1	10	4	60	24	8	3	2	1	254
Total discharges (n = 1,628)	1,150	71	20	1	86	5	293	18	69	4	10	1	1,628
Total of study group (n = 2,019)	1,150	57	20	1	86	4	293	15	69	3	10	0	1,628

Source: Child Care Review Service.

Table 5.9. Number of Spells in Care by Reason for Entry

	First Spell		Second Spell			Third Spell		
	Total	Discharged	No. returning	% of total	Discharged	No. returning	% of total	Discharged
Abuse/neglect	576	411	87	15	49	11	2	8
Status offense	666	630	175	26	155	33	5	3
Juvenile delinquency	14	12	2	14	2	1	7	0
Voluntary placement	482	373	81	17	67	23	5	21
Uncategorized	281	262	47	17	35	9	3	7
Total	2,019	1,688	392	19	308	77	4	39

Source: Child Care Review Service.

of stay in their first spell, were more likely to reenter care than other children in the study group: over a quarter reentered care, and they account for 45 percent of all study group reentries. Abuse/neglect entrants and those who enter care on a voluntary agreement reentered care at rates of 15 and 17 percent, respectively.

Time from Discharge to Reentry

Among youth who have second spells in care, two-thirds reenter within one year of discharge (figure 5.4). Status offender entrants who reenter care are more likely to do so within a year than youth who originally entered on abuse/neglect petitions or voluntary placements, an expected finding given the vagaries of the status offender court process. For those children who did reenter care within one year, most reentered within the first six months after their discharges (figure 5.5). Status offender entrants reentered at their highest rate in the third month after discharge, with their reentry rate declining thereafter. Other groups demonstrated a more consistent rate of reentry throughout the year.

Figure 5.4. Years between First Discharge and Reentry into Care ($n = 392$)

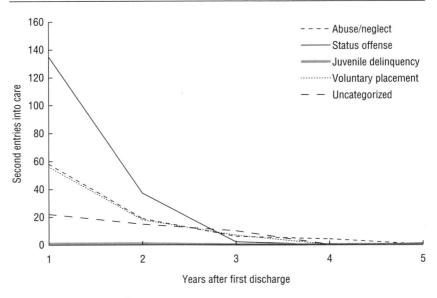

Source: Child Care Review Service.

Figure 5.5. Reentries within One Year of Discharge
(*n* = 263, 67 percent of second entries into care)

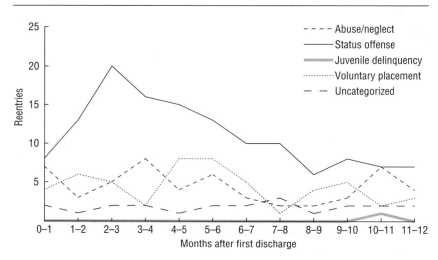

Months after first discharge

Source: Child Care Review Service.

Changes in Reason for Entry across Spells

Researchers also analyzed how frequently reasons for entry changed
when a child reentered care (table 5.10). Reason for entry showed a high
level of consistency. Over two-thirds of abuse/neglect and status offender
entrants who reentered care did so for the same reason, as did nearly
60 percent of those voluntarily placed. However, the greatest overlap is
between status offenders and voluntary children. Of the status offenders
who reentered care, 22 percent reentered through voluntary agreements.
Of the children who first entered care through voluntary agreements and
subsequently reentered, 20 percent reentered through PINS petitions.

Placement Cost

To estimate the cost of care by reason for entry, researchers calculated the
average number of days spent in each placement type *over all spells* through
May 1, 1999 (table 5.11). Considering all spells allows researchers to project average lifetime costs per child regardless of the number of reentries.
Multiplying congregate care days by $170 a day and foster boarding
home and kinship costs by $40 a day produced an average cost per youth.[13]

Table 5.10. First Reason for Entry by Reason for Reentry

	Abuse/ neglect	Status offense	Juvenile delinquency	Voluntary placement	Uncategorized	No legal action	Total
Abuse/neglect	57	4	0	13	12	0	86
Status offense	2	121	2	39	13	0	177
Juvenile delinquency	1	0	1	0	0	0	2
Voluntary placement	5	17	0	51	13	0	86
Uncategorized	4	4	1	12	3	0	24
No legal action	0	0	0	0	0	16	16
Total	69	146	4	115	41	16	391

Source: Child Care Review Service.

To calculate the cost per day, the researchers divided the average cost per youth by the average number of days in care. Because some youth had not finished their stays in foster care, these numbers should be seen as the five-year cost of this group, not the lifetime cost.

The handful of juvenile delinquent placements have the highest average placement cost ($102,530), followed by voluntarily placed children ($93,660). This represents 44 percent more than the average early adolescent entrant ($65,171), and easily out-distances status offender and abuse/neglect entrants. The cost for voluntarily placed children reflects the relatively long length of stay and that two-thirds of these days are spent in congregate care—the most expensive placement type. The cost of status offender entrants is also revealing: on average, they cost just 12 percent less than abuse/neglect entrants despite their brief median length of stay. Virtually all status offender entrants spent their entire stay in congregate care; not a single youth entered a kinship placement. A large percentage of status offender costs is created by the small percentage of such youth permanently placed in foster care.

Discussion

Since this study was exploratory, it did not seek to prove or disprove specific hypotheses. In addition, the authors did not have the opportunity to examine case file materials, which limits the conclusions they can

Table 5.11. Estimated Placement Cost by Reason for Entry

Reason for entry	n	Still in Care		N	Time Spent in Care (average number of days)						Average total cost	Average daily cost
					Congregate		Foster Boarding		Kinship Home			
		n	%		n	%	n	%	n	%		
Abuse/neglect	576	206	36	944	186	20	409	43	349	37	$61,905	$65.57
Status offender	666	61	9	339	314	93	26	8	0	0	$54,420	$160.53
Juvenile delinquency	14	3	21	650	589	91	60	9	0	0	$102,530	$157.74
Voluntary placement	482	127	26	748	490	66	236	32	23	3	$93,660	$125.21
Uncategorized	281	34	12	379	242	64	113	30	24	6	$46,617	$123.01
Total	2,019	431	21	3,060	1,821	50	844	32	396	18	$65,171	$105.63

Source: Child Care Review Service.

draw. Nonetheless, the mass of data in the results provides the basis to offer an initial typology of early adolescent cases.

The data suggest three patterns in adolescents' pathways through the foster care system. The patterns are linked to the reasons children enter care. The researchers named the patterns "quick turnarounds," "repeaters," and "longtermers," based on short stays in care (less than two months), reentries into care, and lengthy stays in care (from entry in 1994 through May 1999), respectively. Of the early adolescents in the 1994 cohort, 57 percent experienced the foster care system in one of these ways; the remainder entered care only once and stayed longer than two months but less than the entire period.

Quick Turnarounds

Quick turnarounds are early adolescents who enter foster care only once and are discharged within two months. Quick turnarounds account for 25 percent of the study group. Over one-third (35 percent) of the status offender entrants can be classified as quick turnarounds, compared with 15 percent of the voluntaries and 11 percent of those placed as a result of abuse/neglect petitions. With an average age at entry of 14.4 years, quick turnarounds are five months older on average than the rest of the early adolescent group.

Four of five quick turnarounds are discharged to parents or relatives, with virtually all the remainder discharged to AWOL (16 percent) or administrative action (2 percent). Length of stay statistics show that most quick turnarounds stay for much less than two months. Seventy-three percent stay in care for 30 days or less, and almost 50 percent for 10 days or less.

Despite the short time these children spend in foster care, they consume a noticeable amount of resources. Three-quarters of these children are first placed in congregate care, one-quarter in foster boarding homes, and less than 1 percent in kinship homes. Quick turnarounds occupy the equivalent of 20 congregate care beds for an entire year, at a cost of $1.2 million. Though in care for a short time, the group accounts for 121 AWOLs and have an extraordinary AWOL rate of 13.8 per 1,000 care days. Opening and closing cases and searching for AWOL children are labor intensive (see chapter 6). Thus, the true cost of managing the quick turnarounds is considerably higher than the one calculated here.

It appears that families and the Family Court may be using foster care as respite care. Respite care can be an effective intervention in many instances.[14] The foster care system, however, is neither intended for nor designed as a respite care resource. This suggests that child welfare officials—likely working with the status offender system and mental health agencies—may want to consider developing specialized respite care programming.

Designing such a program would require more research on the presenting problems of the quick turnaround population. Such research would focus on determining whether specific markers could help status offender and child welfare staff identify this group when it is first is considered for foster care. As chapter 7 discusses, many status offenders systems, including New York City's, focus their operations on connecting youth to services quickly in the hope of diverting these children from foster care. Part of this research would involve learning more about these childrens' families and what services might have allowed them to keep their children at home without a foster care stay.

Repeaters

Repeaters are foster children who reenter care at least once following a discharge. The study group contains 393 repeaters, or 19 percent of the total. Almost all these children reenter care only once. Over 25 percent of status offender entrants are repeaters, compared with 17 percent of voluntary placements and 15 percent of abuse/neglect entrants. With an average age of 13.7 years, repeaters are three months younger on average than the group as a whole.

Over two-thirds of repeaters enter congregate care as their first placement, and an even higher share (79 percent) enter congregate care at the start of their second spell. Most repeaters (57 percent) spend all their time in congregate care, while only 8 percent reside exclusively in foster boarding homes and 1 percent in kinship homes. Eighty-two percent are discharged home following their first spell, and 9 percent are discharged to AWOL. Of those discharged a second time (75 percent of all repeaters), only 62 percent go back to their parent(s), and 21 percent are discharged to AWOL. Repeaters spend an average of 141 days in care during their first spell and 377 days during the second spell, a 267 percent increase. Overall, repeaters have an AWOL rate of 2.4 events per 1,000 days in care, or 70 percent higher than the average for the whole study group. In addition, 26 percent of repeaters enter juvenile detention facilities, a rate 70 percent higher than the study group as a whole.

The rate of return to foster care for this group suggests a focus on "aftercare" programs—services available following family reunification.

Aftercare services should be designed generally for an adolescent population but need to have the flexibility to enable a custom plan to be developed for each family. In the past few years, some jurisdictions have experimented with Multidimensional Systemic Therapy, Functional Family Therapy, and Adolescent Portable Therapy as aftercare services, though the results from these initiatives are not yet definitive.

Longtermers

Longtermers are adolescents who remain in foster care without a discharge from their first entrance in 1994 through May 1, 1999, the end of the study period.[15] While these youth account for only 13 percent of the study group, they are of particular concern because of the lack of permanency, the cost of the foster care they experience, and the diminished likelihood of positive outcomes after such a long stay in care. Half of these youth enter care through abuse/neglect petitions, and one-third enter on voluntary placements; this translates to roughly one of every four abuse/neglect entrants and one of every five voluntary placements in the study group. Only 11 percent originally come into care on status offender petitions (this constitutes only 5 percent of the status offender entrants). With an average age at entry of 13.4 years, longtermers are seven months younger on average than the group as a whole.

On average, the child welfare system spent $150,471 on each of these 270 children, or $40.6 million through the five-year period, and this number will increase. Longtermers consume 468 bed-years of congregate care, 489 bed-years of foster boarding home care, and 244 bed-years of kinship care. Congregate care costs account for 74 percent of the total amount spent on providing services to these children. In other words, though longtermers spend more time in family-type care, congregate care consumes the vast majority of resources.

This group stands out in two other ways. These children appear to come from homes where caseworkers viewed a trial discharge as unlikely to succeed and youth rarely ran away from care. Only 6 percent ever experienced a trial discharge. While one-third of the group has at least one AWOL event, 24 children (9 percent of all longtermers) account for 62 percent of the total number of AWOLs. The group as a whole has only .58 AWOLs per 1,000 care days.

The deadlines imposed by the federal Adoption and Safe Families Act in late 1997 give child welfare staff incentives and mandates to move kids out of foster care more quickly. ASFA has helped speed time to permanency in many jurisdictions and in many subgroups of the child welfare population—especially younger children. The increased use of treatment foster care and other innovations in many places has reduced reliance on congregate care for teens. Still, adolescents make up an increasing percentage of the foster care census. Developing quicker and more stable pathways to permanency will remain a challenge.

Conclusion

In New York and in many other jurisdictions, adolescents are an increasing proportion of the foster care census. This chapter focused on the different avenues that adolescents enter foster care. It found that how a young person enters foster care affects the pathway he or she will follow while in care and how he or she will leave care.

The strength of this research lies in the large numbers examined and the ability to follow what happens to youth over time. However, future research in this area might delve more deeply into the specific circumstances that lead to placement and discharge and how these circumstances might affect service plans, placement choices, and other aspects of the foster care experience. For example, the research in this chapter shows that youth who enter care through abuse or neglect stay in care longer than youth who enter through voluntary agreements, but researchers do not know much about why that difference exists. The difference might be related to the mechanism of entry: in theory, a youth voluntarily placed might be reunified with her family more quickly because voluntary agreements have fewer legal restrictions for returning a child than abuse/neglect petitions. Alternatively, the longer lengths of stay might be explained by the different circumstances and characteristics of the families and children involved. Examining case files and speaking with caseworkers and the families would help put the analysis presented above in context.

The research suggests that cross-cutting issues play a role in what happens to adolescents that enter care. This chapter, for example, does not discuss why status offenders might have such divergent outcomes in care or what could be done about them. Chapter 7 tackles this question. Nor does the chapter address issues that arise when youth in care enter the delinquency system—an issue discussed in chapters 8 and 9. Understanding how the foster care experiences of youth differ by how they enter the system, however, sets the stage for these discussions.

6

Youth Who Chronically Leave Foster Care without Permission
Why They Run, Where They Go, and What Can Be Done

When I had got sent upstate [to a congregate care facility], first I was trying to figure out how to get out of there . . . it was scary. I didn't want to be there . . . It
seems like a nightmare now . . . And that Saturday morning I got up. Two of the
girls was going AWOL so they were telling me that I could leave with them . . . We
ran out . . . we were running through people's backyards. I came through and
there goes the van from my place. They was telling me to get in the van. I was so
scared. I kept on running . . . I had to sit in the cemetery for two hours 'cause
I was scared to get up. They came in the cemetery looking. That is when I had
to go. I fell into a lake. I came out . . . I was scratched up, bruised up . . . I found like
the train . . . And I ended up getting on the train, on the Metro North. I had to
hide in the bathroom 'cause I didn't have no way [no money] to get on the train.
—Heidi, age 15[1]

This chapter explores several issues related to youth who leave foster
care without permission, commonly referred to as "going AWOL."[2]
A common fear among the adults responsible for foster children who go
AWOL is that they will return to an abusive home where they will be at
risk of further maltreatment. Another fear is that AWOL youth end up
living on the streets, homeless and without resources. Desperate, these
children may become involved in prostitution, drugs, and other dangerous activities.

Despite these risks, many basic questions concerning AWOL foster
youth have received little attention from researchers—a gap that the study
in this chapter seeks to ameliorate. By examining some administrative

data and speaking with kids about their experiences and motivations, the study focuses on some basic questions: Who goes AWOL from foster care? Why do foster youth go AWOL? Where do they go, and what risks do they encounter while AWOL? The literature on children and youth who run away from home may provide some clues to these questions, but there has been little work directly comparing runaway youth with AWOL foster youth.

There are also many questions about how child welfare and the other systems inevitably drawn into AWOL situations react. How do child welfare staff respond when youth go AWOL? How can child welfare agencies handle this issue more effectively? What role do police and school officials play when a youth is reported AWOL? This chapter provides some tentative answers to some of these questions. Before outlining the methods and findings of this study, a review of what is known about AWOL places the rest of the chapter in context.

Understanding the Problem

Youth who go AWOL present some of the most difficult challenges to foster parents, child welfare staff, police, school officials, and other adults charged with ensuring their well-being. AWOL youth may be in danger if they run back to an abusive home or to another hazardous situation, and since AWOL youth are unlikely to be in school, their education is disrupted. Police may assist in finding AWOL youth and returning them to care, but reporting youth to the police often undermines the fragile trust developed between staff and the youth they serve. And while staff may not want to involve law enforcement, child welfare policies usually mandate a missing persons report when youth go AWOL for more than two days. In some cases, youth who AWOL may be leaving a foster care situation because they have legitimate safety concerns (Biehal and Wade 2000). If child welfare staff members fail to identify and act in these situations, the youth will continue to be in danger, and another AWOL is all but inevitable.

To complicate matters further, agencies are legally liable for youth in their care—even when they are AWOL. If harm comes to a youth, child welfare agencies may be sued on charges of negligent supervision.[3] However, child welfare staff can implement few restrictive measures. Best practices, ethics, and the law prevent foster care facilities from resembling secure facilities such as jails or prisons. In practice, foster parents and congregate care staff usually must rely on their powers of persuasion and their relationships with the youth in their care to prevent AWOLs.

In addition to the danger youth may encounter, AWOL events create a host of intra- and interagency problems. For foster care providers and child welfare agencies, an AWOL event often triggers a wave of reporting requirements to the child welfare agency, police, parents, and others. Diligent efforts must be made to find the missing youth by child welfare staff. Police must spend time filling out missing persons reports, looking for AWOL youth, and returning them to care. Schools need to be notified. Other service providers, whether privately funded agencies or government-run runaway shelters, also spend time and money on youth who AWOL from foster care. When a youth repeatedly goes AWOL, efforts to find and return him or her to care can be costly and frustrating to all involved. In some cases, this frustration may lead to slow or ineffective responses—leaving youth at risk for longer periods. Taken to the extreme, older youth may be discharged as a result of going AWOL, which may disqualify them from a range of benefits they would otherwise receive.

Youth who go AWOL are also at risk of a placement transfer. A youth returning to foster care after an AWOL may find that his or her foster parents are unwilling to take the youth back into their care. More often, a group home may have filled the youth's bed if the AWOL lasted more than a few days.[4] Losing a bed may mean staying at an emergency placement facility until a new placement is found—and AWOL youth may be labeled "hard to place" because of this history. The new placement also means developing relationships with new caregivers and housemates. Depending on the location of the new placement, a transfer may require registering at a new school.

Despite these potentially serious consequences, AWOL has received relatively little attention from researchers. Much of the existing research has been conducted in Britain, and the available data on AWOL foster children and nonfoster youth running away from home are of low quality.

According to the research, AWOL is both a marker and a cause of other problems. One study finds that though many youth placed in foster care show a marked improvement in school attendance, youth who go AWOL enter care with worse attendance records than their fellow foster youth and attend school less after placement (Conger and Rebeck 2001). Among foster youth who are arrested, judges are more likely to detain foster youth with an AWOL history than those who have never gone AWOL.[5] Youth placed in foster care through status offenses, referred to as persons in need of supervision in New York State, go AWOL more often than foster children placed for other reasons (see chapter 7 for more information on status offenders).[6] One study reports that youth who go AWOL tend to be age 15 or older, and nearly three-quarters of all AWOLs are reported from group homes (Ross 2001). As the cohort study presented in chapter 5 of this book shows, AWOLs are often concentrated among a small number of youth: although 40 percent of the cohort went AWOL at least once, only 3 percent of the cohort went AWOL more than twice, and they accounted for 54 percent of the entire cohort's AWOL events.

Adolescence alone is often cited as a primary reason for AWOL behavior. Indeed, "running away" is a term almost unique to adolescents: younger children are referred to as "missing" or "lost." But nonfoster youth who run away cannot have AWOL records—going AWOL is unique to those youth in foster care. Certainly, adolescence is a turbulent time characterized by resistance to authority, exploration of self-identity, and anxiety about social position (Steinberg and Morris 2001). A Centers for Disease Control study estimates that nationwide about 16 percent of adolescents have run away from their homes for at least one night in the previous year (Adams et al. 1995). While transitioning to adulthood is difficult under most circumstances, it can be especially challenging for foster youth who have experienced abuse, neglect, or other problems with their biological families (Moffitt 1993).

But developmental changes alone are not a satisfying explanation for AWOL activity. Most youth never run away, and most youth in foster care do not go AWOL. Researchers have found that foster youth who go AWOL have emotional or psychological problems that began before they entered foster care (Fine 1985; Klee and Halfon 1987). Foster care placement is a traumatic experience that can trigger a range of behaviors (Hochstadt et al. 1987; Salahu-Din and Bollman 1994). Regarding youth in foster care who leave without permission, one researcher asserts that "the failure of many state programs to extend screening, counseling, and other rehabilitative services [essentially, 'treatment'] to runaways and potential runaways results in a higher rate of running behavior among foster youth than among other youth" (Ryan 1993, 279–80).

While AWOL behavior has psychological roots, many foster youth have mental health issues but do not go AWOL. Little research captures the voice of foster youth. One of the few examples is a two-year study of run-aways in California, where researchers asked youth if anything could have changed their minds about running away. The 11 percent of the sample who were foster youth stated that they would not have run away if long-standing problems related to their placement had been resolved or if an alternative placement had been offered (Miller et al. 1980).

This gap in the research has real consequences for policy. Knowing more about why foster youth say they go AWOL would provide sugges-tions for service reforms. In addition, the proximate causes of AWOL may be easier and less expensive to address than deep psychological ones. The lack of knowledge about what happens when foster youth are AWOL leaves managers to guess the risks youth face. Finally, there is lit-tle information to guide the development of best practices on the part of foster care providers.

A Study of AWOL in New York City

To learn more about absences without permission, researchers inter-viewed 30 youth with AWOL histories who were in foster care at the time of the research, as well as 17 staff who worked at 11 different facilities. The research focused on youth age 15 to 20 who ran away repeatedly from congregate care. The youth were randomly selected from a group of all youth with these characteristics generated from child welfare administrative data.[7] The study sought to learn more about three issues: the factors foster youth identify as contributing to their decision to go AWOL, youth experiences while AWOL, and how facilities work to pre-vent and respond to these situations.

The youth in this sample differed in some respects from most youth in the foster care system and even from the majority of youth who AWOL. Nearly two-thirds entered care as a result of a status offense or a voluntary placement, rather than for abuse or neglect, compared with just over half for other youth who go AWOL (table 6.1). PINS petitions and voluntary placements often stem from a parent's inability to control a child and from concern about dangerous behaviors. In addition, 17 of the 30 teens interviewed reported running away before entering care. Studies in Britain have suggested that running away before placement is strongly associated with AWOL behavior while in care (Rees 1993; Stein, Rees, and Frost 1994; Wade and Biehal 1998). The youth in this study

Table 6.1. Comparison of Study Sample to Chronic and Single AWOLers

	Sample (n = 30)	Chronic AWOLers[a] (n = 692)	Single AWOLers (n = 848)
Gender	female: 24 (80%) male: 6 (20%)	female: 328 (54%) male: 286 (46%)	female: 445 (52%) male: 403 (43%)
Age at first placement (years, mean/median)	15.3/15.0	13.2/14	14.1/15
Facility type	Institution: 11 (44%) Group residence: 2 (8%) Group home: 11 (44%) AOBH: 1 (4%)	Institution: 312 (50%) Group residence: 49 (8%) Group home: 214 (35%) AOBH: 39 (6%)	Institution: 356 (42%) Group residence: 104 (12%) Group home: 265 (35%) AOBH: 91 (11%)
Reason	Abuse/neglect: 5 (20%) PINS: 6 (24%) Voluntary: 10 (40%) Unknown: 4 (16%)	Abuse/neglect: 5 (36%) PINS: 93 (16%) Voluntary: 213 (36%) Unknown: 72 (12%)	Abuse/neglect: 259 (32%) PINS: 128 (16%) Voluntary: 301 (37%) Unknown: 15 (14%)
Number of AWOLs (mean/median)	6.4/4.0	4.7/3.0	1.0

AOBH = agency-operated boarding homes

PINS = persons in need of supervision

a. Chronic AWOLers are children in foster care who, according to the CCRS, had at least two AWOLs from congregate care during their most recent spells in foster care as of January 1, 2002.

had also experienced more placement transfers than most youth in foster care (Ross et al. 2001).

The study sample consisted mostly of girls (80 percent) and ranged from 15 to 20 years old with an average age of 17. Most of the sample entered foster care after age 13. One-third first went AWOL within 6 months of being placed in foster care, another third between 6 and 12 months, and the final third a year or more after placement. This final third was usually placed in foster care before the girls turned 13. The youth had between 2 and 19 AWOL reports, and the length of the longest AWOL ranged from two days to six months.[8] Table 6.2 further describes the characteristics of the sample.

For the adult sample, researchers interviewed 17 staff members from 11 facilities: seven different contract congregate care facilities and four group facilities run directly by the child welfare agency. These individuals included the director of the facility and/or one frontline staff member who had substantial daily contact with the youth. The researchers sought viewpoints from professionals in different roles to elicit diverse views about AWOL policies and activity at their facilities. The adults were chosen as part of a purposive sample, which relies on the identification of individuals and groups who are likely to possess specialized knowledge (Bernard 1994). In particular, the researchers tried to include staff from facilities of varying sizes and levels of restrictiveness, and with varying reputations regarding the extent of their AWOL problems.

This methodology has some limitations. The findings may be representative of a population of youth who have a history of *chronic* AWOLs,

Table 6.2. Characteristics of Participants' AWOLs (*N* = 30)

	Number	Percent
Number of AWOLs		
Fewer than 5	14	48
Between 5 and 10	7	24
More than 10	8	28
Longest AWOL episode		
1 week or shorter	13	45
1 week–1 month	4	14
1 month–3 months	6	21
Longer than 3 months	6	21

but they may not apply to youth who have only one AWOL or to the foster care population in general. Since each youth was interviewed only once, interviewers did not have the opportunity to develop a long-term rapport. In this sense, youth may have self-censored the information they divulged based on their own level of trust and their individual personalities.

Table 6.1 shows a cross-sectional sample drawn from New York City's child welfare administrative database. The sample differs from the majority of youth who AWOL in a few key ways, including gender and age at placement. The older populations, including girls placed in mother-child facilities, generally were more likely to return researcher phone calls and attend scheduled interviews. Although the sample differs from the chronic AWOL populations on these measures, the group offered researchers the advantage of speaking to youth who had outgrown the urge to AWOL. This allowed researchers to find patterns in the changes in their attitudes, life circumstances, and placement that stopped them from going AWOL.

Why Youth Run from Foster Care

> It was like my whole freedom was taken away. I was in the middle of nowhere,
> I was all the way in Hastings, I didn't know nothing about upstate [New York],
> and I didn't like it. —Jeanette, age 19

For the youth in this study, running from care was often an attempt to seek relief from some aspect of the foster care system. Their motivations for running can be separated into problems at placements that "pushed" them to run, and family- and friend-centered factors that "pulled" them toward going AWOL. Other studies of youth going AWOL from foster care have also cited these two kinds of factors (Ackland 1981; Miller, Eggertson-Tacon, and Quigg 1990; Payne 1995; Wade and Biehal 1998). While some of the New York City data likely reinforce what foster care professionals might anticipate as motivations for youth going AWOL, other areas youth cited were unexpected and not well documented in the literature.

Problems at Placements

Twenty-five of the 30 youth interviewed identified problems at their placements as a cause for at least some of their AWOL activity. These problems were rooted in the youths' own behavior, their perceptions of systemic or organizational problems at the facilities, or serious problems with peers or staff members. For 13 of them, placement problems overlapped with their desire to see family and friends as primary reasons for going AWOL. Researchers grouped placement-centered reasons for going AWOL into two main categories—frustration with the system and social stress—as youth repeatedly used the words frustration and stress to explain why they went AWOL.

Certain aspects of the foster care system provoked immediate frustration, while others built up over time. For example, many youth expressed a feeling of constant boredom that contributed to an overall belief that they were languishing in their placements. Boredom usually became most acute on nights and weekends and during the summer, especially in facilities that restricted access to the outside or required youth to be under constant adult supervision. Supervision policies are set by individual contract agencies and the type of placement. For example, some group homes allow youth to sign themselves out of the facility for social activities, such as going to the movies. In contrast, some large facilities in the New York City suburbs do not allow residents to leave their cottages for unscheduled activities unless accompanied by an adult supervisor.

Boredom can lead to alienation among adolescents (Tolor 1989). Many youth who reported that they were bored also said that they did not feel connected to the peers or adults at their facilities. The residents' boredom put an onus on facility staff to provide activities and entertainment, and many residents were critical of their performance. Michael, age 17, explained his usual weekend experience at his suburban campus-based placement:

> Basically . . . you are in the house . . . Fridays and Saturdays we rarely go on activity.

> All day we on campus, bored in the house, so we go outside, get high, whatever, hang out with the girls, do this or that. And really, when we don't feel like hearing them out, like "Why was you unaccountable?" . . . we go AWOL for the whole weekend so we don't have to deal with it.

Desiree, age 17, who was also in a campus-based placement, had similar feelings:

> Sometimes I feel I am in a lock-up facility 'cause we are really not allowed to go anywhere during the week. Only on the weekends we could go home to our family if we are allowed to or if you are on a certain amount of weeks of positive you could go on day passes and stuff. Otherwise, you can't go anywhere. Most of the time staff don't want to go outside 'cause either they are just tired or they feel there

is no reason to go outside, so you can't go anywhere. We sit in here all day and do nothing. Most of the time I'm sleeping if I have to be in here.

Some staff members acknowledged boredom as a major factor that pushed youth to AWOL.

We understand that the program is boring for them, that they want to go and hang out.—Inez, child welfare specialist, group home

Other factors also contributed to running from care. Some youth reported that they knew little about the progress of their case; this contributed to their frustration and sense of languishing in care. Some claimed that they were not receiving proper treatment or evaluations or that they could not pursue career opportunities. Others suspected that facility staff members acted deceptively when communicating about their cases. Camilla, age 18, depicted her turmoil by saying, "I was fed up! I wasn't getting no psychiatrist evaluation like they said I was. I wasn't being processed for leaving. I was fighting a lot." Tara, age 17, was similarly critical of her facility's staff:

I did everything for myself. If I didn't have the support system outside of the group home I wouldn't have—I would not have known what steps to take as far as getting into school, as far as getting a job, as far as finding therapy for myself.

One child recounted that staff encouraged him to go AWOL to pursue a promising trade apprenticeship because the apprenticeship's hours could not be reconciled with the facility policies at his placement.

Attitudes toward rules and authority become more unfavorable as adolescents age, specifically during high school years (Levy 2001). As children transition into adolescence, their reasoning skills increase and they have a greater tendency to question authority. Further, when adolescents obey the rules set by an authority figure, it has less to do with their responding to or respecting the authority than the youths' degree of internal acceptance of the rules (Smetana 1998). Therefore, if adolescents agree with the rules being set, they are more likely to follow them, regardless of who set them.

Not unexpectedly, the increased demands and restrictions youth face upon entering care are related to immediate frustrations. Demands include chores and other responsibilities. Restrictions are permanent rules, such as curfews, or punishments, such as limits on watching television or going outside. The number of permanent restrictions varied according to facility type. The most restrictive placements were the highly structured residential treatment centers (RTCs), where the higher levels of supervision are in place to serve youth who are felt to need more intense services.

Several youth mentioned their difficulty in adjusting to a more structured environment. Jessica, age 16, a resident in a group home, stated, "Like the staff telling you to do this, telling you to do that, do your chores, or you didn't do your chores, you missed a spot here, you missed that spot." Resistance to restrictions took on greater prominence when youth grew older or when restrictions were applied to young people already testing the system. Emma, a 20-year-old, explained why she didn't ask staff for permission to leave. "Yeah, because you have to ask for everything in this house. Twenty years old, I don't think you should have to ask for juice or food, but you have to. So it is like you are a little-ass kid." Adrian, age 18, agreed:

> If you do a chore you get five minutes outside, what's five minutes going to do for me? I'm basically 18, you know what I mean? . . . With me, I want to be able to step out the door, go find a job, or become something in my life.

Several youth explained that restrictive punishments, especially when levied for what they saw as minor violations of facility rules, such as smoking, exacerbated their desire to leave. Isabel, age 17, was one such youth:

> Yeah, they are strict, and you have people in here that are like 18 or 19, and they are giving us restriction. And that means we can't go outside, like it was a nice day like it is today, we can't go outside, and that makes a person want to AWOL. That's why I break restriction and I used to AWOL, because they didn't let my family come here when I was on restriction.

Many youth reported social stress related to placement. Few of the youth interviewed said they felt connected with their peers or with the staff at their facilities. Reasons given for this disconnection ranged from age and personality differences to distrust to outright animosity and violence by both peers and staff. A few youth mentioned that sexual incidents played a role in creating stress and prompting them to run from care. For example, Camilla told interviewers that the sexual activity occurring at her facility created a negative environment for her:

> Yes, you pick up all the negativity . . . there was a lot of sexual activity up there. A lot of people had babies with other residents up there and sharing lots of diseases like chlamydia and gonorrhea and herpes, 'cause they wasn't teaching them about sex.

Jessica recounted how she thought of going AWOL for the first time after being sexually assaulted by another resident in a group home four days before her 13th birthday. She did not initially report the incident and said that many staff did not believe her when she did. Only after several requests was she transferred to another facility. Jessica added that she last AWOLed after being returned to the same facility years later, when a boyfriend she described as "really crazy" and abusive forced her to pack her things and leave with him. Jessica feels that the sexual assault contributed to future problems, as she later became seriously involved with drugs and entangled in abusive relationships. Her story also represented a worst-case scenario; no other child reported being sexually assaulted while in care or reported that such incidents were common. Sexual issues also became a major pull factor drawing young people out of care, as discussed later in this section.

Overall, the youth portrayed environments where stealing, bullying, and fights were common, including some instigated by study participants. Heidi told interviewers, "I used to leave because people was taking my stuff, I just didn't like the group home." Andrea, age 19, added:

> I'm having a lot of problems with the girls in this house. You know, one of the girls calls me Spic and stuff like that. And it is very uncomfortable when they are threatening your child, and when they are stealing your stuff, they spitting in your food.

In a few cases, youth perceived staff as taking part in bullying, physical abuse, or sexual misconduct with the residents. Sally, age 17, said:

> The staff in there, they are supposed to be there to help us, but what they really do is cut us down, they curse us down, they even fight us. And like the male staff be having intercourse with the other females. . . . [Apart from a few staff members] . . . everybody else, they don't care about the kids, they just go up there, do whatever to get their money. But I never really liked it up there, that's why I always used to run away. . . . I got bullied a lot of times, by boys, by girls, even staff I got bullied by. So I got tired of it and I left.

Camilla explained that the staff at her facility left her to fend for herself after she was involved in fights with other girls. "The staff wasn't providing me with any help, any security, like these girls really want to kill me. I just be dead, 'cause the jealousy and animosity was getting real, it was getting stronger and there was nothing they were doing about it." Michael summed up his opinion of facility staff this way:

> 'Cause that is what my mother used to do to me. She used to always put me down and that used to make me feel bad. And half the staff say they know what it's like, but they come here with their problems. Come here, curse at kids, get mad, take

out their family problems or whatever. This really ain't a good place for them to work, and that is part of the reason that a lot of kids go AWOL.

In the worst incident involving staff, Isabel described the events surrounding her first AWOL:

There was a rumor going around that I was having sex with someone and I was like 10 years old . . . I wasn't doing nothing and the staff took a hockey stick, like a plastic hockey stick, and she was beating me with it. I mean, actually beating me. I got mad and packed my stuff. That's the first time I left.

Some staff members acknowledged that youth faced threats to their safety within group-living situations. Kirsten, the director at a diagnostic reception center, mentioned a primary push factor being a feeling of danger within the placement:

When a kid is unsafe he is going to run and it shouldn't be that way. But you know, sometimes, as you hear about homeless people, they feel safer on the streets in front of the church than they do in the shelters. And so if a kid doesn't feel safe in school, at home, where he is living . . . sometimes there are young people that have no sense of support other than [on the streets], and that is not always a positive place to be.

Taken together, the chronically AWOLing youth described themselves as being bored and under constant pressure and stress living in congregate care, and they felt that going AWOL was a logical response to their situations. Certainly, for some youth, part of this pressure was rooted in their own behavior, be it fighting with peers or breaking facility rules. But the overall outcome was the same. As Emma stated, "I know what I do when I feel stressed. If I feel stressed and overwhelmed, I am definitely going to AWOL. I have no reason to stay here and listen to it any more."

The Pull of Family and Friends

Seventeen youth told interviewers that their desire to see family or friends influenced their decisions to AWOL. For 13, this draw included negative feelings toward their placements. For the other four, it was the primary reason for all their AWOLs. The situations that led them to AWOL to family and friends did not fit a single pattern. Youth more often AWOLed to see friends than to see family.

Many AWOLs were tied tangentially to sexual issues, such as going to see boyfriends and girlfriends. Interviewers also learned that complications regarding home passes are often related to AWOLs. Overall, teens

AWOLed because they missed family, friends, and boyfriends; they wanted to stay out past curfew; they wanted to leave with other teens; and they had family crises and events.

Youth commonly expressed a general sense of not fitting in at their placements combined with strong feelings of missing their families, friends, and old neighborhoods, which were often a significant distance from their facilities. In describing her first AWOL, Lola, age 17, simply stated, "I ran away . . . because that was the first time being away from my family, and I didn't get along with the other kids that was there. So I just left and I went back to my grandma." Sally, in a facility in Yonkers, continued to AWOL for this reason throughout her time in care, saying, "I miss my friends that I had in Brooklyn, so I usually go AWOL just to see them . . . When I had my time . . . I'd go back to the group home." Andrea summed up the situation simply and powerfully by saying, "I miss my siblings, and I wanted to be home with them. You know, you are not home until you're home."

Among this group, policies about granting home passes were a recurrent issue. While some youth overstayed home visits while on passes, they often said that they did not consider these AWOLs. They were more accurately extensions of their visits, from which they planned to come back before they lost their beds. Others felt that facility staff unreasonably denied them passes in an attempt to keep them from their parents or because their destination was not with a family member. Not getting a home pass was particularly hard during holidays and weekends when other youth had permission to leave. Isabel voiced these frustrations by saying,

> They give you a day pass from 10 [a.m.] to 10 [p.m.]. What is that?! You can't go out. And on a holiday you can't go out on an overnight . . . You want to be there to open presents with your family and have Christmas dinner . . . and chilling and talking about things.

Several youth stated that they began AWOLing after being denied passes but that they did not continue AWOLing after being allowed home consistently. Sometimes youth who were continuously denied home passes because of AWOLs became trapped in a cycle of having to run away to see their families or friends. Andrea believed that her AWOLs might have led to her receiving weekend passes. "Yeah, matter of fact I didn't have weekend passes. I started AWOLing and that is when they started giving me weekend passes. You know what I am saying? I had to AWOL to get weekend passes."

A handful of youth explained how a family crisis or the influence of another resident led them to run from care. In the first scenario, the child usually could not get a home pass. In the second, a youth new to a facility was brought along on an AWOL with another child in order to meet his or her friends or family. One family crisis mentioned several times was girls becoming pregnant and seeking out the comfort of their mothers or boyfriends at some point during the pregnancy. Andrea explained:

> I wanted to be home with my mother on weekends . . . and I don't think I was allowed it . . . Once I got pregnant, that's when I started AWOLing . . . I was pregnant and I needed my mother, and I would stay for months and months and months.

Olga, age 17, described her last AWOL, which was a combination of family crisis and a friend-influenced AWOL:

> The last time I ran away . . . I went with this girl named Faith 'cause her father was in the hospital and they wasn't letting her go to a home visit or even see her father, and her father needed an operation. So I went with her to the hospital.

Sometimes the connections made during these latter AWOL events led to more episodes of running away. But most often, AWOLs in these situations did not become a consistent reason for a child to run from care.

Breaking curfew constituted another reason for AWOLing, especially among older teens. Many believed that if they were late for curfew it would be considered an AWOL anyway. Many youth did not think that breaking curfew should be considered AWOLing. Kim, age 20, proposed this view:

> To me, going AWOL is, in my opinion, leaving the facility for days at a time. You are not coming back. You are not calling. That is AWOL. If I came in a little bit after 2:00, now we're considered AWOL. If I came in at 2:01 [in the morning] every day, they're going to say, "Oh, she's AWOL every day, you know."

Usually, youth who broke curfew were at parties, with friends, or even at home and sometimes did not realize that their curfews had passed. In one case, a girl told interviewers that she had overslept at her boyfriend's apartment and quickly realized that she was now AWOL. In this sense, she did not mean to intentionally AWOL. A similar incident happened to Christina, age 18:

> Last time . . . wasn't an intentional AWOL. I went to my sister's house for a weekend. She lives in Virginia and she drove me up there and she didn't have money to bring me back down. So I wound up staying an extra three days and they [said I was] AWOL.

Issues surrounding sex also pull youth to go AWOL. Studies have documented that a history of being in foster care is associated with high-risk sexual behavior and increased rates of pregnancy and sexually transmitted diseases (Becker and Barth 2000; Carpenter et al. 2001). Further, one study conducted in Baltimore found that the average age at which the foster youth in their sample first had sexual intercourse was 12.7 years, with 69 percent sexually active before the age of 15. Seventeen percent of the girls in the sample had been pregnant, and more than a quarter did not use a condom during their last sexual encounter (Ensign and Santelli 1997). No youth in the New York City sample spoke explicitly about AWOLing to pursue sexual activity, either with romantic partners or for prostitution, but sexual activity was implicated in a number of ways.

In several cases, girls broke their curfew or ran to see their partners, who ranged from boyfriends to fiancés to the fathers of their children. Six girls in the sample were in mother-child placements, and two had more than one child.

Some girls stated adamantly that they would not AWOL for a boyfriend, but for others the draw was about creating or maintaining a new family. Michael was one of the few boys who AWOLed to see a potential partner. He told interviewers, "The reason why I went 'cause I wanted to see this girl who I had met on the weekend before with my cousin. I went to work with her one of the days when I went AWOL just to try to spend some time with her." Caroline, age 18, went AWOL to her boyfriend, the father of her child, and experienced something similar to the independence of having her own family, saying, "I was with my boyfriend . . . When I was there . . . my son, my daughter had everything she needed, milk, everything, clothes, all that." In some cases, however, girls in mother-child facilities stopped AWOLing because of threats to the custody of their children from ACS.

Several girls mentioned that some residents practiced prostitution near where they lived, and that this accounted for some girls going AWOL:

> Yeah at [the placement], they be doing whore strolls, they be on whore strolls. . . . it happens a lot. They call [the placement] the whore house . . . and the placement, they be going AWOL, but the guys be taking the girls out of there and they become their whores and stuff.—Caroline

> I did experience that in [the placement]. A lot of girls, they were hookers. —Emma, age 20

Other girls mentioned that they knew girls in foster care who became involved in prostitution while AWOL. Desiree said:

> I met a girl that used to be here when she was 14 years old and now is 21 . . . she had got arrested for prostitution 'cause she said once she went AWOL she didn't know what to do, she ended up with a pimp and now she can't get away from him.

However, the girls interviewers spoke with adamantly denied their own involvement in prostitution. These contrasting statements suggest that some girls were not comfortable disclosing their own activities or that they might have been perpetuating rumors about the prevalence of prostitution among girls from some facilities. Additionally, certain facility staff thought that some girls AWOL and engage in prostitution:

> I don't know why [some girls prostitute], but I can only assume it is for the money, the attention. They way other young ladies may put it out to them . . . when they meet girls who are getting sneakers, the jewelry, having money and things like that, it seems like a good deal to them and then it is also like a freedom . . . they team up with the girls, they hang out, they go outside . . . I don't believe they know the seriousness of it.—Jane, child welfare specialist, group home

The Experiences of Chronic AWOLers

> I had hopped out of the van and my staff didn't even bother to chase me, he knew that I was leaving 'cause I had my bag and all he said back at the house was, "Are you going to go AWOL?" And I said, "Yup." And then he said, "You shouldn't go AWOL." . . . He knew that I was going 'cause he saw me getting into the van with my bags, and I just hopped out of the van and he said this isn't a good move for you. I kept walking and he just had to act like he was trying to stop me. But really he didn't care, he was like, "Do whatever you want, I don't care."—Michael

As Heidi's story at the beginning of this chapter shows, some youth may face dangerous situations when purposely running away. Youth in this study reported a range of experiences in leaving their facilities, from simply walking away to having to come up with more creative means of escape. Jeanette told interviewers, "There's no gates or anything like that. Nobody could hold you down, so I just left." Others also described the ease with which they left:

> I know how to get out of there. All you do is just walk down the stairs and like if somebody come in you could walk out. . . . they just buzz the door and you leave.
> —Rolanda, age 15

How would you leave? [Interviewer]
Pack my stuff, tell everybody, "see you later," and walk out the door.
And the staff didn't try to stop you? Did they know you were going? [Interviewer]
I used to let it be known.
About how many times did you do this? [Interviewer]
So many, I can't even count.—Camilla

Other youth had a more difficult time in leaving the facility. Jessica, who was in an upstate facility, said that she had to "walk to the train station and get on the train and hide out in the bathroom and just get to New York City." Others had similar tales:

We had to go over the barbed wire. Now this was hard, but it was a tree . . . so we had to pull ourselves up and it is like an escape. And we had to jump down from the tree. I think we climbed the gate, but we couldn't touch it at the top because it had barbed wire. So we had to pull ourselves up on the tree and then we had to drop ourselves all the way back down.—Emma

When Friday comes, everybody gets into the vans to go home and I snuck into the back of the van . . . so I am sitting in the back of the van with my bag . . . Then they [the other kids with legitimate home passes] got out, they let me out. . . . They just let me out of the van and I went into the train.—Randi, age 17

AWOL Destinations

Youth running away from group home care appear to be less likely to have slept on the streets than those running from a family home (Rees 1993; Wade and Biehal 1998). Interviewers asked the youth in the New York City sample where they were most likely to go while AWOL. Most indicated that they consistently had a specific destination in mind before leaving. Very few suggested they had nowhere to go, and only three youth said they had spent even one night on the streets during their AWOL.

Youth identified three main destinations—family, friends, and boyfriends/girlfriends—though they are not mutually exclusive. Most youth have stayed with all three at one time or another, sometimes within a single AWOL. Although the researchers initially thought that most youth left to be with family, these youth visited friends most. Often, AWOL youth feared that their family would know they were AWOL and make them return to foster care. Joey, age 17, told interviewers that he did not go to his mother's because "I know my mom is going to take me back, so I didn't go straight to my house. I went to a friend's house." Lola's grandmother found out that she lied about being on a weekend pass and made her go back to the facility. Lola told interviewers, "She made me come back because she said she could get in trouble because they would call it harboring kids . . . she wouldn't let me stay and I had to come back up here." Thereafter, she also started going AWOL to friends' houses.

Some youth lied to family members to avoid being sent back to care. For example, Vanessa, age 17, told her grandmother that she had permission from the facility to be at her house, that she had called the facility and they said it was okay. Additionally, when staying with family members, youth often bypassed their parents or grandparents and went to stay with extended family members such as aunts, uncles, or cousins. In these cases, relatives knew the child's AWOL status but let them stay regardless.

> I tell her [her aunt]. I am very honest with stuff. And she like, "they let you out?" No, they ain't let me out. I am almost grown and do my own things so she [aunt] always respected that. . . . let me come in when I want.—Camilla

> So I ran away and I started living with my cousin for the whole entire summer . . . she was mad [about the AWOL], but she let me in.—Sally

When staying with friends, youth did not have to worry about their AWOL status as much as they did with families. Either their friends knew they were AWOL and did not care or they hid their foster care status from friends or friends' parents. Bernice, age 15, told interviewers that her friend's father just thought she was "hanging out and staying over" and did not know she was AWOL from foster care. Rolanda said about her friend's parents, "I don't even think that they knew we was in a placement." Sharon also went to a friend's house. She told interviewers that the friend's mother did not know she went AWOL from foster care, adding that if the mother knew "I'm pretty sure I wouldn't have been there." Olga said that sometimes she "would go around my block in the Bronx. . . . So I would go sleep at their [friends'] house. Their mother is nice, but their mother is not thinking anything. And I be like, 'no I am living with my father, he let me come out here.' . . . I would lie to them."

Almost one-third of the study sample said that they stayed with boyfriends, who often took care of them financially. Camilla slept at her boyfriend's house every night while AWOL, and he gave her money and took her to the movies. Olga's boyfriend took her to the movies, took her out to eat, and drove her around to see her friends. In some cases, the boyfriends came to the facility and helped the girls go AWOL:

> I called him [her boyfriend] and said to pick me up. I was on the phone and people kept trying to rush me off the phone . . . and I got frustrated. . . . So he realized

that and he was like, "You know what, I am just going to come get you and just get you out of that house."—Sharon, age 17

Why did you want to go AWOL? [Interviewer]
Because he [her boyfriend] convinced me.—Vanessa
He convinced you to go? What did he say to convince you? [Interviewer]
He said, "I want you to stay with me for the night." That's what I like.—Vanessa

For girls such as Jessica, staying with boyfriends was a precarious situation. She told interviewers that when she was 15,

> I had a boyfriend and he was like really crazy. He used to abuse me and stuff like that. He made me leave the group home. Like he went to my group home and he packed up my shit and I had to live with him. I just stayed there. I was like the little wife. I don't know. Stayed there, cooked and slept, whatever. . . . I was getting drunk and high every day.

What Happens When Youth Go AWOL: Evaluating the Level of Risk

Determining the risks youth face while AWOL is difficult. One might assume that youth who have gone AWOL more frequently and for longer periods of time might place themselves in increasingly risky situations. One prior study, however, suggests that there is little relationship between a child's history of going AWOL and the level of risk encountered in a specific AWOL incident (Wade and Biehal 1998). No one pattern can be used to predict troublesome incidents, though common sense dictates that within a single incident the destination and length of the AWOL may affect exposure to risk. For example, a youth who goes AWOL for two days to her grandmother's house would probably be less likely to encounter risk than one who AWOLs for three months and is bouncing from friend to friend or spending significant time on the streets.

Information gleaned from the narratives of youths' AWOL experiences can be used to divide youth as having experienced low, medium, or high risks while AWOL. The researchers categorized youth who said they stayed around the house, watched TV, and hung out with friends or family in the low-risk category. The researchers put youth who spoke about casual drinking and marijuana use or consensual sex in the medium-risk category. The researchers considered an AWOL experience high risk when a more specific, serious incident occurred, such as drug dealing, serious drug use, arrest, assault, and gang involvement. The criteria for these categories are subjective, and the authors relied only on the stories that the youth told interviewers—and some may have exaggerated or deemphasized the level of risk encountered. Nonetheless, the categories provide a basic framework for understanding risk while AWOL. Based on the information provided by the youth, slightly more than one-third of the sample fell into each of the high- and medium-risk categories, while less than one-third fell into the low-risk category.

The researchers found little relationship between a youth's riskiest incident and the number of AWOLs in the youth's history. While a higher percentage of youth in the medium- and high-risk groups had longer AWOLs on average than those in the low-risk group, the researchers do not know whether the specific incident that pushed them into those categories occurred during their longest AWOL. Further, while youth who have a higher number of AWOLS are probably more likely to encounter risk over the course of their entire AWOL histories, the researchers found no association between the characteristics of a single AWOL event and a youth's AWOL history. This may suggest that all the youth in the New York City study could be equally likely to encounter risk during any given AWOL episode, a belief consistent with other research.[9]

AWOL Stories

The youth in the low-risk category often reported uneventful AWOL experiences. They went AWOL to visit close family or friends and spent the time "hanging out." When asked what they did while AWOL, these youth generally reported few risk-taking behaviors. For example, Bernice told interviewers that she "didn't really do anything. Just sat there and watched TV." Jeanette would "go outside. Not really do much." Olga said that she "went to Brooklyn. I went to Brooklyn, see my friends. Hanging out. . . . Then we came inside her house and we watching a movie. Just chilling."

One issue to keep in mind, however, is that more than half the youth with low-risk AWOL experiences were placed in foster care because of abuse or neglect; there may be some risk involved with youth returning to and spending time in households that authorities determined were abusive or neglectful. For example, Aaron entered foster care because his mother abused him while she was intoxicated. When he turned up at her house while AWOL, he told interviewers about her reaction. "In a way she was happy [to see him], in a way she wasn't. And when she was sober she wanted me home, but when she was drunk it was a different story."

Youth placed in the medium-risk category told stories of casual drinking and drug use and some fighting, as well as unwanted sexual advances. Yolanda told interviewers that when she was AWOL she would do "stuff that I wouldn't do on my home pass . . . that's what I would do. Well, we were like smoking and drinking." Other youth described experiences they had with drugs and alcohol while they were AWOL:

Well, I would AWOL and go to my friends. We drank, things like that, party out. . . . getting drunk, getting high.—Tara

Well, when I first AWOLed I wanted to go smoke marijuana and hang out and drink . . . we drinking beer and we thinking we grown . . . we just chilling, laying back and there was these guys there. I wasn't getting with nobody, and these girls started getting intimate with each other so then one of the girls looked at me and say, "I want to fight you." I got up. . . . she came outside. I just punched her, boop. —Isabel

We went to a Valentine's party . . . I used to smoke weed and I would smoke it often and we went to this party and there were a lot of guys there. After the party we left and went to this guy's house . . . I didn't really feel comfortable but I was going because I can't just leave . . . the guys, they were like, they were a little older and they were, like, asking, "Do you want a drink, do you want a smoke?" And we were, like, "no." Everybody was high and everybody was drinking already at the party . . . So they were like trying to team up, like pair off, right . . . So I felt kind of uncomfortable, not that anything had happened to me . . . but if they wanted to, they probably could have taken advantage of us because we were all drunk, and we were smoking. We were intoxicated, period. You know what I am saying? —Kim, age 20

While nothing happened to Kim that night and Isabel's fight did not result in serious injuries, other youth experience far more serious incidents while AWOL. Eleven youth in the study sample mentioned at least one dangerous situation they encountered during an AWOL. A few young people told interviewers of serious drinking and drug use. Some research suggests that many youth in foster care go AWOL specifically to get drunk or high, and a few youth in this sample fit that pattern (Wade and Biehal 1998). Michael told interviewers that he often went to his uncle's house while AWOL and that this uncle introduced him to marijuana:

I went AWOL to go hang out with my uncle and his friends . . . he was really like my biggest fatherly figure in my life . . . he is the reason why I started smoking weed. . . . I was 12, he said he would rather me try it with him than try it with someone else. Tried it with him and then every time I would hang out with him I would start smoking weed.

What's a typical day like [while AWOL]? Hang out. Don't come home 'til like five
in the morning . . . smoke weed and drink . . . used to be all day. Every time I
AWOL, I would smoke [marijuana] all the time.—Caroline

I was in a friend's house, just like doing everything, getting high. I wouldn't call it
fun any more . . . because it was just all like associated with drugs, just to get
high. . . . try to get some money from this kid . . . or go see whoever is getting their
paycheck, you know, and get high.—Karen, age 17

In addition to using drugs, a few teens got involved in selling drugs
while AWOL. For example, Karen said that she sold drugs to make money
while she was AWOL. Jessica told interviewers that while she was living with
her drug-dealing boyfriend during an AWOL incident, he taught her how
to process crack cocaine that he would later sell:

I made my money. I sold my dope, my crack. . . . I made it and cracked it up, you
know.—Jessica
Was it your boyfriend who got you into that? [Interviewer]
He told me one day, did I know how to chop up crack. I was like, "no." So he
teached me and just made me start chopping up crack and putting it in the vials.
He made me grind the dope and shit and make it.

While Emma did not want to get involved with drug dealing, she went
AWOL with a friend intent on dragging her into that lifestyle:

I was in my teens. Not 16, under 16. We went to 42nd Street. [Her friend]
wanted to be a drug dealer. I didn't want to be a drug dealer. I don't know why I followed her, you know. . . . So we went to 42nd Street. She wanted to sell drugs. . . .
Stayed in a hotel with this guy. This guy, he kept pushing up on me. I didn't like
it. I wanted to go home . . . I didn't have any more money to go home . . . She
thought she was going to be some kind of big time Italian drug dealer but her ass
wasn't. She was selling crack. And I told her if the cops catch you, you are going
to be in a shit hole. She doesn't care. I mean she had plans, she had big plans. . . .
I mean . . . drugs everywhere; he was doing drugs, crackhead hookers, crackhead
men looking like women. I had no reason looking at that, I was exposed to a life
that wasn't me at an early age. And it was very, very scary 'cause I didn't know what
to do with myself.

In addition to involvement with drugs, some youth were involved in
violent encounters while AWOL, leading to injury or arrest.

I beat up this lady . . . I just threw her across the room and beat the shit out of her.
While I am beating her up the cops came and I am still beating her up . . . well they
took her to the hospital and me to the precinct. They asked me my Social Security
number and the silly fool like me gave them my Social Security number. They said,
"You got a warrant." . . . They found out that I was a missing persons report . . .

and they called [her facility] and they said they was going to come get me that night. They never made it up there. [The police] was calling them all night and they never came. They kept on saying, "Yeah, we're on our way." They never came . . . I am in a cell with this grown lady who is in there and has been charged with attempted murder.—Camilla

This guy, I had a fight with . . . 'cause he was drunk, I was drunk. It was over some stupid shit and he hit me with a stick.—Caroline

Like last year, no the year before last, when I went AWOL, and I was staying with my friend, there was a guy that lived on her block that liked me and I didn't like him because he was an older man and I guess, he figured I was around his age, but I tried to tell him I wasn't old enough for him he wouldn't leave me alone and I would get harassed by him every night, one night he followed me into her building, I got scared. . . . Then two days after my birthday I ended up getting into a fight with him. He was 26 and I was only 16 . . . he just hit me and he started fighting . . . I don't know he just turns around and smacked me again . . . and my friend told me to just leave so I just left.—Desiree

Michael inadvertently got involved in gang violence while AWOL:

I AWOLed and went to my cousin's house . . . and he is in a gang, he is Crip, and when I was hanging out with him I had went to the store and then there was a gang of Bloods, there were five of them. I guess that they seen me a few times and thought I was Crip too because I rack a lot of blue clothes 'cause I like blue and gray and white, black and so I got jumped, I got jumped back and I had a busted nose . . . I was lucky 'cause they would have tried to kill me but I went back into the house and told my cousin what happened and he has a gun so he went crazy he went outside, I went with him 'cause I was trying to stop him. At first I was saying if you are going to go outside looking for them let's go get some people with us 'cause . . . so he went crazy . . . And I went upstairs and he came back with blood on his hands, and . . . he said he just stabbed somebody just because he didn't know who it was who had jumped me because they wasn't there but he said he assumed that it was one of them and luckily he didn't get caught or anything but the kid didn't die. When I left a few days later I got approached by one of them [gang member] . . . I really talked my way out of it.

Two girls in the study told interviewers they became pregnant while AWOL. As the result of her being AWOL, Emma did not get the prenatal care she needed:

I tried to go see a doctor. I couldn't see a doctor because every time I went to a doctor's appointment or something they would have to call [the facility] to get my Medicaid number. [The facility] never wanted to give it to them because they wanted me to come back from AWOL. So eventually I got too far along in my pregnancy.

One encouraging piece of information learned from the interviews is that most youth return to care voluntarily after an AWOL. Almost two-thirds of the sample went back to the facility of their own volition; slightly fewer than one-third had to be brought back by either the police or another involved party.

Most youth who voluntarily returned to care said the primary reason was that they were tired of being AWOL. For example, Karen told interviewers, "I don't know, I just got, like, real sick and tired of doing the same thing every day . . . and I was like, screw it. So I came back." Lola explained that she simply comes back when she is ready. When she "finishes hanging out. That is what I leave for." Sharon said she returned because, "I had to come back, you know. I didn't want to mess myself up."

How Do Different Facilities Respond to AWOLs?

The heaviest burden for dealing with adolescents who AWOL falls on the primary foster care providers. They are compelled to track and sometimes search for the youth, to counsel those who are at risk of running, and, perhaps hardest of all, to create strategies and procedures that prevent youth from AWOLing in the future. To add stress to this responsibility, staff in congregate care facilities may have to deal with multiple youth who have gone AWOL during the same period, sometimes daily. This section discusses how facility employees perceive AWOLs in general. It further examines the way staff view the problem of dealing with youth who chronically go AWOL.

How Agencies Respond to AWOLs

The staff interviewers spoke with generally articulated policies consistent with the official child welfare agency policy on AWOLs (see appendix A.6). When staff members were asked how they defined AWOLs, only one interviewee at a Manhattan group home misidentified the official definition, suggesting that an AWOL occurred at 72 hours rather than 24 hours. Most agency staff said they informed the child's caseworker of an AWOL if the child missed the morning census. Others said they considered a youth AWOL if he or she missed curfew. There may be some difference between what policy dictates, what these staff members consider an AWOL, and how often they actually report AWOLs. Many acknowledged a struggle between being flexible with a group of adolescents who often break curfews and reporting AWOLs as soon as a youth is discovered missing. Veronica, a site supervisor at a Bronx group home, commented, "It is always a question for us when you talk about AWOLs versus . . . just breaking curfew."

In a study of youth absconding from secure facilities, Milham, Bullock, and Hosie note, "Absconding . . . leads to anxiety among the staff as it threatens the containing functions of the home, chills the institutional climate, and puts the absentee at risk" (1978, 70). In reacting to the problem and in trying to prevent it, the staff were doubtful that they could prevent AWOLs and frustrated with unsuccessful attempts to stop the problem. However, most staff remained committed to trying different strategies to prevent AWOLs and to responding constructively to AWOL events that had already occurred.

Preventing AWOLs

Staff told interviewers they attempted to prevent AWOLs by creating a hospitable and supportive environment. In several cases, facilities offered activities and recreational trips to try to keep residents occupied and interested in staying at the group home:

> We have activities. We have groups. We have sleepovers and slumber parties where they can . . . just have fun. [We try to keep] a program diverse enough to keep them interested in the facility as much as we can.—Virginia

> The best policy is to have a program that the kids want to be in. So we do a lot of programming for kids to expand and develop their interests.—George, director, RTC

Staff also commonly referred to behavior modification as a strategy for preventing AWOLs. This involved a system of rewards—both formal and informal—whereby residents earn privileges based on their behavior. Individuals who did not AWOL earned greater privileges and independence:

> We've got a level system, an achievement system.
> And does each level give them certain privileges? [Interviewer]
> Yeah . . . More money in their allowance, you know, certain perks—they can go on certain trips. A little bit more freedom.—George

Several staff commented on the effectiveness of extending curfews and making weekend home passes as available as possible to prevent AWOLs from occurring:

> We can provide them with weekend passes so they can stay the weekend with their family members . . . or a family friend . . . so they don't AWOL.—Inez, child welfare specialist, group home

Some staff also mentioned their practice of holding group counseling sessions at times when going AWOL commonly occurs, such as around holidays when some young people cannot visit their families. The sessions discuss the dangers of going AWOL and the frustrations that might cause the behavior:

> We talk about AWOLing . . . during "community meetings." We say OK, holidays are coming up, girls are going to see other girls go home.—Veronica

When a Youth Returns from AWOL

When preventive strategies failed and a child ran away, staff discussed responding to individual AWOLs in very similar ways. Every staff person mentioned counseling youth a day or two after their return to the facility. The sessions collect information on where the youth had been and any risky or unhealthy behaviors experienced, and counsel the youth on the dangers of running away.

> Basically we counsel them . . . let them understand the dangers of being out in the street like they are. Our perception of the streets and their perception of it differ. —Roger

In most cases, staff members restrict youth privileges as a consequence for going AWOL—sanctions given as part of the behavior modification system mentioned above:

> If you are in a single room and you continue to AWOL, we take away that privilege from you and you go to double occupancy.—Cleo

> Privileges that are normally given [are restricted]. Maybe he will not have the use of the phone. He might be kept from going on an . . . outside activity.—Roger

The study sample mentioned close supervision as another common reaction to AWOL. Staff from residential treatment centers often referred to confining a child to a cottage or a room with close scrutiny from a staff member.

> [Restriction] means that you can't leave the cottage other than to go to school, go to meals, and . . . go to work. Then you get off restriction when you negotiate your way off with your supervisor and make a commitment about future responsibilities about AWOL. So we believe the best way to do it is to make the resident most responsible.—George

When asked about the effectiveness of any one policy, staff often expressed their frustration with working in an open setting and with the difficulty of countering the desire of many of the youth to leave. This is particularly true of the staff members who work closely with the youth.

> We try to counsel them, but [with] a lot of them we are not successful. So they still AWOL out there anyway.—Inez

> We cannot physically lock them in or out. So it is not much that we can really do. We can talk, talk, talk, talk, and sometimes it will work and sometimes it won't. —Jane

Such pessimism about the use of sanctions is in line with research on congregate care staff in Britain, which finds that staff often give out punishments because that have few tools to prevent an AWOL, even though staff realize the punishments are generally ineffective (Wade and Biehal 1998).

Some interviewed staff claimed success with strategies that combined counseling, activities, and the systems of rewards and consequences in a way that could be refined based on an individual's needs:

> I really in my heart after being here for so long thought that you know if they felt better about themselves and had things to do, that would decrease the AWOL and the curfew violations, and that is exactly what has happened. And that involves actually more structure and consequences on one hand and on the other hand a lot of support and encouragement.—Kirsten

Dealing with Chronically AWOL Youth

The study sample often self-identified as youth who ran repeatedly. Even when staff knew that such youth were at risk, most expressed little confidence in predicting when they would AWOL. This was especially true of the frontline staff who worked one on one with the youth in their residences. However, the people interviewed reported some common signs that a youth planned to AWOL—including carrying a packed bag or dressing particularly well. They commonly cited vigilance and close scrutiny of youth who regularly ran away.

> It is just us documenting their every movement and covering ourselves. We know what the child is wearing, if the child carried a bag, any detail, because we never know when the child is going to AWOL. I mean, the child might know at that moment, but we don't.—Jonathan

Although staff looked for these signs, many reported feeling powerless to prevent a youth going AWOL if youth wanted to leave:

> There is really not much that we can do. We can't, like, close or lock the door or hold them back.—Inez

> Well, I will always say our hands are tied when it comes down to the AWOL. This is the door, they can come and go.—Jonathan

Some spoke, however, of their determination not to let the youth leave:

> I am not going to allow you to run out the door when I know you are getting ready to leave. So I am going to watch you.—Meadow

Although staff acknowledged the difficulty of dealing with youth who chronically AWOL, no one mentioned discharging youth to AWOL as a common practice. Instead, staff spoke of attempts to find a more appropriate placement:

> It might be that we are not the right setting, so it might be a matter of, we need to contemplate, depending on the status of placement, whether we can try to work even more adamantly to get him sent back home or to a setting that is more conducive to him.—Veronica

> The most severe [response to repeat AWOLs] is a meeting which is on a division level . . . This is perhaps not the most appropriate setting. They might need something more structured and therapeutic.—Anne

Discussion

The information that this study gleaned from both youth and facility staff points to several areas where improvements may lessen a youth's desire to AWOL. Many suggestions are already practiced in facilities that provide care to foster youth.

Some youth will run from foster care regardless of a facility's policies or actions. At the same time, many motivations for going AWOL that youth described are changeable aspects of the foster care experience. For example, the overwhelming number of comments interviewers received expressing boredom among residents at congregate care facilities raises a real but manageable concern. Other research studies concur that steering youth away from boredom and other situations that may prompt AWOLs is a matter of providing proper diversions (Wade and Biehal 1998). The youth the interviewers spoke with, however, felt that their activities often depended on the whim of their supervisors instead of their needs.

While the study did not evaluate congregate care programming, the information gathered suggests that foster care providers should pay close attention to scheduling engaging and enjoyable activities, especially during weekends and summertime. Researchers in London have found that some facilities prevented AWOLs by identifying a youth's leisure activities and interests as part of the assessment process when he or she entered care, then building activities related to those interests into the individual's care plan (Parker et al. 1991; Ward 1995). Carrying out these plans requires a degree of organization, quality time spent with residents, and low staff turnover—and the latter is often an issue in congregate care facilities.[10] Further, efforts to socially integrate youth with peers outside foster care may be beneficial, especially to those youth who reside in more isolated campus-like facilities. Studies have indicated that allowing youth to make friends and participate in excursions off campus may help them develop individual, positive social relationships outside foster care (Wade and Biehal 1998).

The finding that sexual issues contributed to some AWOL activity presents a similar area for possible intervention. Foster youth as a group are more sexually active than their nonfoster peers.[11] Considering the risks associated with sexual activity, including sexually transmitted diseases, pregnancy, prostitution, and related AWOL risks, foster agencies could benefit from reviewing how their facilities address sexual education issues. For example, one study showed promising results from the implementation of a new pregnancy/HIV/STD prevention curriculum customized for youth in foster care (Becker and Barth 2000).

The study did not set out to examine engaging in sexual activity for money among foster youth, and no youth in this study admitted to doing so. However, several participants raised the issue, which is cause for concern. Many respondents reported that exchanging sex for money often took place near group care settings. Facility managers should make sure that staff members pay attention to the activities in the surrounding area that may pose a risk to the youth. Managers should also ensure that staff members know the proper procedures for reporting this activity to the police and child welfare authorities. Nationally, few programs work with youth exploited in the commercial sex industry, though some models have developed in the past several years.[12]

The relationships between foster youth and their peers and between youth and the facility staff lie at the core of many motivations to go AWOL. Many youth felt no connection to other youth or adults at their facilities, and some reported negative relationships that included repeated theft of personal possessions, bullying, and fights. When bad situations festered, youth ran from their placements.

In this respect, close monitoring and involvement in peer situations by frontline facility staff could reduce a youth's perceived need to run away. Remediation measures could range from conflict resolution techniques to moving a particular youth to another house or floor at a facility. Poor relations with staff members represent a more complex problem, but youth should be aware of the procedure for reporting inappropriate staff behavior.

When a youth returns to foster care following an AWOL, the early reaction of staff members may affect a future decision to run away. Other research shows that when young people return from an AWOL, they may appreciate a caring, sensitive response, including displays of emotion and concern, rather than anger or irritation (Abrahams and Mungall 1992; Newman 1989). Some youth in this study said they felt the urge to AWOL when they believed the staff performed only the minimum work required to keep their jobs. When emotional ties existed between youth and staff, youth sometimes felt guilty about going AWOL and leaving people who cared about them.

Without a strong relationship as a foundation, other forms of control are likely to fail. Child care staff may find it beneficial to trace where individual youth went during their AWOLs and to assess the associated risks (Wade and Biehal 1998). If done sensitively, gathering this information upon the youth's return helps build the feeling that adults in their lives care about their well-being.

In a related area, youth in this study felt frustrated and disempowered over the progress of their cases. Youth often claimed that they did not receive promised services, received little information about their cases, felt misled about changes to their placements, and did not have enough contact with family members. This suggests that more openness regarding case information and attentive case management can help remedy some aspects of the AWOL problem.

Sometimes, a youth's misbehavior brought restrictions that curtailed his or her freedom to leave the placement, creating the sense that foster care workers care more about punishment than youth development. Adolescents in and out of foster care frequently oppose punishment, but in some cases, the use of sanctions in dealing with AWOLs may be counterproductive and reinforce negative behaviors. For example, one girl told interviewers that she AWOLed because staff denied her home passes as a punishment for past AWOLs. For her, punishment became part of a vicious cycle of going AWOL, being denied a home pass as a result, and having to AWOL again to see her family.

Of all preventive options, increased flexibility may be the most complex but also the most effective strategy in diminishing the desire to AWOL. People still in care past the age of 18 especially felt that fixed policies unnecessarily conflicted with aspects of their daily lives. Some had children or were engaged to be married and found curfews inappropriate and demeaning—especially when enforced by staff members of a similar age. Other older residents found that job training and educational opportunities were put at risk when staff applied AWOL rules rigidly. Many wanted separate policies for older adolescents and younger ones. For them, the rigidity of the AWOL rules undermined the legitimacy of rules generally. More flexible rules tied to each individual's ability to handle more responsibility might increase compliance.

Younger teens who AWOL present a more complicated problem. While younger youth felt disappointed and frustrated at the policies surrounding passes for home visits, it is impossible to tell from interviews if this feeling came about because of policies or the nuances of their individual cases. They pointed to many features of the home pass system they disliked, such as being unable to list family friends or relatives as their destination. These changes require caseworkers to carefully assess the potential risks involved, since younger youth can and do encounter high-risk situations. However, when the destination is known to the caseworker and is considered low risk, extending home passes to allow for special events or allowing home visits for crises or emergencies may help prevent AWOLs for younger youth who consistently overstay home visits. For youth who cannot go home for weekends or holidays, it may be useful to increase family contact, such as phone calls and onsite visits, and to provide special activities with other residents.

The youth had few concrete ideas when asked what would have stopped their AWOLing. The older youth that were interviewed said they simply reached an age at which they tired of running. Their decisions to stop going AWOL came after many absences and the cumulative effects of punishments and unpleasant experiences. A few girls began to recognize the adult responsibility of caring for their own children and feared that going AWOL might jeopardize their custody. Others, like Olga, simply began to see their own future potential:

> [Going AWOL] is not getting me anywhere. And after a while I just started getting bored, in and out and in and out, and I'm not getting really anything from

it. There is really nothing out there for me, I feel like there is something in here for me—like the school, my bed and everything, all my belongings, is all here . . . It was this one morning I decided I am going to wake up and I am going to school, I'm going to do what I have to do, and I am going to try to get me a job. So I got me a job and I am going to school . . . and everything is working out fine.

Conclusion

Many of these recommendations made to reduce the incidence of going AWOL amount to improving congregate care facilities generally. If a method were developed to stop youth from going AWOL, but the youth continued to be bored and disconnected, that solution is untenable and unstable. Keeping track of the environment surrounding a facility is something that staff need to do whether AWOL is an issue or not. Many dedicated staff in child welfare and other agencies work long hours to make life better for youth in group facilities.

They are fighting an uphill battle. The weaknesses of congregate care for youth have proved remarkably difficult to address in a range of situations, be it foster care, juvenile detention, or military style "boot camps." Poor pay, trying work conditions, and the challenge of working with youth who have often endured years of maltreatment lead to high turnover among caseworkers, house managers, and other frontline congregate care staff. Concentrating youth who are each facing multiple life challenges in one location may create many more obstacles to healing—obstacles that lead some youth to run away.

Following years of dissatisfaction with group care facilities and a declining foster care census, New York City's child welfare agency made a concerted effort to close congregate care facilities starting in 2003. Many of these facilities were group homes that had high rates of youth going AWOL. By 2005, 473 congregate care beds were eliminated with another 121 scheduled for closure.[13] These efforts, combined with reforms that aim to decrease the number of status offenders placed in foster care (see chapter 7 of this volume), may be the best hope for reducing the incidence and risks of foster youth going AWOL.

New York City Policies on Absences without Leave

N ew York City's child welfare agency defines an AWOL child as one "who is in the care and custody, or custody and guardianship of the Commissioner of the Administration for Children's Services and is placed in a licensed foster care facility, direct or contracted, and who disappears, runs away or is otherwise absent voluntarily or involuntarily without the consent of the person(s)/facility in whose care the child has been placed" (New York City Administration for Children's Services 1992).

The policy mandates precise procedures for when a child goes AWOL.[14] When staff members discover that a youth is missing, the assigned case planner/caseworker or agency staffer must be informed. Within 24 hours, the case planner must make a report to the New York City Police Department, the biological parents/caretakers if they are known, the child welfare agency's Division of Legal Services, the case manager, and the case planner (if the child is AWOL from a non-planning agency).

After reporting the AWOL, the case planner must start a search for the child. This may include contacting the members of the child's foster family and biological family, school staff, friends, other adults in the child's life, runaway shelters, and local police officers who work with youth. If the case planner cannot find the child, the case manager is responsible for ensuring that continuous efforts are made to locate the child during each 30-day period after the AWOL is reported.

If the child cannot be found after 60 days, case managers may decide to discharge the child depending on his or her age. Youth who are 18 years or older are discharged. For those between the ages of 16 and 18, the decision to discharge or keep the case open is made on a case-by-case basis. Children under the age of 16 are not discharged to AWOL.

Foster care providers receive payment for an AWOL youth for three days and are expected to hold the placement during that time. Youth who AWOL from congregate care may lose their beds after 72 hours.

Congregate Care Facility Types

New York City child welfare regulations categorize most congregate care facilities by the number of beds they contain, though facilities of similar size may provide different services. In addition, four specialized types of placements can be of any size.

Size Types

Residential treatment centers (RTCs) are campus-like facilities that house 25 or more children and provide various counseling and educational services. Most RTCs are located in the suburbs north of New York City.

Group residences are facilities with 13–24 beds. Relatively few of these facilities exist, and many of them are mother-child placements.

Group homes are facilities with 7–12 beds. They are the most common form of congregate care, and most are located in New York City.

Supervised independent living programs (SILPs) are two- or three-bed placements usually reserved for older, higher-functioning children transitioning to independent living.

Agency-operated boarding homes (AOBHs) are placements with 1–6 beds.

Others: ACS infrequently places children in various specialized (and expensive) congregate care facilities. These include residential treatment facilities (RTFs) for severely disabled or psychologically disturbed youth and noncharitable institutional boarding homes (NCIBs), usually located out of state.

Service Distinctions

Diagnostic reception centers (DRCs) are staff-secure facilities intended as first placements for troubled children entering foster care. DRCs vary in size, and children are not supposed to stay longer than 90 days.

Hard-to-place facilities are placements specially designed to handle more troubled children. The agencies operating these placements receive a higher per diem reimbursement rate.

Mother-child placements are especially equipped to handle foster children with babies and children of their own. Many of these placements are in group residences.

Maternity placements are specially designed to address the needs of pregnant foster children. In general, maternity placements do not allow girls to return following the birth of their baby.

7

Betwixt and Between
Status Offenders and Foster Care

A mother came to the Family Court with two of her eight children and insisted on seeing a judge. She told the probation officer that her 15-year-old daughter and 14-year-old son cause her nothing but trouble and offered these examples: Because the girl told someone at school that her stepfather had slapped her, the police arrested him. The mother also blamed her daughter for her husband wanting a divorce. Her son, who is chronically truant, refused to attend summer school, and has begun smoking pot regularly, never respects her wishes. One day he climbed down the fire escape to visit a friend after she had prohibited him from leaving the house.

E very state has a status offender system—laws, regulations, and court parts and programs targeted at youth engaging in undesirable behaviors but who have not committed a crime that would make them a juvenile delinquent. These teenagers are referred to as status offenders because their status as minors make them of interest—the government does not have the right to intervene in the behavior described in the example above once the daughter is an adult. There are no reliable national estimates of the number of youth involved in status offender systems, but it is safe to say that these systems interact with hundreds of thousands of youth each year.[1]

Many youth who enter status offender systems spend time in foster care. Again, solid national estimates are hard to come by, but those that are available suggest that about 14 percent of status offenders who go to Family Court are placed in foster care (Stahl et al. 2005). However, many others may be remanded to foster care while a judge decides how to resolve the case. It is fair to say that well over 10,000 youth with status offender cases spend some time in foster care—and it is possible that the real number is several times that estimate. In addition, many status offender cases involve parental neglect or abuse; figures from New York City suggest that as many as 40 percent of status offender cases either have open child welfare cases or are reported to the State Central Registry for child abuse and neglect during a case assessment.

The cross-cutting issues involved with status offenders are legion. Depending on the youth, status offender cases may involve the courts, probation, child welfare, the police, schools, and a host of community service providers. This chapter looks at the evolution of the status offender system in New York as it aims to move from a system that relies heavily on judicial interventions and expensive congregate care placements to one that focuses more resources on services that seek to reunify families. This chapter starts with a brief history of status offender policy. The discussion then focuses on reforms in New York by taking an in-depth look at how the system works, the cross-cutting issues that surface, and efforts to solve these issues that show promise but still face challenges.

A Historical Perspective on Status Offenders

At the beginning of the 20th century, the category "juvenile delinquent" was born from the desire to separate children from adults in the criminal justice system. Similarly, in the early 1960s, the category "status offender" was created to separate juvenile delinquents who had committed a crime from truants, runaways, underage drinkers, and others who had broken rules that apply only to children. California was the first state to create a special category for status offenders in 1961. In 1962, New York State passed the Family Court Act, distinguishing juvenile delinquents from status offenders, known in New York as persons in need of supervision. In the years that followed, other states adopted similar status offender laws (Maxson and Klein 1997).

The New York State law defined a status offender as a "person in need of supervision . . . a male less than sixteen years of age and a female less than eighteen years of age who does not attend school in accord with . . . the education law or who is incorrigible, ungovernable, or habitually disobedient and beyond the lawful control of parent or other lawful authority or who violates the provisions of section 221.05 of the penal law, [unlawful possession of marijuana]."[2] The courts later declared unconstitutional the difference in the age cutoff for boys and girls. As a result, until 2001, when New York raised the age limit to 18 for both genders, PINS jurisdiction was limited to youth under age 16.[3]

Status offenders inhabited a system that was troubled from its inception. By the late 1960s, many believed that the justice system exercised too much power over juveniles, particularly status offenders who were not criminals, and that the state often failed to act in the best interests of children. Some children's rights organizations sought to abolish the status offender category altogether. Around the same time, Supreme Court decisions such as *Kent vs. United States* (1966) and *In re Gault* (1967) extended due process rights to juveniles accused of criminal conduct. These decisions made government intervention into the lives of status offenders, who did not have due process rights, that much more peculiar.

In 1967, the President's Commission on Law Enforcement and the Administration of Justice released the *Task Force Report on Juvenile Delinquency,* which reported that status offenders were widely housed in jails and similar detention facilities. The panel called for these youth to be removed from secure custody. The prevailing wisdom was that families and community-based organizations, not penal institutions, should become responsible for these troubled children. The Commission also recommended that lawmakers consider completely eliminating the court's power over status offenders (Marshall, Marshall, and Thomas 1983).

In 1974, Congress passed the Juvenile Justice and Delinquency Prevention Act (JJDPA), which mandated that states deinstitutionalize status offenders (DSO). The law required states to house status offenders and juvenile delinquents separately and to remove all status offenders from secure detention facilities, a provision that became known as the DSO mandate. For states to receive federal funding, they had to develop initiatives that offered young people programs that prevented delinquency, diverted them from the Family Court, and treated individual and family problems.

The DSO mandate had several justifications. Some supporters pointed out that status offenders were not afforded the rights of defendants accused of crimes and so should not face quasi-criminal court processes and dispositions. Others argued that secure institutions—sometimes called "juvenile halls" or "youth authorities"—were not conducive to healthy child development. Still others, with an eye on public budgets, argued that releasing these youth from secure detention promised significant cost savings (Maxson and Klein 1997).

States took various approaches to the implementation of the JJDPA and its DSO mandate. California required status offenders to be removed from detention but provided no money for community services to address the problems that brought the youth to the court in the first place. Some states adopted diversion models and implemented alternative programs such as crisis counseling to keep kids out of courts and jails. Louisiana, Massachusetts, Washington, and Pennsylvania removed status offenders from juvenile court and correctional jurisdiction altogether by transferring authority to welfare agencies, which provided shelter care, foster care, and individual and family counseling. Pennsylvania, Iowa, and Indiana transferred jurisdiction for selected status offenses, such as truancy and ungovernability, to the child welfare section of the legal code (Maxson and Klein 1997).

Not everyone welcomed the DSO mandate. Some working in the juvenile justice system resisted giving up the power to incarcerate status offenders. Both police and court intake workers found other ways to detain some children in this group by charging truants as "trespassers" and runaways as "delinquency suspects." Courts found parental neglect in some cases and justified detention as an act of protection. Some children were apparently placed in psychiatric hospitals, which recorded an increase in adolescent clients with ambiguous psychiatric diagnoses (Maxson and Klein 1997).

Despite this resistance, the new federal law successfully expanded diversion, treatment, and rehabilitation. It removed many inappropriately incarcerated juveniles from institutions, spurred the development of alternatives to incarceration, and provided many young people with services in the community. Every state passed legislation to comply with the federal law. In some states, the law was a catalyst for change. In others, such as New York, it added momentum and resources to local reform efforts already under way.

New York State and Status Offenders

With passage of the Family Court Act in 1962, New York became one of the first states to treat status offenders differently from juvenile delinquents. Yet, by the late 1970s, those who knew the PINS system remained dissatisfied. Many felt that Family Court too often removed children from home for noncriminal behavior and were concerned that the court process failed to address the family problems that led to PINS filings. Critics pointed out that many families were not well served since receiving community services could be frustrating and time consuming. Sole reliance on the court too often delayed or hindered, rather than helped, the delivery of services (Office of the Deputy Mayor 1992).

These concerns prompted legislators to pass the PINS Adjustment Services Act in 1985. The law created a mechanism, commonly known as "PINS diversion," through which young people and their families could receive support from community services without judicial involvement.[4] PINS diversion sought to reduce unnecessary and inappropriate court intervention for troubled children and their families. It also aimed to reduce out-of-home placements by encouraging a broad range of services— mental health services, social services, and others—that could respond to the problems that led to the PINS petition. Planners of the new program hoped it could achieve more desirable outcomes at less public expense, as fewer families formally pursued PINS cases in the Family Court.

Supporters of the Adjustment Services Act believed that families benefited in several ways by avoiding court involvement and receiving services in the community. First, the PINS court process took a long time, requiring both parent and child to attend several hearings. Second, PINS hearings followed the adversarial model, pitting parent against child and often exacerbating family disputes. Third, the court lacked the necessary tools for identifying services quickly for families in need. This led to an overreliance on detention and placement, neither of which adequately met the needs of youths and their families. At the time of the change, a few reformers suggested mandating adjustment services in place of court jurisdiction. But such a move seemed too big a step away from a system that had relied for so long on the court. Instead, the state settled on a statutory scheme that strongly encouraged family-based interventions through adjustment services but kept open the door to court.

At first, the 1985 reform seemed to be a great success; many counties experienced a decline in detention or placement. For example, research in New York City from 1986 to 1988 demonstrated that the new adjustment services dramatically reduced both the number of status offender cases that resulted in placement and the use of court-mandated services.[5]

But in the early 1990s—a period marked by economic recession and budget constraints—those successes proved difficult to sustain as the enthusiasm and funding behind PINS adjustment services deteriorated. By 1999, approximately half of all PINS cases in the state were still referred to the Family Court, and thousands of kids spent time in foster care. PINS cases continued to consume significant detention and placement resources, contrary to the intent of the 1985 reform. By comparison, reforms in Illinois reduced placements from approximately 1,200 a year in the early 1980s to less than 20 a year in the late 1990s. Following a report that documented the availability of court as a barrier to wider use of family-based services in Illinois, the state virtually eliminated court access for status offenders in the early 1980s (Reed et al. 1981). Savings from reduced court costs allowed an expansion of family services and the introduction of respite care for some families in crisis.

The Opportunity for Reform

In the late 1990s, a group of parents living primarily in suburban and rural counties advocated for an increase in the eligibility age in New York State's status offender law. Many of these parents had 16- and 17-year-old children who had run away from home or exhibited other troubling behaviors. When the parents looked for help, they found that their children were too old to qualify for services from the status offender system. It was difficult or impossible to obtain a warrant that would allow the police to return the youth home, and few public services were targeted at this population. In 2000, after several years of advocacy by parents involved in "PINS-to-18" groups, the legislature passed and the governor signed legislation expanding the reach of the status offender system to all youth under 18.

The legislation provided no additional funding to pay for more services. In response to the concerns of city and county officials, some of whom called the new law an unfunded mandate, the state commissioned a study of the new law's impact. That research, based on national trends as well as local and state data from New York, estimated that without changes in the current system, the new law would increase the number of youth entering the system by between 69 and 105 percent (Souweine and Khashu 2001). Additional court costs and out-of-home placements would severely strain the budgets of rural counties and cost New York City millions of dollars.

In response to these concerns, the governor delayed implementing the new age eligibility law for a year, allowing cities and counties to come up with reform plans that would allow them to accommodate more youth at the same cost. To understand the options under consideration, a more detailed understanding of how the system works in practice is needed. Though the next section is written in the past tense, many of the procedures in the system remain the same today, apart from reforms discussed later in this chapter.

The Status Offender System in New York City

The youth who entered the New York City's PINS system before implementation of the PINS-to-18 law were predominantly 14- and 15-year-olds. Almost 20 percent of cases were children with prior PINS cases. Girls and boys entered the PINS system at about the same rate, a gender parity that differs from delinquency cases, which much more often involve boys.[6] Half the youth were African American, and another 39 percent were Hispanic—figures that correlate with the demographics of poverty among youth in New York (Weingartner et al. 2002). According to data from one community service provider, 66 percent of the families of status offenders were headed by a single parent, while another 12 percent of status offenders lived with kin or legal guardians.[7] Many resided in neighborhoods with high rates of unemployment, poverty, crime, substandard housing, and poorly performing schools.

PINS youth were more likely have prior involvement with the child welfare system than delinquency cases. Consistent with other research, a sample of PINS kids from Queens and Brooklyn showed that only 16 percent of the children had any history of delinquency.[8] However, one sample of PINS youth showed that 18 percent of PINS children assessed by a community service provider in 2000 had an active abuse or neglect case—even though families with open abuse and neglect cases were supposed to be barred from filing PINS petitions. Once the assessment process began, the assessment workers, who as social workers were mandatory reporters of child abuse and neglect, notified the State Central Registry of possible abuse or neglect in an *additional* 21 percent of cases.[9]

This raises the question of why parents with open child welfare cases or with the possibility of facing abuse or neglect charges would start status offender cases. Most families go to considerable lengths to avoid contact with the child welfare system. This may be especially true in urban African American communities, where child welfare is often seen as a mechanism to break apart black families.[10]

One answer is that many families are pushed into the PINS system by school officials and the police. Though parents formally initiate almost all of New York's status offender cases, close to half of these parents are referred to the system by their child's school or by the police (New York State Division of Probation n.d.).[11] While school administrators can file PINS petitions, it is common practice in some areas to respond to chronic truancy by asking parents to initiate the process. During focus groups with parents of PINS youth, those who were referred to the PINS system by a school administrator often said that the school had threatened to file an educational neglect complaint unless the parent filed a PINS petition.

Some parents reported that when they asked police officers to return their teenage children who were staying out all night or were gone for days at a time, the police referred them to the PINS system—even though officers have the power to return children without a warrant or the filing of a PINS petition.[12] Though law enforcement agencies file about half of all status offense cases adjudicated by juvenile courts in other states, police in New York City rarely file PINS petitions themselves (Puzzanchera et al. 2000; Weingartner et al. 2002). This occurs in part because police may not understand their authority over status offenders, but also because police are often reluctant to spend their time on runaway youth cases.

When a parent initiates a PINS case, he or she must make one or more allegations about his or her child's behaviors in a petition. Citywide in 2001, the most frequent allegations made by parents were incorrigible or ungovernable behavior, followed by truancy and running away (New York State Division of Probation n.d.). Petitions against girls were much more likely than those against boys to include allegations of running away: 47 percent compared with 27 percent. Interviews with parents suggested that school-related problems, such as disrupting class and acting out, were also common reasons for filing PINS petitions. Less common allegations were stealing, engaging in sexual activity, and threatening or using force. Most parents made more than one allegation, suggesting that by the time they turned to the PINS system, parents and youth were facing multiple challenges.

When a parent, guardian, or other adult decided to file a PINS petition, that person made an appointment to see a probation officer in the county Family Court. When a probation officer first met with a family, the officer checked to see if the child had any pending delinquency, child welfare, or PINS cases—any of which would make the child ineligible for a new PINS case. If the child did not have any open cases, the probation officer listened as the parent or other petitioner described the child's behavior to determine whether the youth met the definition of a person in need of supervision. If so, the officer scheduled a formal PINS interview with another probation officer. That interview usually took place two to eight weeks after the initial intake, largely because probation officers carried as many as 100 cases (Shubik and Khashu 2005).

The case then took one of two routes: the probation officer referred the family to a community-based service provider for assessment or the case went before a Family Court judge. While family-based services were the preferred option, if the child refused to go to services or if the parent insisted on seeing a judge or wanted to get a warrant, the case went to court.

Probation officers initially referred over half of all cases for assessment. The assessments were thorough: the child met two to six times with a social worker to discuss his or her school performance, family interactions, relationships with peers, and emotional and physical health, including drug and alcohol use. Whenever possible, the social worker met with the child's family members for their perspectives on the child's behavior and health. The social worker also reviewed academic, medical, psychiatric, and any other relevant records when available. Drawing on all this information, the social worker created a service plan. Though regulations required that the assessments be completed within 30 days, only a third met that deadline (Weingartner et al. 2002). Many families never completed the process. Among those that did, services began 45 to 120 days after the case was initiated—a long time for families in crisis.

Just under half of all cases went directly to court. Two-thirds of the court cases involved parents requesting a warrant who ordered the police to pick up their children and bring them to court. Once in court, the process took on a more traditional, adversarial legal framework: the petitioner—the parent or guardian—had to prove the allegations in the petition, and the court provided the youth with a lawyer to defend his or her interests. While the case worked its way through the court, the judge decided where the child would live. Most children went home, but in just over a third of the cases, the judge remanded the youth to foster care, usually at the parent's request.

Court cases often dragged on for weeks or months. In one sample of 93 cases that went to court, over half had 4 or more court hearings; one case had 20 (Weingartner et al. 2002). And whether the cases met in court several times or only once, the judge almost always ruled that the parent had proved the allegations. The length of the court process often meant the case went nowhere: among those cases that bypassed assessment, five in every six were dismissed or withdrawn—presumably because of failures to appear at court or parental frustration. Working parents in particular could ill afford to miss work for several days without jeopardizing their jobs.

In the meantime, the children remanded to foster care—almost always living in congregate care facilities—often deteriorated. Most of them entered the PINS system with a history of truancy and became even less likely to attend school regularly after entering foster care. In contrast, the attendance rates of similarly aged kids placed in foster care because of abuse or neglect often improve following placement (Conger and Rebeck 2001).

Keeping PINS youth safe in their placements also proved challenging. Children placed in foster care in conjunction with a PINS case were three times more likely than other children in foster care to run away from placement; child welfare staff called this "going AWOL" (Ross et al. 2001, 19). One study showed that over 60 percent of PINS youth remanded to foster care went AWOL at least once; an ironic, but not surprising, finding given that many parents initiated PINS cases because their children were running away (Weingartner et al. 2002).[13] As discussed in chapter 6, the risks youth face while AWOL vary, with about a third experiencing such high risks as drug dealing or threats and experiences of violence. AWOLs also trigger the filing of missing persons reports with the police, a necessary but expensive process that eats into law enforcement and child care staff resources.

Most PINS youth remanded to foster care were returned to their families within three months, but without receiving services designed to address their issues.[14] Foster care placements were aimed at providing care to abused and neglected children—a group that made up the majority at almost all congregate care facilities at any one time. Services for abused or neglected children were not designed for the short time frames that PINS youth stay in foster care. What is more, most PINS youth did not have documented cases of abuse or neglect and faced different issues that often required a different service orientation.

Finally, despite the short length of stay, the remands were expensive: congregate care placements cost over $185 a day, compared with less than $40 a day for foster or kinship homes. Unlike children in care due to abuse or neglect, for whom the federal government paid half and the state a quarter of the cost, the city paid the whole cost of PINS remands.

With hundreds of PINS youth in care every year, the cost to the city's child welfare system exceeded $10 million a year in per diem placement costs alone. And, a quarter of PINS youth discharged from foster care reentered care, compared with 15 percent of similarly aged youth who entered foster care due to abuse or neglect (Ross et al. 2001).

Reforming New York City's Status Offender Program

The general dissatisfaction with the PINS system among agencies, service providers, and families festered for years. The pending increase in the age limit from under 16 to under 18 years, however, sent New York City PINS officials into crisis mode. Projections showed that left unchanged, the number of youth in the PINS system would increase by 69 to 105 percent (Souweine and Khashu 2001). The projections also suggested that if New York City's status offenders followed national trends, remands and placements in foster care would exceed the overall increase. Data from states that already had 16- and 17-year-olds in the status offender system showed that older youth entered foster care more often than their younger peers. The city's courts, probation, police, child welfare, and community service providers simply could not handle an additional 4,000 to 5,000 youth so quickly, even with a big funding increase.

And new monies were not in the offing. City and state revenues declined in the wake of the September 11, 2001, attacks on the World Trade Center, which meant that maintaining existing funds might be challenging. Even using conservative assumptions that did not include increases in court costs, additional probation officers, additional service use, or capital costs, New York City faced increased expenditures of $15–20 million without changes in the system (Ross et al. 2001).

The confluence of dissatisfaction, increasing burdens, and funding restrictions created a window of opportunity for reform. The city considered three options.

The most progressive reform would replace Family Court jurisdiction with preventive services. Parents initiating status offense cases would be fast-tracked to assessments for community-based services. Family Court judges would no longer hear PINS cases, thus shutting off the possibility of remands or placements to foster care (though short-term respite care could be developed for some families). The savings from lower placement costs would more than make up for the increase in preventive service use. This reform, however, required substantial changes in state law. Having finally passed the PINS-to-18 bill after years of pressure from advocacy groups—whose members saw the prospect of judicial support for parental authority as the prize of their efforts—persuading the legislature to shut off access to court appeared unlikely despite the cost savings.

A second option involved expanding the jurisdiction of the Family Court to include families as well as children. This approach would allow the court to mandate that youth and parents participate in counseling and other services or face judicial sanctions. This reform could address a common problem cited by probation and child welfare staff: parents and youth often refused to participate in services even after thorough assessments found that family interventions were necessary. Some parents placed the blame for behavior problems solely on their child; rebellious youth often reciprocated in their assessment of their parents. While requiring only minor changes in state law, this reform would be the most expensive—and might be seen as replacing parental authority with judicial authority, an outcome that supporters of the PINS-to-18 law did not have in mind.

Instead, the city chose a third option that did not require new legislation and offered the potential to limit costs and target services. A new program, the Family Assessment Program (FAP), sought to connect families to services more quickly and to persuade parents not to insist on going to court by discussing the limits of judicial interventions. By presenting a more realistic view of what parents could expect from the PINS system, program operators felt that only those families that could benefit from what the system had to offer would pursue their cases. By making referrals to community-based service providers in a more timely fashion, the program hoped to defuse crisis situations before they festered into intractable conflicts.

The Family Assessment Program

The Family Assessment Program shifted intake and assessment from probation to child welfare. Instead of seeing a probation officer, families wishing to access the PINS system meet immediately with an experienced child welfare social worker. The social worker assesses the families' concerns and, on the spot, implements next steps and service referrals. All this occurs before probation or court involvement. FAP intakes occur the day the parent walks in, regardless of whether the youth is present.

If the youth is not present, the social worker interviews the parent and arranges for a subsequent interview for the youth within a few days.

When a family enters the FAP office, it is greeted by an administrative worker who runs the family's name through the child welfare and probation data systems to determine if an open case or past history with either agency exists. While waiting for the intake interview, parents fill out a "request for services" form that asks them to describe the issue that has brought them to the PINS system. Similarly, youth complete a "youth response" form in which they are asked why they think they have been brought to FAP and what they think will happen. Once these forms are completed and screening has begun, the family is interviewed by a family assessment specialist, an experienced child welfare employee with a master's degree in social work who shows concern for both the parent's and youth's perspectives and experience. Family assessment specialists interview the youth and parents separately and together. The interviews focus on expectations, family dynamics, and potential services.

For approximately one-third of the families that come to FAP, involvement with the PINS system ends after the initial interview. FAP categorizes these cases as either "refused and withdrawn," meaning the family left after refusing services, or "advocacy and information," meaning the family's interaction with FAP ended after receiving information or other supportive services. By presenting a more accurate picture of what the status offender system has to offer, FAP dispels some common misperceptions held by parents. Some parents think that entering the PINS system will open the door to more authoritarian approaches, such as a tough judge or a "boot camp." By explaining that most youth and parents are referred to counseling (and often other services) and that no boot camps exist, FAP manages expectations and weeds out those cases where children or parents are not interested in what the system has to offer.

In most cases, however, the social worker assesses the family's concerns during the initial interview and immediately implements next steps: a follow-up meeting, a referral to emergency mental health or medical services, a referral to a child welfare contracted– or neighborhood-based provider, scheduling of a more extensive assessment using the agencies doing such work under the prior system, or, in the case of a runaway, referral to probation to begin the process of obtaining of a warrant.

For parents who insist on probation monitoring or court access— parents who previously would have been permitted to go before a judge— probation and child welfare work together to steer the family into services.

If a parent is adamant about going to Family Court after meeting with the social worker, the worker will brief the probation supervisor on the case. Then the probation supervisor and the social worker hold a case conference with the family to reinforce its understanding of the process and to prevent any unrealistic expectations about what court access can provide. According to the social workers and probation officers involved, the family often agrees to have its case remain with FAP following the case conference.

In addition to referring families to services and further assessment, FAP screens out cases more appropriately handled through other programs. If an open probation or child welfare case is discovered during the administrative screening, the family may be referred back to the person already working with them. Families that insist on placement are referred to a child welfare field office for a critical case conference (a conference involving all family members, a caseworker, and other support providers such as school and extended family), which may result in preventive services or a voluntary out-of-home placement. When issues involving abuse and neglect surface during the interview, the specialist informs the State Central Registry.

The Family Assessment Program produced many of the system changes it was designed to accomplish. Table 7.1 shows the referral outcomes for all FAP cases processed from the program's initiation in December 2002 through June 30, 2004. Overall, almost half the families were referred to community-based services or to a more thorough assessment provided by a community-based organization (46 percent). Approximately 12 per-

Table 7.1. Family Assessment Program Intake, December 2002–June 2004

Result of FAP intake	Number	Percent
Referred to child welfare services	1,071	10.8
Reported to State Central Registry	121	1.2
Referred to probation	1,086	10.9
Referred directly to services	1,759	17.7
Referred to thorough assessment	2,764	27.8
Refused services or withdrew case	1,597	16.1
Advocacy or information, or other case closed	1,538	15.5
Total	9,936	100.0

cent of families were referred to another division of child welfare, either because they already had an open case or because the family assessment specialist suspected child abuse or neglect and informed the State Central Registry. Only 11 percent of families were referred to probation for a PINS intake.

Comparing case processing before and after FAP shows dramatic changes—especially since this period coincided with the expansion of the system to those under 18. After FAP was implemented, the number of PINS filings with probation dropped 79 percent. From January 1 through June 30, 2002, the Department of Probation opened 3,345 PINS cases. During the same six-month period in 2004, it opened only 697 PINS intakes.

As a result, juvenile probation officers saw their caseloads drop to 25 youth per officer. This decrease in probation PINS cases has not meant layoffs as some staffers feared, but instead has facilitated a much-needed reallocation of probation staff to other, arguably more significant, assignments more consistent with their law enforcement–oriented skill sets. The PINS cases remaining with probation are often court-involved cases requiring oversight for compliance with court orders.

After FAP was introduced, PINS referrals to Family Court declined by 55 percent. The court heard 1,043 PINS cases from January through June 2002. From January to June 2004, only 474 PINS intakes were referred to the court. The use of foster care has also declined, but not as markedly. During the first six months of 2002, judges issued 343 remand or placement orders in PINS cases. From January through June 2004, the number of remands or placement orders declined to 272. This represents a 21 percent reduction in the use of foster care for PINS cases despite the increase in the pool of youth eligible for the PINS system.

Many of those with experience in the system believe that FAP's less dramatic success in reducing placements is because despite the "upstream filtering" of PINS cases, more challenging cases where few options exist are left. Others, pointing to Illinois's success in stemming placements, argue that these results show that Family Court judges are still unwilling to push back on parents who refuse to take their children home.

The new system has benefits beyond reducing numbers and saving money. Social workers conducting thorough assessments report that the families they work with seem more knowledgeable about the process and more willing to engage. These social workers and probation officers encounter fewer open child welfare cases during assessment or probation meetings, as the FAP administrative screening using child welfare databases is better at turning up open cases than having probation officers ask families. Frontline staff facing less stressful work environments feel they can perform their jobs better. These positives outcomes, however, do not mean that every issue in the status offender system has been solved. Indeed, the system still faces some deep-seated challenges.

Cross-Cutting Issues Remain

Several cross-cutting issues continue to hamper the status offender system in New York City, as might be expected in a system with so many players charged with addressing multiple youth problems. The interagency collaboration that forged a strong bond between probation and child welfare has not been replicated with other agencies. The police and schools account for over half of referrals to the PINS system, yet many police officers and school officials are unfamiliar with PINS and FAP and have only a vague notion of the services available.

The story of one Bronx mother is illustrative. Concerned about her daughter's poor school performance and failure to adhere to curfew, she went to her local police precinct for assistance. There, she said, a police officer instructed her to go to Family Court to seek a "PINS warrant," explaining that a "PINS warrant means that a youth officer goes with her to school and checks up on her to make sure she's doing her homework and is following her curfew and would pick her up if she was out past her curfew and take her to Bridges [secure juvenile detention] just to give her a little taste of reality." Expecting the supervision and law enforcement services described to her at the station house, this mother was frustrated and disappointed to discover that engaging PINS would result in a referral to counseling. In the words of another parent, "There's a lot of information, it's just not accurate information."

Lack of information about FAP extends not only to the agencies referring families but also to the court. Interviews with three Family Court judges revealed that the judges have little if any knowledge of FAP two years after the program's implementation. Given the enormous workload of the court, a lack of information about a relatively new program is not surprising. More troubling, perhaps, is that the judges interviewed also stated that they rarely had detailed information on family assessments or the specific service referrals made in the cases before them. As one judge said, knowing the experience of the family with the system before the court appearance and the results of prior evaluations would allow him to make more informed decisions. Without that information, judges often react to what they hear in the courtroom and thus respond to the forceful arguments of a parent seeking placement.

Under both the old PINS system and FAP, probation conducts intake interviews on runaway cases and then forwards them to court for a "PINS warrant." PINS warrants authorize a located child to be returned to court by law enforcement and, once in court, allow the family to use the PINS system. To gain faster court access, officials from both probation and child welfare report that it is common for parents to falsely claim that their children have run away. Officials note that in some cases involving runaway allegations, the child is staying outside the home at a known and safe location.

To screen out these false cases, all families seeking PINS warrants must first provide a missing persons report from the police department to a FAP social worker. Then the FAP social worker interviews the parent and calls the youth's school, family, friends, or relatives to confirm that the youth's location is unknown. Only after these requirements have been met is the family referred to a probation officer, who then interviews the parent and forwards the case to court.

This process (missing persons report, FAP intake, probation interview, forwarding to Family Court) eliminates many "false runaway" cases. Once a family is identified as an actual runaway case, however, it can take additional hours or days for a warrant to be issued. Because Family Court generally will not accept new cases after 4:00 p.m., probation officers often will not accept runaway cases after the lunch break because these cases will not be processed quickly enough to make it to court before it closes. When this happens, a family anxious about its missing child's safety will be asked to return to court the next day.

Misunderstandings of the process can delay the issuance of a warrant, creating parental anxiety and potentially diminishing the chance of a youth being found. In one instance, a police precinct misunderstood the protocol and refused to provide the parent with a missing persons report. Without that report, FAP would not refer the case to probation for a warrant. Only after the FAP social worker spent hours speaking with the family and with local police was the case referred to court and then only after probation made a special accommodation to take the case late in the day.

Conversations with probation and child welfare as well as observations of FAP families reveal that many families with missing children are under the false impression that a PINS warrant will help speed up the police locating their child. These families may not be seeking the intervention of a Family Court judge, but rather are looking for a way to bring their missing child home quickly. One mother recounted that when she went to fill out a missing persons report, a police officer told her to get a PINS warrant. She was not at all interested in PINS services—she had already arranged for private therapy upon her daughter's return—but based on the instructions of the officer she nonetheless went to the FAP office. When she discovered, several hours into the process of obtaining a warrant, that this would result in her daughter being produced in court, she left in a rage.

To address these problems, child welfare and probation have conducted training and information sessions with police and school officials. The barriers to success are daunting. New York City employs nearly 40,000 police officers and has over 1,000 schools. This size and staff turnover means that any training program would have to be ongoing. Another way to ameliorate these types of cross-cutting problems is to give frontline staff more flexibility, something that bureaucracies are notoriously loath to do. However, as the example of the FAP social worker and probation officer who made special accommodations for the family with a runaway youth demonstrates, granting flexibility often enables a more problem-solving culture to develop.

Conclusion

New York has made its status offender system considerably more rational. Fewer resources are wasted on interventions that have little chance of resolving a family's problems. Though it is not clear how widespread the remaining issues identified are, it is possible and even likely that the longer the FAP program exists, the more staff at other agencies will learn of its operations and value. City officials have taken a proactive approach to solving these problems and publicizing FAP's services, which in itself represents a break from past practice.

While policymakers have made progress grappling with the process issues brought to the fore by the PINS-to-18 legislation, researchers and agency staff have paid less attention to the larger question of how well the services offered by the system resolve status offender problems. Indeed, expanding access to community-based services is a hollow accomplishment unless those services make a difference for youth and families. Assessing the efforts of community-based services, however, is a daunting task because of the wide range of issues that status offenders bring to the table. Chronic truancy, sexual acting out, and substance abuse may each land a youth in a status offender system, but they call for different service programs. A system of performance indicators that measure process and outcome variables—such as child welfare placement, school attendance, delinquency, and criminal justice involvement—might be one way to learn more about the impact of services for status offenders.

Cross-cutting issues in the system, however, will require a sustained effort of communication, training, and administrative flexibility. The number of agencies involved in the status offender system and their diverging orientations mean that only constant vigilance will prevent youth and families from falling through the cracks. The reforms in New York, Illinois, and other localities show that reform can improve systems and save money when the political will exists.

Source Reports
and Methodological Notes

Few status offender systems have comprehensive, reliable data systems that track youth, and even fewer monitor the effectiveness of the services provided. In New York City, information about a single case may be located within two or more databases. Nationally and locally, the literature on the topic is sparse. As a backwater in youth services, high-quality information on various aspects of the status offender system is infrequent.

To ameliorate these difficulties, researchers engaged in a wide range of data collection and analysis. The authors of the reports cited in the chapter analyzed probation, child welfare, and Family Court administrative data from cities, counties, and state agencies in New York. They reviewed 200 case files and observed court proceedings. They interviewed judges, probation officers, police officers, service providers, and child welfare staff as well as city, county, and state officials in charge of various aspects of the PINS system. Focus groups were held with youth and parents who participated in the status offender system. Informal discussions with officials in other states also inform this chapter. Some of the authors participated in meetings and discussions that took place over several months about how to best reform the system.

These activities provided a fine-grained understanding of how status offender systems work in New York State and City, as well as information about how the systems developed in New York and in other parts of the country.

8

Bridging Child Welfare and Juvenile Justice

Preventing the Unnecessary Detention of Foster Children

Timothy Ross and Dylan Conger

In making this appeal for coordination and collaboration among public agencies, I'm not talking about pro forma integration effort—I'm not talking about memoranda of understanding or top-level reorganizations that have autonomous agencies vaguely reporting to a single box labeled "human services." Rather, I'm talking about the much more challenging objective of achieving real working partnerships at the front line.

—Douglas W. Nelson, President, Annie E. Casey Foundation, 1998

Douglas Nelson repeats a common call for public agencies generally and child welfare agencies in particular to coordinate their activities with other human service departments. As previous chapters have documented, child welfare is an especially pressing area for coordination among agencies. In addition to the trauma associated with abuse and child neglect, children and families involved with child welfare agencies often face many other problems, including unemployment, mental illness, substance abuse, discrimination, and homelessness. Several different governmental systems provide services to address these difficulties. Yet, like many other government agencies, child welfare agencies often operate in isolation from other social service providers. This isolation occurs in part because frontline workers are frequently unaware that their clients are involved in other systems, uninformed about how to communicate with other agencies, and unclear about their roles with respect to these other agencies.

173

This chapter examines the hazards created by the lack of agency coordination when youth in foster care become entangled with the juvenile justice system. The chapter then discusses a programmatic response to this problem—Project Confirm—that helped lead to reforms and research studies in Los Angeles, Illinois, and Maryland, among other places. This case study is useful both for its content and as an example of how to evaluate child welfare reform efforts that address cross-cutting issues. The end of the chapter discusses the challenges faced in Project Confirm's first year, while chapter 9 presents the results of an outcome evaluation of this effort.

The Overlap between Child Welfare and Juvenile Justice

The arrest of a foster child requires the involvement of numerous public and private agencies. Confusion about roles, delays in transmitting information, and misunderstandings between frontline workers in the child welfare and juvenile justice agencies may increase the likelihood that arrested foster children are detained in juvenile detention facilities rather than released to foster or kinship parents, guardians, or caseworkers. Project Confirm, a program piloted in New York City by the Vera Institute of Justice and now operated by New York City's child welfare agency, brings together eight state and local agencies to intervene upon the arrest of foster children and prevent their unwarranted detention. Local agencies involved include child welfare, juvenile justice, probation, the Family Court, the police, and the mayor's office. State agencies supporting the program include the New York State Division of Criminal Justice Services and the Office of Children and Family Services. Understanding the scope of what Project Confirm does requires further discussion of the problem and the origins of the program.

Pre-adjudication Juvenile Detention

Juvenile custody rates soared across the country during the 1990s, leaving many juvenile detention facilities, especially those in large urban areas, seriously overcrowded. According to one estimate, the number of children held in locked juvenile justice detention facilities increased fivefold from 1985 to 1995 (Wordes and Jones 1998). In New York City, the average daily population of youth in detention swelled by 60 percent between 1993 and 2000. Such increases have been attributed to the increased use of detention for nonviolent offenders and probation violators (Faruqee 2002; Orlando 1999). In 2001, over 5,000 juveniles were admitted to detention in New York City, where they remained an average of 36 days (Faruqee 2002).

Pre-adjudication detention for juveniles is intended to prevent youth from further offending and ensure their appearance in court. Those who are released while their cases are pending are typically considered at low risk of these activities. Unlike adult court, Family Court judges are also required to take the best interest of a juvenile into consideration when making a detention decision—in other words, to act as a parent. Yet, detention at the pre-adjudicatory phase is not to be used as punishment.[1] An additional consideration informs judges' decisions to detain: whether a "release resource" is present in court, typically a guardian or parent who can take the child home and who can be held responsible for his or her behavior. The presence of an adult is imperative to ensuring the release of juveniles who pose no threat to the community or risk of flight. A youth cannot be released "to the street": an able, willing, and legally authorized adult must be present to take custody of the youth upon release.

In fact, the presence of a guardian at several junctures in the arrest of a juvenile may prevent the use of detention. In New York, when a juvenile (anyone under 16) is arrested for a relatively serious offense, police take him to court, or if court is closed, to a secure detention facility until court opens the following weekday.[2] Once in court, the juvenile meets with a probation intake officer who conducts an interview, ideally with the guardian present, to determine whether to forward the case for prosecution or adjustment.

Cases that require prosecution are then referred to the adult equivalent of a prosecutor (in New York City, the prosecuting agency is known as Corporation Counsel), where the decision is made whether to file a petition to the court. If a petition is filed, the juvenile has an initial court appearance where the judge assigns counsel and decides, with a recommendation from Corporation Counsel, whether to further detain the juvenile in a secure or nonsecure detention facility while awaiting adjudication. According to anecdotal evidence, judges typically follow the Corporation Counsel recommendation to detain. A necessary condition for release is that a responsible guardian is present to take custody.

For decades, advocates and researchers have criticized juvenile detention facilities in New York City and other jurisdictions for their squalid conditions, violence, and abuse toward youth in custody (for example, Hubner and Wolfson 1999; Orlando 1999; and Parent and Abt Associates 1994). In the early 1970s, reformers sued New York City charging that conditions in juvenile detention violated constitutional guarantees against cruel and unusual punishment.[3] Under intense pressure from community groups in 1989, city officials vowed to shut down the sole secure detention center, Spofford, which had "long been considered a symbol of overcrowded conditions and brutality against children" (Faruqee 2002, 3). After the city built two smaller secure facilities, Spofford closed in 1997, with newspaper and magazine articles citing its history of violence, poor sanitation, and lack of services.[4] In 1999, the city reopened the facility with a new name—the Bridges Juvenile Center—but reports of violence and gang recruiting continued amid calls to shift resources away from detention and toward a social service model (for example, Kelly 2004).

Aside from these conditions, other criticisms have been leveled at the use of pre-adjudication detention. Some speculate that it may harm juvenile defendants' educational attainment and income if it keeps them from school and work (Faruqee 2002; Sampson and Laub 1993). Additionally, adolescents in detention cannot demonstrate their ability to obey the law or display other positive behaviors that could lead judges to release juveniles before disposition—the Family Court equivalent of sentences (for example, Cohen and Kluegel 1979). Some argue that pre-adjudication detention may also result in more severe dispositions (Bortner 1982; Fagan and Guggenheim 1996). In a study of all juvenile delinquency cases in a single state, Frazier and Bishop (1985) find that juveniles who were detained before adjudication were slightly more likely than those who were not detained to have their cases result in a formal disposition (rather than an informal disposition, which may result in more lenient sanctions).[5]

Child Welfare for Adolescents in New York City

New York City's child welfare agency has custody of approximately 20,000 foster children, though this number has been as low as 16,000 and as high as 50,000 in the past 15 years. The agency contracts with dozens of nonprofit private agencies that are responsible for recruiting foster families and operating congregate care facilities, such as group homes or residential treatment centers. Approximately one-third of the youth in care are between 12 and 16 years old. Most of these adolescents reside in congregate care, particularly those who enter care during adolescence instead of childhood. Adolescents enter care in various ways. About a third of first-time adolescent entries are because of abuse or neglect, another third are voluntary placements, and most of the remainder enter because of a remand or placement as part of a status offense action (see chapter 7). Less than 3 percent are placed in foster care through the juvenile delinquency system.

Several frontline staff and caregivers are involved in the care of a foster child, and their respective responsibilities can sometimes be unclear when an arrest occurs. Caregivers typically include foster parents, relatives, and/or group home counselors who provide basic subsistence and who may also provide care outside the home, such as taking the child to doctor visits, attending teacher-parent conferences, and acting as the child's guardian in juvenile delinquency cases.

Each child is also assigned a caseworker who is responsible for monitoring the case, such as scheduling meetings with biological parents, assessing the safety and quality of the foster home, and tracking progress toward adoption or reunification with the biological parent. Each case is overseen by a case manager who supervises the caseworker and often makes important decisions regarding the case. Because of the challenging work conditions and low pay, turnover among caseworkers in child welfare agencies is substantial; a 1995 U.S. General Accounting Office study estimated that the annual turnover rate in New York City was 75 percent (GAO 1995). A more recent study credited the agency with substantial improvements in infrastructure that likely reduced this turnover rate (see Lawry and Farber 2007). Still, staff turnover remains an issue in New York and many other child welfare systems. Thus, in addition to confusing lines of parental authority across several caregivers and frontline caseworkers, the people who fill these roles may often change, allowing for further confusion and communication gaps within the child welfare system as well as between child welfare and other youth-serving agencies.

The "Overlap" Problem

In 1996, the Vera Institute of Justice and New York City's child welfare agency sought to examine how interagency communication was affected when foster adolescents were arrested. Vera researchers began by surveying youth entering juvenile detention centers and discovered that foster youth were sent back to detention after their first court hearing at a higher rate than their nonfoster counterparts. An additional review of case records showed no evidence that the foster youth in the survey committed more crimes or crimes of greater severity than the nonfoster survey participants, both factors that might have explained differential detention rates.

Instead, informal interviews with judges, probation officers, detention officials, child welfare officials, and foster youth shed light on the many barriers separating the child welfare and juvenile justice agencies and the possibility that these barriers prevented foster care caseworkers from showing up to court.[6] Responding to the arrest of a foster child requires the involvement of numerous public and private agencies, including the police, child welfare, juvenile justice, probation, contract foster care providers, judges, and juvenile defense and prosecuting attorneys. For children not in foster care, parents are responsible for navigating this system. For foster children, the locus of responsibility is often unclear to frontline staff, case managers, and foster parents. Confusion about roles, delays in transmitting information, and misunderstandings between frontline workers in the child welfare and juvenile justice agencies may increase the likelihood that arrested foster children are detained in juvenile detention facilities rather than released to legal caregivers or caseworkers.

In short, this exploratory research suggested that police, detention, and probation authorities were often unable to track down child welfare caseworkers or foster parents who could serve as release resources. In some cases, child welfare caseworkers and foster parents were not aware that they were responsible for serving this function. Without guardians present in court and at other decisionmaking points, judges were forced to detain foster youth whom they would otherwise release. Those judges interviewed felt that with more information about a youth and with a caseworker in court to serve as a release resource, many foster children would be released to the caseworker rather than detained in juvenile detention facilities. Vera coined the term "overlap problem" to refer to this communication gap between (and within) the child welfare and juvenile justice systems.

Example of the Overlap Problem

The following example is a composite sketch of several cases encountered during the exploratory study of the overlap problem. One evening, the police arrest two 13-year-olds—Jason and Bill—for possessing a joint of marijuana. Bill calls his mother, who, after promising to police that Bill will appear in court the next day, takes him home. Like many foster adolescents, Jason lives in a group home. Embarrassed by his foster care status and fearful that the group home staff will expel him for his arrest, Jason does not tell the police that he is a foster child. When the police ask him whom they should contact to pick him up, Jason gives his biological mother's phone number. The police call, but Jason's mother refuses to pick him up.[7] Because they cannot legally keep Jason longer than three hours at the precinct station, the police send him to a locked juvenile detention facility for the night. The group home staff notice Jason's absence and conclude that he ran away from care.

The next day, Bill and his mother meet with the probation officer and the prosecuting attorney, and mother and child both promise that Bill will be on his best behavior and appear at all court hearings. The prosecuting attorney releases Bill to his mother's custody and continues investigating the case to decide whether to press charges. After Bill appears in court two more times, prosecutors drop Bill's case two months later.

Jason is not so fortunate. After spending the night in detention, he is transported to the courthouse and meets with a probation officer. The probation officer asks for a phone contact and Jason tells the probation officer he is in foster care. The probation officer calls the child welfare agency. But, in an organization of thousands of employees spread out over several agencies, she cannot locate anyone who knows how to find Jason's caseworker. With no caseworker available to consult, the probation officer refers Jason's case to a juvenile prosecutor. Given the nonviolent nature of the offense, the juvenile prosecutor wants to release Jason and schedule a future court date. But since no adult is present to take custody of Jason, the juvenile prosecutor has little choice but to bring the case before a judge. Jason's court-appointed attorney argues for Jason's release, but lacking a child welfare representative to accept him, the judge orders Jason to return to detention to await his next hearing in three days. The probation officer, the juvenile prosecutor, the defense attorney, and the judge, each faced with overwhelming caseloads, turn their attention to the next case.[8]

Jason appears in court two more times. Each time, the judge sends him back to detention because his guardian is absent. After his third court appearance a week later, the judge orders his release to the child welfare agency's emergency children's services, and a transport vehicle takes Jason to the agency's emergency placement unit. Like many private foster care placements, Jason's group home is paid per diem, and after three days of absence, the agency placed another child in Jason's bed. With no bed for Jason, the placement office scrambles to find a new group home for him. Jason's arrest makes placing him difficult, and he spends two nights in the placement office before moving to a new group home known for taking "hard to place" children.

Child Welfare Consequences of the Overlap Problem

Pre-adjudication detention of a foster child can affect both the child and the involved public agencies detrimentally. In addition to the social and economic costs to the youth of being detained—unsafe or squalid conditions of facilities, inability to demonstrate good behavior to the court, and possible missed education and employment—there are potential welfare consequences. Foster youth who are detained for several days may lose their foster care placements, especially if they live in congregate care facilities. The private agencies that operate most group homes in New York can hold the bed for a missing foster youth for up to three days. But if the juvenile's whereabouts are unknown, the agency usually fills the bed with another child. A youth leaving detention then experiences the disruption of moving to a new home in a new neighborhood and developing a relationship with new caretakers. A change in placement also may weaken or destroy relationships with important adults in the children's lives, such as their biological parents, child care staff at the facility they leave, and peers, potentially resulting in antisocial and delinquent behavior (Runyan and Gould 1985; Widom 1994). Because of the disruption new placements cause, federal foster care guidelines identify reductions in placement changes as a key goal for child welfare agencies (HHS 2000).

A related concern is that youth released from detention may be sent to emergency placement facilities because they have lost their foster care placements. Most child welfare managers and officials view emergency placements as undesirable because in addition to creating instability in children's lives, they require extensive and stressful personnel time to locate new placements. Additionally, until the opening of a new 100-bed facility in New York City, youth in emergency placement facilities occasionally faced overcrowding problems that created uncomfortable spaces for children and poor working conditions for staff.

Secure detention costs New York City more than $300 a day per bed compared with between approximately $25 and $200 a day for foster care (as of 2006). In addition, while the federal government pays for

50 percent of foster care costs, no corresponding funding match applies to secure detention. This comparison alone reveals the financial burden associated with housing foster youth in detention facilities rather than in foster homes. Even further costs are generated during the period the child welfare agency pays a contract foster care provider to hold a child's bed while the youth resides in detention, a situation that can result in total costs of $500 per day.

Project Confirm as a Solution to the Overlap Problem

Project Confirm was launched in July 1998. Within three months of startup, the program expanded the target population to include not only children in foster care but also those under court-ordered supervision—cases in which children are not removed from their homes but are monitored by the court because of allegations of maltreatment. Project Confirm included supervision cases because the child welfare agency maintains legal responsibility for these children. The program uses two primary strategies to reduce the overlap problem: notification and court conferencing. Project Confirm augments these components with other activities that distribute information, such as community conferencing and information sessions with frontline workers in the involved agencies. Figure 8.1 is a diagram of the program's logic model.

Notification

Project Confirm starts with a notification system. Juvenile detention intake workers phone Project Confirm whenever the police admit a minor to a secure juvenile detention facility. A Project Confirm screener then searches the child welfare system's main administrative database to ascertain the foster care status of the arrested youth. If the screener identifies a foster child, the screener contacts a liaison at one of the private agencies that provide most foster care for New York City children and the probation officer assigned to meet the minor in court. The agency liaison, in turn, instructs the caseworker to call Project Confirm for instructions. Through notification, Project Confirm seeks to increase the appearance rate of child welfare representatives, who have a legal responsibility to attend hearings and the authority to accept custody of children released by the court. By increasing the appearance rate, notification also

Figure 8.1. Project Confirm Logic Model

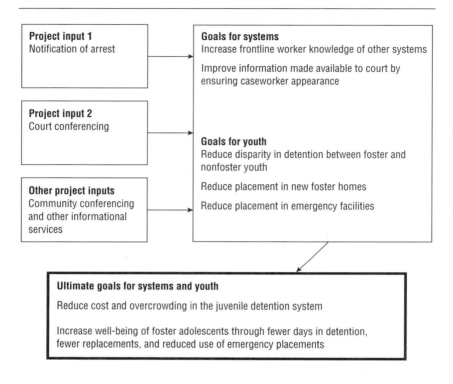

attempts to improve the information available to juvenile justice professionals deciding about these delinquency cases.

Court Conferencing

Following notification, Project Confirm employs court conferencing to ensure that when notified of an arrest, child care workers and their counterparts in the juvenile justice system know the role the law requires them to play when addressing a case involving a foster child. A Project Confirm field coordinator meets a foster care caseworker at court, introduces the caseworker to the probation officer in charge of the case, and guides the caseworker through the entire process from the probation interview to the hearing before the judge. By connecting child care workers with the Family Court system, court conferencing seeks to give probation officers and prosecutors more knowledge about the child, to give judges the opportunity to ask child care workers questions, and to ensure that in the event of a release, a person authorized to accept a foster child is present. In this way, field coordinators also play a role in holding foster care providers and juvenile justice officials accountable. By law, caseworkers must show up at court and must accept custody of a released child.

Community Conferencing and Other Information Services

Project Confirm performs several other services not directly related to its primary mission of reducing unnecessary detention. The program is seen as an "information Switzerland," a neutral party that can broker data and connect people from agencies and departments that have historically had either little contact or adversarial relationships. Frontline workers and policymakers in child welfare and juvenile justice frequently consult with Project Confirm staff when they have questions about how other agencies work.

If a child is released, for example, Project Confirm field coordinators often schedule a community conference with the minor, the child welfare representative, and other involved parties to provide information about what to expect at the next hearing. At the meeting, a field coordinator explains the court's action, answers questions, explains how the youth needs to prepare for future hearings, and explains the legal obligation to appear on the next court date. Field coordinators use community conferences to ensure that all parties know the result and implications of a court hearing and to impress upon the youth that he or she is ultimately responsible for taking the appropriate actions.

Project Confirm leverages its expertise in both the juvenile justice and child welfare systems to generate additional contacts that allow the program to intercede in cases that might otherwise escape its notice and to build and improve upon relationships with the numerous actors involved in the overlap problem. The program frequently works with the child welfare placement office to find solutions for hard-to-place children involved with juvenile justice, especially cases in which foster children experience multiple transfers between child welfare and juvenile justice. In addition, the program fielded more than 350 phone calls from juvenile justice detention staff concerning juvenile offender cases not in Project Confirm's formally defined target population during its first year. The project also receives occasional calls from the police, the probation department, and private foster care agencies on other cases not in the target population despite the fact that the program is not set up to receive referrals on these cases.

A reexamination of Jason's case helps to illustrate how the program works in practice.

Jason's Case under Project Confirm

Following the introduction of Project Confirm, the processing of Jason's case changes significantly. The morning after Jason enters detention, Project Confirm notifies Jason's caseworker and instructs her to call Jason's probation officer. The probation officer asks the caseworker several questions about Jason's behavior and history, and though he could release Jason to the caseworker, he decides that a juvenile prosecutor should review the case. Later that day, the caseworker meets a Project Confirm field coordinator at court. Together, they meet with the juvenile prosecutor, who decides to release Jason to the caseworker with a return to court scheduled in a month. Jason returns to his group home, and his caseworker schedules a counseling session aimed at addressing drug use and delinquency issues.

If the juvenile prosecutor had decided to bring the case before a judge, the Project Confirm field coordinator would explain to the caseworker her responsibilities. These duties include taking custody of Jason if he is released and attending Jason's future court hearings if he is detained. The field coordinator also explains the juvenile detention visitation policy, asks the caseworker if Jason needs any medications, and passes that information along to juvenile detention officials if Jason is detained.

Regardless of the outcome of the case, Jason's future is determined by his behavior and history instead of by his foster care status. In the event of release, Jason retains his placement at his group home, where child care workers can hold him accountable for his behavior. If the staff members from the group home decide that the home's services do not match Jason's needs, caseworkers can arrange a transfer to a new placement in an orderly and legal manner.

Overcoming Implementation Challenges: The First Year of Operations

Well-designed programs often founder as a result of obstacles in implementation. Implementation problems especially plague complex programs like Project Confirm that involve changing the behavior of frontline workers in multiple agencies. To assess the program's implementation, the researchers matched the program's extensive administrative database with records from child welfare and juvenile justice. This allowed them to determine program coverage rates, referral rates, and other indicators of program implementation. The researchers surveyed frontline staff at juvenile justice, child welfare, and foster care contract agencies to determine their satisfaction with the program and to identify problems these staff encountered. To further understand the challenges the program faced, the researchers interviewed several middle managers and sat in on program staff meetings. The following paragraphs summarize the key findings from this research.

Though Project Confirm needed to overcome several implementation obstacles, the program reached most of its implementation objectives in the first year of operations (July 1998 to June 1999). Measures of implementation, such as the percentage of children juvenile justice intake workers checked on to determine their foster care status and the percentage of children eligible to receive services who actually received them, were at or above 90 percent. Under the program, the percentage of foster children released from court at their first hearing, 45 percent, matched the release rate among the general population.

The surveys of frontline workers and middle managers in the partnering government agencies revealed high satisfaction rates with the program. In addition, the commissioner of child welfare and the City of New York nominated Project Confirm for the prestigious Innovations in American Government award administered by Harvard's Kennedy School of Government. The researchers consider the implementation effort successful. The sections below show some of the evidence used to come to this conclusion and describe the project's approach to implementation.

Juvenile Detention Intake Worker Referral Rate

Juvenile justice intake workers must phone Project Confirm whenever the police admit a youth charged with juvenile delinquency to juvenile detention facilities. To make sure this happens, Project Confirm compares the number of phone calls it receives from the intake workers with the number of official admissions recorded. Dividing these two numbers produces a referral rate: if intake workers called Project Confirm on 5 cases, but 10 youth entered detention, the referral rate would be 50 percent. During its first year, Project Confirm fielded calls regarding

1,718 of a possible 1,804 juveniles, resulting in a referral rate of 95 percent. The rate increased consistently over the course of Project Confirm's first year, registering 84 percent at startup and exceeding 95 percent in the last few months.

Program Coverage

The program coverage rate, the number of children served divided by the number of children in the target population, is also an important indicator of implementation (see Rossi and Freeman 1993). During Project Confirm's first year, 16 percent (295) of the 1,850 children who entered detention overnight were eligible for screening and notification services because they either resided in foster care placements or received court-ordered supervision at the time of their arrests.[9] The program provided screening and notification services to 90 percent (266 of 295) of the children in the target population. The 29 children who did not receive services either came to the attention of Project Confirm too late for notification or fell into the category of supervision cases before Project Confirm started officially working with such cases. These high program coverage rates provide strong evidence that Project Confirm implemented its program model successfully.

As explained below, Project Confirm phased in court conferencing during its first year, so only 44 percent (131) of all cases were eligible for court conferencing. Project Confirm conducted court conferencing in 104 (79 percent) of these cases. In 24 of the remaining 27 cases, a conference did not take place because probation officers, the juvenile prosecutor, or the police released the child to the caseworker early in the morning (usually with Project Confirm's prompting).

Caseworker Appearance Rate

Although the notification component operated citywide from the start of the program, Project Confirm quickly found that notification alone did not motivate all caseworkers to come to court. Before the institution of court conferencing, Project Confirm discovered that in over 25 percent of cases, caseworkers did not appear in court despite notification. The program could not ascertain whether a caseworker appeared in an additional 15 percent of the cases. Thus, Project Confirm initiated court conferencing and gradually expanded its use citywide by spring 1999. Notification combined with court conferencing increased the caseworker appearance rate to 93 percent. This change suggests that caseworkers may feel more comfortable attending court with someone to guide them through the process. In addition, knowing that someone might hold them accountable for not appearing in court may have increased caseworkers' sense of obligation or fear of workplace disciplinary action.

Program Participants and Short-Term Outcomes

Most of the 266 youth served by the program entered foster care on abuse or neglect petitions (58 percent), and a sizeable proportion (23 percent) entered as status offenders.[10] The remaining youth came into care as voluntary admissions (17 percent) or juvenile delinquents (1 percent).[11] Compared with other foster children of the same age, detained youth are more likely to live in congregate care facilities such as group homes, diagnostic facilities, or residential treatment centers. More than half (58 percent) of detained juveniles lived in congregate care upon arrest, compared with less than 40 percent of the entire foster population age 13 through 15.

Of the children screened for Project Confirm, those who were in foster care and served by the program did not differ from those who were not in foster care ($N = 1,423$) on age and race,[12] but they did differ on gender. Almost 33 percent of the detained foster children were girls, compared with only 17 percent of the nonfoster children.

The children served by Project Confirm achieved release from court 45 percent ($n = 120$) of the time—the same rate as all children admitted to juvenile detention facilities by the police in 1998.[13] Children were released in only 30 percent of the 47 cases where the child welfare representative did not appear, but the rate rises to 48 percent in the 194 cases where the child welfare representative did appear—a statistically significant difference ($p < .05$).[14] These numbers reveal the importance of the child welfare representative's presence at Family Court when probation officers, prosecution attorneys, or the judge deems release appropriate.

More than 90 percent of released children avoided emergency replacement or other undesirable outcomes such as going AWOL or being temporarily housed in youth shelters. Of the 102 children released, 72 returned to their original foster care agency, 18 returned to a family member, and 4 went directly to a new foster care agency. Only five children went to the emergency placement unit to await replacement following release. One child went to a private youth shelter, and two children went AWOL following release.

Government Partner Perceptions

To gauge reaction to and perceptions of Project Confirm, the researchers surveyed more than 40 randomly selected juvenile justice intake staff, probation officers, child care workers, and supervisory staff at private foster care agencies that had contacts with the program. The results suggest that Project Confirm succeeded in the challenging task of establishing positive relationships with these frontline workers and that Project Confirm staff possess a strong reputation for their knowledge, courtesy, and efficiency.

On a four-point Likert scale of "very negative," "negative," "positive," and "very positive," 70 percent of the frontline workers reported very positive interactions with Project Confirm staff, and an additional 28 percent categorized their exchanges as positive. On a similarly scaled question, 78 percent agreed or strongly agreed that the project is worth their time and effort, whereas 17 percent had no opinion, and only 5 percent responded negatively. Frontline staff indicated that they approved of Project Confirm because it enabled them to perform their jobs better by providing needed information in a timely and friendly manner. Of the 31 workers who felt qualified to judge the level of communication between child welfare and juvenile justice, for example, all but two respondents reported that communication improved with Project Confirm. Researchers also interviewed eight middle managers in the partnering agencies who reported similar positive perceptions and satisfaction with Project Confirm.

Future Challenges

Although Project Confirm reached many of its implementation objectives the first year, it faced future challenges. The program intercepted only foster children who were arrested after court hours and sent to detention by the police. Children arrested during court hours and brought before a judge the same day are usually not referred to Project Confirm and may appear without a caseworker present. To prevent this problem, Project Confirm needed to receive notification of juvenile arrests directly from the police. Generating these calls requires coordinating with one of New York City's largest agencies: roughly 40,000 officers work in the New York City Police Department's 76 precincts. In its second year, the program succeeded in having police headquarters issue an order mandating cooperation. But despite Project Confirm staff attending roll calls and making other outreach efforts, the size and competing priorities of police prevented this part of the program from being successfully implemented.

Another challenge involves the future functioning of the program. Ultimately, Project Confirm seeks to change the knowledge and behavior of the partnering government agencies so a separate program is no longer necessary. If the agencies incorporated the Project Confirm model, juvenile justice intake staff and the police could phone or send electronic messages to child welfare directly following an arrest or entry into detention. All child welfare caseworkers and foster care providers would need to know their responsibilities when foster children are arrested. They would also be required to know the legal processes associated with juvenile delinquency proceedings.

Project Confirm faces several obstacles in helping the agencies reach this ideal. High turnover among caseworkers hinders efforts to train these employees (Special Child Welfare Advisory Panel 2000). Caseworkers need training in many areas, and because only a small proportion of all foster children ever experience arrest, training in this area will probably not be given the priority that Project Confirm desires. Even with knowledgeable caseworkers and technology that enables electronic information exchanges between frontline workers, someone within the child welfare agency will need to determine the foster care status of arrested children and provide the appropriate contact information.

Discussion

Project Confirm is a compelling example of the type of frontline partnerships that Douglas Nelson calls for at the beginning of this chapter. Despite recommendations by scholars and other observers, however, programs that help coordinate multiple agencies are uncommon (Morgan 1995). This is not surprising: new programs must overcome many hurdles, such as acquiring funds, hiring and training staff, locating space, equipping offices, and establishing standard operating procedures.

Engaging several agencies in the work of a new program multiplies the number and complexity of these implementation problems. Without an established position in departmental hierarchies, for example, cross-agency programs may trigger turf battles both within and across agencies and have their requests for information and cooperation ignored by frontline workers (Pressman and Wildavsky 1984; Wolff 1998).

Implementing a new program that works across several agencies requires obtaining the cooperation of many people occupying the full range of positions, from top executives to frontline staffers. Before its launch, Project Confirm gained the approval of top executives in each of its government partners. It also mobilized mid-level managers to aid in the program's development, while avoiding conflicts with unfriendly actors capable of blocking or undermining the program. Indeed, Project Confirm garnered this support despite the increasingly punitive environment surrounding juvenile justice, an environment that militates against programs aiming to reduce the use of juvenile detention (Anderson 1998; Elikann 1999; Hemmens 1998).

The aspect of Project Confirm's implementation that stands out most prominently, however, is its ability to change the behavior of frontline staff. Program innovations usually require modifying the behavior of public employees who carry out the day-to-day business of government. Altering standard operating procedures and behaviors on the front lines, even with direct orders from senior executives, can be extraordinarily difficult (Allison 1971). Project Confirm's ability to succeed at this task is a prime reason for the program's successful implementation.

After a supervisor issued a formal order mandating a change in either standard operating procedures or informal behavior, Project Confirm deployed its frontline worker strategy to make sure the change actually occurred. The strategy evolved throughout the implementation and depended in part on the frontline workers involved and the specific operational changes needed. Still, three common elements of the strategy are apparent: building relationships with frontline staff that help create a sense of shared mission and an expectation of cooperation, providing tools and assistance that enable frontline staff to complete Project Confirm–related tasks with minimum cost, and holding them accountable if cooperation does not occur. To carry out this strategy, Project Confirm used multiple tactics, including conducting training sessions, holding on-site face-to-face meetings, serving as an information resource to frontline workers in various agencies, and relentlessly following up on every child's case and each request for information. Project Confirm's work with juvenile justice intake workers highlights these techniques.

Project Confirm requires that juvenile justice intake workers call the program whenever a child enters detention, and a mid-level juvenile justice manager issued an order mandating these calls. When the program started, Project Confirm staff called each of the three juvenile detention facilities every morning to make sure that the number of calls Project Confirm received on its answering machine matched the number of children that entered the facility the previous night. The program developed a database to record critical information about each call it received. When the morning calls uncovered cases not reported to Project Confirm, the program's staff noted the failure to call in the database.

To improve the call rate, Project Confirm staff made midnight presentations to the night staff at each intake facility. The training sessions helped establish personal relationships between the intake workers and Project Confirm staff members, outlined the reasons the calls were important, and reinforced the expectation that the program should receive a call on every child. Many intake workers responded to the presentation by pointing out they felt that some foster children were detained unnecessarily and expressed enthusiasm for efforts to address this problem. To make remembering to call Project Confirm easier, Project Confirm staff hung posters in each intake office, prompted juvenile justice officials to include a check box on their intake forms labeled "Project Confirm called," and asked that the agency's employee orientation and training sessions include the obligation to call Project Confirm in its procedures manual and in orientations.

To hold the intake staff accountable, Project Confirm generated "failure to call" reports from its database and relayed them frequently to the mid-level manager in charge of the intake staff. The manager personally followed up on the reports. To further ensure that the program identified every failure to call, Project Confirm matched its database with the juvenile detention entry database every three months. The matches revealed that morning intake staff did not report every case in response to Project Confirm's morning calls. The program forwarded these reports to the juvenile justice manager for follow-up.

Once Project Confirm hired staff to answer their phones 24 hours a day, the intake workers talked to Project Confirm staff regularly. The frequent contact led to stronger personal connections to the program that helped blunt any resentment generated by the failure-to-call reports.

Having live staff also allowed the program to serve as a resource to the intake staff. The program provides medical and school information concerning detained foster kids that would otherwise require the intake staff to track down caseworkers.

These efforts have resulted in a call rate that consistently exceeds 95 percent. Having changed the standard operating procedures of juvenile justice frontline staff, Project Confirm now expends few resources ensuring their compliance. The program similarly addressed challenges in working with other frontline workers and achieved comparable results. The importance of successfully engaging these employees should not be underestimated: ultimately, Project Confirm seeks to enable frontline workers to act in ways that eliminate gaps between agencies without special programs or extra efforts on the part of managers.

Conclusion

The unnecessary detention of foster children is a problem worth addressing in its own right: locking up some of society's most vulnerable members simply because they are foster children should not happen. The importance of Project Confirm, however, may reside as much in the example it sets for program implementation and multi-agency collaboration as in the direct services it provides.

If the integrated services model that many informed observers prescribe is a prerequisite for improved child welfare services, then advocates and policymakers must decide how best to reach that goal. Dictates from high-level officials or judicial mandates are necessary but insufficient conditions for child welfare agencies to improve collaboration with other child-serving agencies (Doss and Idleman 1994; Hagedorn 1995; Nelson 1998). To establish a truly integrated child welfare system may require replicating programs like Project Confirm across many service areas such as education, job training, health, and income maintenance. Project Confirm's success in bridging the administrative and programmatic gap between child welfare and juvenile justice should broaden the vision of child welfare managers.

9

An Outcome Evaluation of Project Confirm

Dylan Conger and Timothy Ross

Chapter 8 discusses the challenges faced by foster youth who are arrested and the government agencies that must respond when such an arrest occurs. It describes a program, Project Confirm, designed to remedy these problems and reduce the bias against foster youth in juvenile detention decisions. As noted in that chapter, Project Confirm overcame the most common obstacles to implementation. But did it reduce the disparity in detention rates between youth in foster care and those who live with their parents or guardians?

It may seem intuitive that a program that addresses a problem identified by exploratory research, that has a logic model with a strong conceptual base for solving the problem, and that solved the most common implementation obstacles must have succeeded in its mission. Yet success for programs with these characteristics is not guaranteed: many have no effect on the outcomes they seek to change, and some have unintended effects that make the problem worse (Moos 2005; Rhule 2005). Indeed, relatively few social service programs have undergone rigorous evaluations that find significant positive results (Elliott 1997).

This chapter presents results from an evaluation of Project Confirm. Program efforts to reduce disparities in detention decisions succeeded, but not for all groups. The program eliminated the detention disparity between foster youth and their nonfoster peers among low-level first-time offenders—in fact, after Project Confirm, youth in care arrested for the first time on low-level charges were detained less frequently than their nonfoster peers facing similar charges. The program effects also varied by race and ethnicity, as well as geography. The disparity between foster youth and their nonfoster peers, however, increased for foster youth facing higher-level charges—an unintended effect that the program sought to address following this research.

Outcome Evaluation Method

Chapter 8 discussed youth in foster care entering the juvenile justice system. The issue to understand here, then, is the methodology used to evaluate Project Confirm. As discussed in chapter 1, there are many challenges in conducting research in cross-agency issues in child welfare. These challenges are often magnified in program evaluations.

Gold standard research designs, such as random assignment to a control or treatment group, are rarely available in either criminal justice or child welfare settings. Children in foster care and people in detention facilities receive special treatment under federal research ethics guidelines.[1] These guidelines reflect concerns raised by a history of research that treated children, detained populations, and "wards of the state" unethically.[2] In addition to the genuine concerns of officials for the youth in their care, many decisionmakers have legitimate concerns about the politics of research on these vulnerable populations.

To pass muster in the academic community, program evaluation designs must meet scientific standards and acknowledge weaknesses where they exist. At the same time, to have an effect on policy, any complex mathematics involved in the statistical procedures used in evaluation must be translated into language that officials understand. This evaluation of Project Confirm seeks to explain the results in ways that many audiences will understand.

Research Questions

The evaluation of Project Confirm sought to answer several questions: Did Project Confirm reduce the disparity in detention rates between nonfoster and foster youth? By how much? Did the program reduce the disparity in detention more for some groups than for others? Specifically, since court officials have few reasons to detain youth facing low-level charges and with minor delinquency records other than the absence of a release resource, Project Confirm may have a larger effect on these types of cases than on more serious cases. Researchers also wanted to know if the program had differential effects by gender, race, and county of arrest.

Because of data constraints, the evaluation focused only on decisions made by court personnel to detain youth who had already spent at least one night in juvenile detention facilities because they were arrested when court was closed. These cases are called "police admits" to juvenile detention—those youth arrested after the court was closed, taken to juvenile detention by the police, and brought before a judge the following the next day. Project Confirm focused its efforts almost exclusively on this population during its first year: police admits accounted for over 90 percent of youth who received services from the program.[3] Project Confirm did not provide a significant amount of services to "court admits" to detention (those youth who are arrested, appear in court the same day, and are then taken to juvenile detention) until its second and third year of operations.

Design

Project Confirm provided services citywide, prohibiting the use of a comparison group of similar youth experiencing arrest during the same period but not served by the program. The best comparison group available consisted of youth who became involved in the juvenile justice system immediately before the program's start date. This quasi-experimental design, therefore, compared the cohort of police admits before the implementation of Project Confirm (January 1997 to August 1998) with the cohort of police admits after Project Confirm overcame some initial implementation problems (September 1998 to September 1999).[4]

In essence, the evaluation compares four groups. The first two groups are foster youth arrested before introduction of Project Confirm and foster youth arrested after Project Confirm. The design also includes two cohorts of nonfoster children—those detained before and after Project Confirm—to control for overall trends in release rates from juvenile detention. To estimate the effect of Project Confirm, the evaluation compares the difference in detention rates between foster youth and nonfoster youth before and after Project Confirm's implementation.

Data and Sample

Researchers created an analytic database by matching records of administrative data from the New York City child welfare and juvenile justice systems. The researchers matched identifying information on all juvenile detainees from the three-year time span (1997–99) to child welfare records with different combinations of name, date of birth, and other identifying characteristics. This technique identified which teens who went to detention also resided in foster care at the same time. The database included all variables stored in the juvenile detention records on detainees, including their admission and discharge dates, charge levels, county of jurisdiction, and placements in juvenile prison. The database also included children's child welfare records with information on placement dates, movements between foster homes and agencies, the number of times they went on unauthorized absences from these homes, and the types of homes in which they lived.

The sample included 4,611 juveniles detained between 1997 and 1999.[5] Thirteen percent (583) of the youth resided in foster care at the time of their arrests. The youth in foster care included a greater percentage of girls, youth listed by juvenile justice staff as black, and youth whose cases were heard in Queens and Staten Island than the group not in foster care (see table 9.1).[6] Correspondingly, there were fewer whites and juveniles with cases in Brooklyn among foster than among nonfoster youth. The young people in the two groups were similar in age, charge level, and previous detentions—the variables that should be most important to a judge in making a decision to detain.

Analysis Strategy

The evaluation sought to find out the impact of the program itself, not other factors that might have explained differences in how often youth were detained before and after the program. For example, if the foster youth arrested *before* Project Confirm had many more serious felony charges than foster youth arrested *after* the start of the program, detention rates might decline after the program started—but have nothing to do with the program itself. By "controlling" for different factors, researchers are able to better pinpoint the effect of the program. At the same time, they are able to understand how much these factors—demographics, charges, court county—affect detention rates.

The chapter authors used logistic regression to analyze the data. Logistic regression is a multivariate statistical method often used when an outcome has only two possibilities—such as approves or disapproves, yes or no, or, in this case, detained or released. Logistic regression analysis produces results that include odds ratios. Odds ratios estimate the change in

Table 9.1. Differences between Foster and Nonfoster Cases

	Foster care	Nonfoster care	Percentage-point difference
Number of cases	583	4,028	
Percentage who are:			
Female	28.1	17.1	11.0***
Black	69.8	64.4	5.4**
Hispanic	28.1	29.6	−1.5
White	1.7	4.3	−2.6**
Age 13 or older	95.5	94.8	0.7
Percentage charged with:			
Below C-felony	58.7	55.1	3.6
C-felony or above	35.3	38.2	−2.9
Warrant	6.0	6.7	−0.7
Percentage never detained before	73.6	76.4	−2.8
Percentage of court cases in:			
Brooklyn	25.4	29.8	−4.4**
Bronx	24.2	25.4	−1.2
Manhattan	20.8	22.1	−1.3
Queens	20.8	16.8	4.0**
Staten Island	8.9	5.9	3.0**

Note: Chi-square test was used to test for statistically significant differences between foster and nonfoster juveniles.

*significant at 10%; **significant at 5%; ***significant at 1%

the chances of the outcome occurring for a specific variable after controlling for all other variables. For example, one would expect that having a prior felony arrest record, after controlling for all other variables, would increase the odds of being detained. Appendix A.9 contains a more technical discussion of how the authors used this method.

Results

To set the stage for the analyses, table 9.2 shows the percentages of foster and nonfoster youth who were detained before and after Project Confirm's implementation. Before the program, 55.5 percent of arrested

Table 9.2. Detention Rates of Foster and Nonfoster Juveniles before and after Project Confirm Implementation, by Seriousness of Case

	Before Project Confirm		After Project Confirm	
	Number of cases	Percent detained	Number of cases	Percent detained
All cases				
Foster	353	55.5**	230	56.5
Nonfoster	2,480	48.3	1,548	50.9
Less serious cases				
Foster	158	44.3**	106	34.9
Nonfoster	1,058	33.3	698	38.7
More serious cases				
Foster	195	64.6	124	75.0**
Nonfoster	1,422	59.4	850	60.9

Notes: Tests of statistical significance refer to difference between foster and nonfoster juveniles. "Less serious cases" refers to juveniles who were charged with below C-felony crimes and who had never been previously detained; "more serious cases" refers to juveniles who were charged with above C-felony crimes or who had been previously detained.
*significant at 10%; **significant at 5%; ***significant at 1%

youth in foster care were detained, compared with only 48.3 percent of arrested nonfoster youth, a statistically significant difference and evidence that children in foster care were indeed detained at higher rates. Moving down the column to the next few rows shows the foster/nonfoster difference in detention rates among the less serious cases (lower charges) and more serious cases (higher charges). Among the less serious group, youth in foster care were detained at significantly higher rates, but no foster care disparity is indicated for more serious cases. The next two columns reveal the differences after the program was implemented. For juveniles as a group and for the less serious offenders, the foster/nonfoster difference is statistically insignificant, indicating no disparity. Yet among the more serious cases, a large difference appears in the *opposite* direction expected after the program's introduction: youth in foster care are detained at a much higher and statistically significant rate.

Are these raw differences in detention rates driven by differences in the presenting charges and characteristics of the juveniles? And can the changes in these patterns be attributed to Project Confirm or to changes in the characteristics of the youth? Answers to these questions are found in table 9.3, which provides the estimated odds-ratios and confidence intervals around these ratios from the logistic regression used to identify program impact.

The odds-ratio on the foster care variable is statistically significant and positive, providing evidence of differences in detention between foster and nonfoster youth before the program was implemented. All else equal, being in foster care increased the odds of detention by approximately 35 percent. The odds-ratio on the post-program variable indicates a general increase in detention rates between the two periods. The odds-ratio on the treatment variable—the interaction of foster care and post-program—is statistically insignificant, indicating that there was no change in the foster care disparity following the introduction of the program.

Table 9.3. Odds-Ratios and Confidence Intervals from Logistic Regression of Detention, All Cases

	Odds-ratio	Confidence interval on odds-ratio
Foster care	1.348	1.059–1.715**
Post–Project Confirm	1.170	1.020–1.341**
Foster care × post–Project Confirm (treatment)	0.973	0.663–1.428
Never detained before	0.254	0.217–0.298***
Charged with below C-felony	0.530	0.467–0.602***
Female	0.958	0.814–1.127
Age 13 or older	1.169	0.884–1.544
Black	0.917	0.696–1.209
Hispanic	0.987	0.738–1.319
Court in Bronx	2.241	1.885–2.664***
Court in Manhattan	3.019	2.525–3.610***
Court in Queens	2.098	1.735–2.536***
Court in Staten Island	1.217	0.922–1.605
Intercept	1.348	1.059–1.715***
Number of observations	4,611	
Chi-square likelihood ratio test	641.98 ($p < 0.0001$)	

Note: For the court county variable, the county left out is Brooklyn.

*significant at 10%; **significant at 5%; ***significant at 1%

Other variables in the model yield expected relationships: no prior detentions and lower charges (below a C-felony) reduce the likelihood of detention, while demographic traits (gender, age, and race) have no relationship to detention. There are also significant differences in the detention rates of the various court counties.

In sum, this means that before the program started, youth in foster care had a much higher chance of going to detention (35 percent) than youth not in foster care, and such factors as charge level, age, gender, and race do not explain this difference. In general, youth with less criminal history and who committed less serious acts were detained less often, whether they were in foster care or not. Some counties send more youth to detention than others, even when those youth have the same characteristics.

Program evaluators expected Project Confirm to have a larger effect in less serious cases since the absence of a release resource is one of the few reasons to detain juveniles with minor records. Table 9.4 provides the odds-ratios on the two most relevant variables from regressions estimated separately for the less serious cases and the more serious

Table 9.4. Odds-Ratios and Confidence Intervals on Foster Care Variables from Logistic Regression of Detention by Seriousness of Case

	Odds-ratio	Confidence interval on odds-ratio
Less serious cases		
Foster care	1.542	1.093–2.203**
Foster care × post–Project Confirm	0.562	0.321–0.985**
Number of observations	2,020	
More serious cases		
Foster care	1.212	0.882–1.666
Foster care × post–Project Confirm	1.662	0.971–2.848*
Number of observations	2,591	

Notes: "Less serious cases" refers to juveniles who were charged with below C-felony crimes and who had never been previously detained. "More serious cases" refers to juveniles who were charged with above C-felony crimes or who had been previously detained. Regressions also include dummy variables indicating whether detained after project Confirm, gender, race, age, and court county.

*significant at 10%; **significant at 5%; ***significant at 1%

cases. Among the less serious cases, the estimated odds of being detained were approximately 54 percent higher for foster than nonfoster children before the program was launched. These odds were substantially reduced (by half) following the program. Thus, while the program showed no effect for foster juveniles in aggregate, it had a much stronger effect on foster youth charged with less than C-felonies and no prior detentions, a group that makes up 46 percent of the population eligible for program services.

Table 9.4 also shows that the opposite occurred among juveniles with more serious records: teens facing charges of a C-felony or above or who came before the court on warrants from prior arrests, or with a previous detention. Among these youth, there was no disparity in detention between foster and nonfoster juveniles before the program; yet, the odds of detention for foster youth relative to nonfoster youth *increase* following the introduction of Project Confirm.

Evaluators also examined the change in the foster care disparity according to gender, race, and court county to see whether the foster care disparity and the program effect differed for these subgroups (table 9.5).[7] Perhaps the most striking numbers in the table are the extensive differences in the foster care effect before Project Confirm began. This analysis shows that the disparity was greatest for foster children who were female, who were listed as Hispanic, and whose cases were heard in the Bronx or Manhattan. Additionally, for several subgroups—boys, those youth identified as black, and youth with cases heard in Brooklyn, Queens, and Staten Island—there was no foster care disparity before Project Confirm. The odds-ratios on the treatment variable (foster care and post-program status) indicate that in most cases, the risk of detention declined after the program was implemented; however, the effect was only statistically significant (and marginally so) among those listed as Hispanic. Among this group, the risk of detention for foster youth (which was almost two times higher than the risk for nonfoster youth) was cut in half following program implementation.

In sum, some foster youth were detained more often than others. Foster youth who were girls, who were listed as Hispanic, or who went to court in specific counties were detained much more often than similar children who were not in foster care. Project Confirm reduced substantially the "penalty" for being in foster care among these youth. Foster youth with more serious cases, however, were more likely to be detained after Project Confirm started.

Table 9.5. Odds-Ratios and Confidence Intervals on Foster Care Variables from Logistic Regression of Detention by Gender, Race, and Court County

	Odds-ratio	Confidence interval on odds-ratio
Male ($n = 3{,}759$)		
Foster care	1.197	0.907–1.581
Foster care × post-Confirm	0.991	0.634–1.550
Female ($n = 852$)		
Foster care	2.020	1.230–3.317***
Foster care × post-Confirm	0.811	0.376–1.753
Black ($n = 3{,}000$)		
Foster care	1.162	0.872–1.550
Foster care × post-Confirm	1.223	0.770–1.945
Hispanic ($n = 1{,}356$)		
Foster care	1.855	1.164–2.957**
Foster care × post-Confirm	0.508	0.247–1.044*
Court in Brooklyn ($n = 1{,}349$)		
Foster care	0.822	0.478–1.416
Foster care × post-Confirm	1.661	0.765–3.610
Court in Bronx ($n = 1{,}162$)		
Foster care	1.982	1.203–3.268***
Foster care × post-Confirm	0.745	0.340–1.633
Court in Manhattan ($n = 1{,}012$)		
Foster care	1.739	1.034–2.924**
Foster care × post-Confirm	0.676	0.275–1.658
Court in Queens ($n = 796$)		
Foster care	1.130	0.665–1.919
Foster care × post-Confirm	1.051	0.445–2.478
Court in Staten Island ($n = 290$)		
Foster care	1.116	0.485–2.567
Foster care × post-Confirm	1.073	0.283–4.066

Note: Regressions also include all relevant control variables.

*significant at 10%; **significant at 5%; ***significant at 1%

Discussion

As in all studies, the evaluation methodology has some limitations. Because it compares groups before and after Project Confirm, the chapter authors cannot say whether some other factor not included in the analysis caused the changes identified. This weakness reduces the authors' confidence in attributing changes in detention rates solely to Project Confirm. While the evaluation did not identify any new policies or demographic changes that may have affected foster and nonfoster youth differently during the period studied, such changes could have occurred. The authors minimized this possibility by restricting the pre–Project Confirm group to youth detained within the year and a half before the program, although they had information on youth who were detained several years earlier.

The authors were unable to include some information that might have influenced detention decisions and thus affected the results. These omitted variables include school attendance, arrests that did not result in detention, and other factors that were not recorded in the available databases. The authors are also missing a key intervening variable: whether an adult showed up in court, and, if so, what role the adult played in the detention decision. Without this information, the authors cannot be certain that the foster care disparity before Project Confirm occurred because youth lacked release resources and that the presence of resources following Confirm led to the decline in the disparity for some groups. That concerns about the lack of release resources prompted the development of the program gives the chapter authors some confidence that pre-program disparities were related to this issue.

Despite these limitations, the study contains enough information to evaluate the effectiveness of Project Confirm. In short, the study indicates that the program had no effect on disparities in detention between foster and nonfoster youth overall but had widely varying effects for subgroups of the population. To understand these findings, the chapter authors met with program staff and reviewed the observations and notes collected during the program's implementation. A closer look at some of the reasons judges detain juveniles helps interpret the results of the evaluation.

The Importance of Unauthorized Absences from Foster Care

Examining the program's effect separately for juveniles with minor and more serious records reveals the source of the modest overall effect.

Project Confirm substantially reduced the disparity for youth facing low-level charges and with no prior detention history. In contrast, the program appears to have created or increased the disparity for youth facing higher-level charges, facing a warrant, or dealing with a prior detention history. What explains the increased disparity in these cases? Answering this question requires a more comprehensive understanding of the foster care disparity, what Project Confirm does, and the limits of the program's intervention.

Project Confirm intervenes in the juvenile justice process primarily in two ways: by ensuring the presence of a responsible adult to take custody in the event of release and by providing additional information that might not otherwise reach court officials. Having a release resource unambiguously overcomes one obstacle to release—*not* having a release resource is one reason court officials may detain juveniles.

Providing more information, however, may increase or decrease the chances of release depending upon the facts made available. Given that court officials look for signs that an offender poses a risk of flight or danger to the community or himself, knowing a youth's full history may increase the chances of exposing information that heightens such fears. One such piece of information is a youth's history of running away from his or her homes; at least one study, albeit dated, confirms that a prior runaway incident increases the likelihood of detention among the general youth population (Sumner 1970). For foster children, a record of unauthorized absences from foster care may do the same. According to many program staff, some court officials detain juveniles with even one previous instance of running from care, commonly referred to as going AWOL.

Among the 583 foster youth in this sample, detention was much higher among youth with at least one AWOL event recorded in child welfare data than among youth with no AWOL events recorded, 64 and 50 percent, respectively ($\chi^2 = 11.5$, p-value < 0.001). Administrative data on AWOL should be interpreted carefully, as not all AWOL events are reported or recorded. On the other hand, those that are not reported or recorded are less likely to come to the attention of the court.

AWOL events may play only a small role in cases involving misdemeanor or minor felony offenders with no prior record. Aside from the lack of a release resource, there are few reasons for court officials to detain juveniles with minor records; the expense of detention facilities provides a further disincentive for their use. Although juveniles facing low-level charges may have an AWOL history, prosecutors may be less likely to request such information than they are in more serious cases. Therefore, ensuring that a release resource is present in court should all but guarantee equal treatment between foster and nonfoster teens, even for foster juveniles with AWOL records. Following this logic, Project Confirm should and does have a strong effect on reducing the disparity among youth with no prior detentions facing minor charges.

In contrast, the presence of a release resource for youth charged with more serious offenses or with a prior record, while a necessary precondition for release, may not be sufficient. In such cases, the juveniles' school and home lives may weigh more heavily in prosecutors' determination of the risk of further offending or failing to appear in court. An AWOL record is almost certain to be revealed in these cases and may be interpreted as a sign that the youth will not show up to the next court hearing.

AWOL records might explain why a foster care disparity is not eliminated by simply ensuring that caseworkers come to court. But what explains the apparent *increase* in the disparity for the more serious offenders following the introduction of Project Confirm? Through conversations with program staff, the chapter authors identified two ways that the program may have increased detention for youth in care facing more serious charges: by changing *who* appeared in court and by increasing prosecutors' knowledge of the kinds of information that could influence judicial decisions to detain youth in foster care.

Conversations with court personnel and child welfare staff suggest that when an adult showed up in court on behalf of a foster care youth before Project Confirm, the adult usually was a group home child care worker, foster parent, or biological relative. Because these adults are less likely than a caseworker to know about a youth's runaway history, the adult rarely revealed AWOL events to court officials. Caseworkers, on the other hand, have more extensive knowledge of a child's foster care history, including his or her runaway records. Project Confirm may increase the likelihood that court officials learn of AWOL events by getting well-informed caseworkers to court instead of, or in addition to, the other adults that sporadically appeared in court before the program.

A second possibility is that prosecuting attorneys are now more likely to ask about a youth's AWOL history when determining whether he or she should be detained. While some prosecutors may have used AWOL records as an indication of risk before Project Confirm, others might not have requested AWOL information until the program began to spread awareness about the foster care population. Some prosecutors may now request AWOL information routinely upon learning of a juvenile's foster care status and base their decisions largely upon the teen's history of unauthorized absences.

One way to learn more about the impact of having an AWOL record in more serious cases is to remove foster youth with AWOL records from the analysis of more serious offenders and then re-examine differences in detention rates among those youth arrested following the program's launch. Among this subsample of 922 youth, the difference in the percentage of foster and nonfoster youth with serious records who were detained became statistically insignificant; 69 percent of foster youth versus 61 percent of nonfoster youth ($\chi^2 = 2.03$, p-value = 0.154). This suggests that the increase in detention for these foster care cases may be partially explained by changes in information about AWOL records. Bringing caseworkers to court for juveniles facing high charges with prior records, but no AWOL history, may equalize their risk of detention relative to similar youth not in foster care.

In short, by improving the quality of information made available to the court, Project Confirm may have increased the disparity in detention between foster and nonfoster youth charged with higher-level offenses or with prior detentions. Project Confirm appears to have increased what court officials believe is necessary detention for one particular group of foster juveniles.

Differences in Program Effect by Gender, Race, and Court County

The evaluation findings also reveal that the foster care disparity and Project Confirm's effect varied substantially according to race, gender, and court county. Before Project Confirm, girls faced a large foster care disparity that the program's introduction did not eliminate, while no such disparity existed among boys. Additionally, the program reduced the foster care disparity among youth listed as Hispanic but had no effect on the large disparities in the Bronx and Manhattan. What explains these differences, and how should they be interpreted?

The authors discovered that a relatively large foster care disparity existed among cases involving girls before Project Confirm, some of which may be explained by the high AWOL rates among foster girls. In the evaluation sample, 59 percent of the girls had a prior AWOL event recorded, compared with 41 percent of boys ($\chi^2 = 15.3$, p-value < 0.001). These AWOL differences may also explain why Project Confirm did not remove the disparity against girls in foster care. The authors conducted further analysis of the female population and found that there was no foster care disparity among girls without AWOL records following the introduction of Project Confirm; the rate of detention among girls in foster care (without AWOL records) and nonfoster girls was 41 and 43 percent, respectively, a statistically insignificant difference ($\chi^2 = 0.069$, p-value $= 0.792$).

The high level of disparity and Project Confirm's effect on the disparity for foster youth listed as Hispanic suggests that having a caseworker present for this population is especially important. Unlike girls, the pre-program disparity against those listed as Hispanic in foster care is not explained by higher AWOL rates. Were this the case, the program would not have been able to eliminate the disparity as it did. Instead, program staff reported that some youth listed as Hispanic had language barriers that limited communication with court officials. It is also possible that some youth listed as Hispanic may come from cultures that have negative experiences with law enforcement agencies that may further limit communication. This difficulty may have been exacerbated if these foster youth had foster parents, relatives, and other potential release resources with limited English language skills. Therefore, having a caseworker in court who could interpret the process may have made a substantial difference for this subgroup.

Disparities in detention decisions varied tremendously according to court county, though the AWOL rates of teens in foster care did not. Observations and conversations suggest that the varying court cultures contributed to differential detention rates independent of Project Confirm. In essence, the threshold for detaining youth varied from county to county, and the program did not change this baseline.

Conclusion

The juvenile justice and child welfare systems intersect in many ways, yet they do not always coordinate their efforts. The arrest of youth in foster care is one such incident that most requires such coordination and may not always receive it. The analysis described here suggests that despite Project Confirm's efforts, foster youth continue to enter detention at disproportionate rates, and court officials still detain many foster youth at higher rates than their nonfoster peers arrested on similar charges.

Project Confirm's successful work with low-level offenders shows that this state of affairs is not preordained. Exploratory analyses and follow-up discussions with program staff suggest that the work that remains may center less on providing new services, and more on shaping interpretations of AWOL records among court officials and studying the likelihood that teens who AWOL will fail to appear in court or commit crimes in the interim.

Following the completion of this study, child welfare officials in New York City agreed to institutionalize Project Confirm within their agency. After a period of technical assistance from the program's operators, child welfare staff assumed control of the program. The program continues to assist foster youth caught up in the juvenile justice system—evidence that the cross-agency issues that affect children and youth in foster care can be addressed.

Technical Description of Analytic Strategy

The chapter authors used logistic regression to determine the size of the foster care disparity before and after Project Confirm, controlling for legal (juvenile justice) and extralegal (mostly demographic) variables. The model is as follows:

$$\ln\left(P/(1-P)\right)_i = a + b_1 F_i + b_2 PC_i + b_3 FPC_i + b_4 X_i + \varepsilon_i$$

where P is the probability of being detained, F is foster care status (1 = foster care, 0 = nonfoster care), PC is detained before or after Project Confirm implementation (1 = after Project Confirm, 0 = before Project Confirm), FPC is the interaction between F and PC (in other words, the "treatment" variable capturing those foster youth who received program services), X is a vector of nonredundant covariates, ε is the error term, and i indicates juveniles. If a foster care disparity existed before the program, the chapter authors expected the coefficient for the foster care status variable (b_1) to be positive, substantial in magnitude, and statistically significant. If changes in detention rates occurred between the two periods, the coefficient on the pre-post Confirm variable (b_2) should be statistically significant in either direction. The effect of Project Confirm on the foster care disparity is found in the coefficient on the interaction of foster care and the pre-post Confirm variable (b_3); a statistically significant negative coefficient would indicate that the disparity declined.

The vector X includes two legal variables that tend to play a large role in pre-adjudication detention decisions—charge level and prior arrests that resulted in detention (Bailey 1981; Pawlak 1977). The model also includes court county because individual counties have their own court cultures, politics, philosophies, and standards; the authors expect this is as true in New York City's five counties as in any other jurisdiction (Cohen and Kluegel 1979; Feld 1999; Pawlak 1977; Schwartz, Barton, and Orlando 1991).[8] Standard demographic variables—age, race, and gender—are also included to control for the possible influence of some extralegal factors on detention decisions.

To further examine if the program affected groups differently according to the severity of their records, separate models were estimated for juveniles charged with misdemeanors or minor felonies and no prior detentions (referred to as "less serious cases") and for juveniles charged with C-felonies or above, and those with warrants or with prior records of detention (referred to as "more serious cases"). Subgroup program effects were also examined by gender, race, and court county.

Sensitivity Analysis, First Two Months of Project Confirm Operations

As described in the text, the design treats the first two months of program operations as "pre-program" to estimate the effect of the program after implementation obstacles have been overcome. The authors did, however, estimate the model using two alternative approaches. The first approach includes these first two months of program operations in the "post-program" group. The second approach omits the first two months of program operations from the entire regression. The following appendix table provides the odds-ratios from the two approaches along with the odds-ratios reported in the text (table 9.3). As shown, the results are similar irrespective of the approach taken.

Table B.9.1. Odds-Ratios from Logistic Regressions of Detention Decisions

	First two months of program operations treated as post-program	First two months of program operations omitted from analysis	First two months of program operations treated as pre-program
Foster care	1.36**	1.37**	1.35**
Post–Project Confirm	1.17**	1.18**	1.17**
Foster care × post–Project Confirm (treatment)	0.95	0.96	0.97
Never detained before	0.25***	0.25***	0.25***
Charged with below C-felony	0.53***	0.53***	0.53***
Female	0.96	0.94	0.96
Age 13 or older	1.17	1.19	1.17
Black	0.92	0.92	0.92
Hispanic	0.99	0.97	0.99
Court in Bronx	2.24***	2.30***	2.24***
Court in Manhattan	3.02***	3.04***	3.02***
Court in Queens	2.10***	2.13***	2.10***
Court in Staten Island	1.22	1.19	1.22
Observations	4,611	4,443	4,611

Notes: In column 1, the pre-program group includes juveniles arrested from January 1997 through June 1998 and the post-program group includes those arrested from July 1998 through September 1999. In column 2, the pre-program group includes juveniles arrested from January 1997 through June 1998 and the post-program group includes those arrested from September 1998 through September 1999. In column 3, the pre-program group includes juveniles arrested from January 1997 through August 1998 and the post-program group includes those arrested from September 1998 through September 1999.

*significant at 10%; **significant at 5%; ***significant at 1%

10

Solving Cross-Agency Challenges

This volume began with a discussion of the different cross-cutting issues that affect child welfare and other human service agencies. The past several chapters have demonstrated how the typology of cross-cutting issues discussed in the first chapter—tunnel problems, information flow, diffusion of responsibility, and unloading "problem cases"—can harm children and their families and often frustrate frontline staff and managers of government agencies. There are also many lessons in this work about factors that help mitigate cross-agency challenges. This chapter identifies the common themes in the solutions developed in New York City for several cross-cutting issues in child welfare.

Mitigating Cross-Cutting Issues

The research and programmatic remedies to cross-cutting issues have four common themes: one person or unit needs to have responsibility for addressing the issue; that person must have a range of resources—political support, access to specialized staff, as well as a budget—that can assist many agencies in fulfilling their missions; initiatives addressing cross-cutting issues must develop new standard operating procedures across agency boundaries that codify problem solving; and strong managers are needed to tackle these complex problems—half-hearted efforts will not suffice. This chapter highlights the lessons that come from the previous chapters and shows how these practices address each problem discussed in the typology of cross-cutting issues.

Establish Responsibility

Mitigating cross-agency issues first requires that one person or entity becomes responsible and accountable for the problem. Staff in most human service agencies face greater demands on their time than they can ever meet.[1] Even a cursory look at the headlines shows that child welfare agencies in particular are frequently understaffed and overwhelmed with high caseloads and backlogs of work. This chronic condition gives managers and staff legitimate reasons for avoiding cross-cutting issues that can arguably be laid at the doorstep of other agencies. Making someone responsible for managing a cross-cutting problem is a necessary, though insufficient, part of a solution.

Several chapters in this book provide good examples. To address police–child protective worker coordination, New York City's child welfare agency established an Instant Response Team coordinator to liaise with police officers and detectives in each borough. Within the child welfare agency, a criminal justice coordinator supervised this group and was responsible for making the program work. The agency also created a Children of Incarcerated Parents Program to manage issues between child welfare and criminal justice (discussed in chapters 3 and 4). Project Confirm initially used a different mechanism—a demonstration program developed by a nonprofit—to assign responsibility for juvenile justice/child welfare issues, but the theme is consistent: one person became responsible for the problem under discussion.

Assigning responsibility tackles several of the cross-cutting problems previously identified. One of the first items on the agenda of someone assigned responsibility for a cross-cutting problem is learning what data exists about the problem—prompting a discussion of information-sharing concerns. Diffusing responsibility and unloading problem cases becomes more difficult, or at least more obvious, when doing so directly undermines someone else's job. Finally, in the best situations, the person responsible for the problem develops a more holistic view of the issue. This broader vision can facilitate "outside the box" solutions that help frontline staff develop a range of services instead of sending all their cases down the same service tunnel.

Provide Resources That Can Be Used
to Solve the Problems of Other Agencies

Simply assigning responsibility for problems alone does little to resolve them. A responsible party needs resources. Child welfare agencies, however, rarely have the luxury of "throwing money" at problems. Appeals to the better natures of budget officials and staff at other agencies are ineffective at garnering resources to solve cross-cutting problems. Every human service agency wants more funding, and most have compelling arguments for why their needs—for counseling services for victims of domestic violence, for low-income housing for homeless veterans, for heating bill assistance to homebound seniors—trump the needs of other agencies. So given the intense competition for limited resources, how can child welfare agencies think creatively to provide the resources needed to solve cross-cutting issues?

The examples in this book suggest that solutions to cross-agency problems can save money, but other resources, such as political capital and small amounts of specialized staff time, are also important. Those resources that can be used to help solve the issues faced by multiple agencies—with an eye toward longer-term cost savings—offer child welfare agencies opportunities to solve cross-cutting problems that simply asking for more money will not.

Resources that help solve the problems *of other agencies* are crucial. Project Confirm, though funded by child welfare, also helped tackle a problem faced by juvenile justice officials: expensive and overcrowded detention facilities. By working to ensure that child welfare caseworkers appeared in court, the program also helped juvenile probation officers, juvenile prosecutors, and Family Court judges by providing an information resource and a release resource. Providing these resources, in turn, allowed Project Confirm to ask for favors from these actors—and improve services for youth in foster care.

Project Confirm could produce the caseworkers in court in part because the commissioner of child welfare signed a letter informing contract agencies that their caseworkers were obligated by the terms of their contract to appear in court following the arrest of a child on their caseload. Financially, insisting that the private foster care providers live up to their obligations cost the child welfare agency no more than the time to prepare the letter—though staff at Project Confirm spent considerable time cultivating key foster care provider staff so the letter would not provoke a backlash. As is often the case in solving cross-agency issues, *political* capital is often as valuable as financial capital. Project Confirm had political value for child welfare officials and other agencies. Though juvenile justice did not pay for Project Confirm, juvenile justice officials highlighted the program in their section of the Mayor's Management Report—a yearly public document scrutinized by elected officials and the press.

Aspects of the Family Assessment Program discussed in chapter 7 also demonstrate how resources invested in solving the problems of other agencies can help a program solve cross-cutting issues. Social workers that quickly assess families entering the status offender system are the primary cost of the FAP. By diverting cases away from probation and the Family Court, FAP saves these other agencies money. In the case of probation, this allowed the agency to reduce caseloads by reassigning probation officers. The program also reduced the status offender caseload for the Family Court. FAP imposed a real cost on the child welfare agency in the form of additional staff, but savings in other agencies helped create political support for the program. Projected savings in placement costs offered the possibility that child welfare would recoup the initial outlays for the social workers.

The absence of resources to solve cross-agency issues associated with children leaving foster care without permission ("going AWOL"—see chapter 6) helps explain the persistence of that problem. To the police, AWOL foster children are a subset of missing persons—a population that police often find exasperating. Missing persons and AWOL cases consume significant staff time, rarely result in arrests, and often turn out to involve chronic noncriminal disputes that are on the fringe of what many police officers view as their law enforcement responsibilities. Foster care agencies have few resources to help the police solve AWOL cases, which may be seen by police as an example of the child welfare system unloading problems onto law enforcement.

Small amounts of specialized staff time are another resource with limited cost that can improve a cross-agency effort's effectiveness. Specialized staff time investments are often "one-shots"—a one-time use of resources that do not require requesting an increase in the agency's budget. The Instance Response Team program, for example, received help from lawyers who drew up the memorandum of understanding (MOU) concerning information sharing among child welfare, the police, and prosecutors. The MOU helped facilitate information flow to the IRT program and met the ongoing needs of other agencies that had difficulty receiving certain information they needed to meet their agency's goals before the MOU.

Conversely, limiting the ability to draw on specialized staff can have negative repercussions. The IRT program did not receive assistance from child welfare's management and information systems professionals. As a result, the criminal justice coordinator—a dedicated manager with no training in database protocols or statistical analysis—made do by creating his own spreadsheets. While the spreadsheets provided some useful information, minor adjustments to the database design that would have required a few hours from a database professional would have produced a more effective management tool.

Having resources that help solve the problems of other agencies helps break down the logic of the four types of cross-cutting problems. An initiative that offers an agency an alternative option to the regular service tunnel makes "tunneling" less likely. Many frontline staff and middle managers are aware of and frustrated by cross-agency problems and will embrace solutions if the resources needed to solve the problem are provided. In some instances, transferring a difficult case to another agency may still happen—as when an arrested child in foster care is still detained even when his or her caseworker appears in court—but the transition happens more smoothly and generates fewer problems. Having a range of resources also allows for a quid pro quo: the new initiative provides the resources, and the agency staff accessing those resources provide information and accept responsibility they might otherwise avoid in some situations.

Establish Standard Operating Procedures with Other Agencies

Providing a person responsible for solving a cross-agency problem with resources is important because it allows the person to bargain with staff at other agencies. This type of bargaining, however, cannot be sustained if it is done repeatedly over individual cases. There are usually too many cases and not enough time for senior managers to engage in daily bargaining sessions.

Instead, managers need to use their bargaining authority to change the way organizations operate in their bailiwicks. Bureaucracies run on standard operating procedures, or SOPs: in a given situation, there is a standard response. Bureaucracies usually create SOPs that rely on their own staff; indeed, agency managers cannot do otherwise without reaching across bureaucratic boundaries. This is the essence of the tunnel problem. Sometimes SOPs call for the staff to hand off a case to another agency but rarely demand follow-up with that agency—creating a diffusion of responsibility problem if the receiving agency refuses the handoff.

Establishing new SOPs is the heart of solving cross-agency issues. It is hard work. The examples in this book and in other cross-cutting work suggest four lessons for establishing new SOPs. First, new ways of operating are rarely possible without top-level support. None of the initiatives discussed in this book could have taken place in the absence of approval and encouragement of commissioners at several agencies. Without the enthusiastic support of senior executives at the affected agencies, new initiatives to solve cross-cutting issues are unlikely to craft new procedures needed to address those problems.

A second lesson is that written procedures trump oral understandings. New SOPs require a written format for several reasons. Many human service agencies, especially child welfare agencies, have high staff turnover rates, and painstakingly negotiated arrangements may be lost when a key official or staff member leaves. Another reason is that having a written document allows staff to hold each other accountable—if a protocol calls for one action and a different action is taken, managers have greater leverage to address the issue when it is in writing. Negotiating written protocols often leads managers to identify and address previously unforeseen problems. And once managers and senior officials have invested the time and political capital in creating new SOPs, they have a greater vested interest in seeing those procedures carried out. Finally, many cross-cutting problems are embedded in existing written SOPs.

In the case of the IRT program, the new protocol spelled out in excruciating detail the response each agency would take in different situations. More severe injuries, precisely defined, call for the involvement of higher-ranking police officers. The creation of FAP involved generating flow diagrams that spelled out how status offender cases were to be handled and the events that triggered the involvement of probation, police, child welfare, and the courts. Project Confirm used the child welfare commissioner's letter to make going to court an SOP for contract agency caseworkers and a written order from an associate commissioner in juvenile justice to have detention intake staff call Project Confirm every time a new detainee entered their facility.

A third lesson is that managers need reliable data that show the level of compliance with the new SOP. A constant concern faced by people working on issues created by children in foster care with detained or imprisoned parents is that no reliable data exist on the scope of the problem. The regulations and official SOPs on the books require that child welfare caseworkers, corrections staff, and others act to minimize issues related to visitation, communication, and other cross-agency issues. For many reasons, however, there is no reliable data collection system for identifying foster children with incarcerated parents. This means that managers and advocates can only point to ad hoc situations of non-compliance with SOPs.

Conversely, Project Confirm used individual-level data matching to determine if a detention intake worker had called the program when a youth entered detention and to see if a caseworker had appeared in court—activities required by the SOPs of the agencies involved. The data allowed Project Confirm to identify specific instances of noncompliance with the new SOP that allowed supervisors to hold frontline staff accountable. Frontline staff received a clear message that noncompliance with SOP could have consequences.

A fourth lesson is that changing SOPs is facilitated by building personal cross-agency relationships between frontline staff and middle managers. As the discussion of the IRT program showed, as police and IRT coordinators got to know each other through combined trainings and working on cases, communication and satisfaction with the program grew stronger. Those aspects of the program where personal relationships did not develop—such as between a rotating cast of hospital social workers and child protective workers—showed signs of strain and conflict. Project Confirm's director reported that even with executive support, resources that solved agency problems, written SOPs, and data-driven accountability, the compliance of detention intake staff with a new SOP did not rise to acceptable levels until Confirm staff journeyed to the Bronx for a midnight presentation complete with coffee and doughnuts.

In examples where new SOPs took root, the development of personal relationships changed the experience of executing the new procedure. Frontline staff may resist new SOPs because they perceive the new method as another uncompensated responsibility imposed through a fear of disciplinary action in the event of noncompliance. The new SOP may be perceived as a challenge to workers' autonomy, and, to some workers, it may imply poor past performance. In the best scenario, building personal relationships changes the frontline workers' experience of the new SOP to one of helping people they know do a job that benefits children, youth, and their worker's agency. Compliance is easier to achieve when staff feel a sense of achievement or purpose by complying.

Establishing new SOPs addresses each of the four cross-cutting issues directly. FAP reduced the tunnel issues in the status offender system by creating new SOPs that offered quicker access to more services. After ensuring compliance with new SOPs that identified arrested youth as in foster care, Project Confirm collected and disseminated data so all parties had access to the size and scope of the problem. The IRT program mitigated diffusion of responsibility problems by identifying the roles played by specific staff in a range of situations. Each of these efforts made unloading problem cases riskier: doing so could undermine cooperation with other agencies that people came to rely on for help in carrying out their jobs.

Establishing and enforcing new SOPs takes time, persistence, and patience. It also takes skill and savvy, which brings us to the final lesson for solving cross-cutting problems.

Invest in Strong Management

Public administration texts often call for better management, but many officials find this advice frustrating. Strong managers are successful and successful efforts have strong managers; this truism is not especially helpful. The argument here is that the lessons from this discussion provide leads on the types of people likely to succeed in solving cross-cutting issues. In other words, what have we learned about the qualities of successful managers of initiatives aimed at mitigating cross-cutting problems?

People responsible for mitigating cross-cutting issues need political skills to bargain with staff from other agencies over which they have little or no formal authority. They need to know how to "manage up" to gain access to specialized staff time. They need to understand the strengths and weaknesses of the data they examine—or know how to gain that capacity in their staff. They need to know how bureaucracies work and be able to persuade others that it is in their interest to cooperate with them.

This list of skills suggests three qualities that people responsible for solving cross-cutting issues should have. Initiatives to address cross-cutting issues need to be led by people who have the credentials—be they educational, organizational, or experiential—that make them credible to staff in their own and other agencies. For some, this may be a high-level position in the organization that commands respect. For others, it may be years of experience in the trenches or strong educational credentials. Managers that do not have the credibility to interact with agency executives in child welfare and other human service agencies will not be able to solve problems.

Second, managers addressing cross-cutting issues need to have substantive knowledge of the child welfare field and ideally of other fields with which they will interact. Learning the complexities of a new field on top of addressing cross-cutting issues puts tremendous pressure on a person entering a new position. Project Confirm's director spent over a year planning the program, during which she met with officials and frontline staff at eight different agencies. She also had prior experience working with runaways at Covenant House and defended juveniles in Family Court. This range of experiences and knowledge helped her persuade officials and staff at other agencies of the value of cooperating with Project Confirm even though as the employee of a nonprofit she had no formal authority over any of her government colleagues.

Finally, strong managers in cross-cutting initiatives must have the social skills to develop a network of cross-agency relationships and understand how politics affects decisionmaking. Managers need to enjoy sharing credit and to see or create opportunities to reward partners and frontline staff in other agencies. An ever-present awareness of how decisions and actions will be perceived by a range of partners is needed to detect and avoid the minefields of turf wars, conflicting role definitions and legal obstacles.

Conclusion

Though there is no simple recipe for solving cross-cutting issues, this book shows that it is possible to mitigate these problems and improve the lives of the young people and their families that rely on child welfare services.

A skeptic might conclude, however, that the conditions described above are so challenging that initiatives to solve cross-agency issues are bound to fail more often than they succeed. Achieving executive-level consensus across human service agencies in defining an agenda, a problem, and a solution is not a common occurrence in government. Giving talented staff the resources needed to develop new ways of working across agency boundaries, however, improves the chances of success. Even after all this work has been done, there is still no guarantee against an unforeseen hurdle sinking the effort. As Machiavelli wrote in *The Prince:*

> It must be considered that there is nothing more difficult to carry out, nor more doubtful of success, nor more dangerous to handle, than to initiate a new order of things. For the reformer has enemies in all those who profit by the old order, and only lukewarm defenders in all those who would profit by the new order, this lukewarmness arising partly from fear of their adversaries, who have the laws in their favour; and partly from the incredulity of mankind, who do not truly believe in anything new until they have had the actual experience of it.[2]

Cross-cutting issues in child welfare are not easily resolved. If they were, a book addressing why they occur and what might be done to address them would hardly be necessary. At the same time, successfully tackling cross-cutting issues offers real benefits to the children and families that child welfare agencies serve. Success leads to rewards for the leaders and managers who have the initiative, creativity, and skill to implement reforms. And once a new order that solves these problems succeeds, undoing that new order faces the same tough challenges as instituting the new way of doing things once did.

It is my hope that the examples and ideas in this book will encourage more child welfare officials to take on these tough challenges. I hope that the knowledge provided here will make success easier to attain. As ever, the youth and families that rely on government for safety and assistance desperately need services that work together to help them take steps to leading productive and fulfilling lives.

Notes

Chapter 1. Cross-Cutting Issues in Child Welfare

1. Parts of this chapter draw upon a working paper written by Timothy Ross and Dr. Joel Miller for the Youth Transitions Funders Group. For additional discussion of cross-cutting issues, see http://www.ytfg.org.

2. For a discussion of ASFA, see Gendell (2001). CAPTA marked the first major federal effort in the field. See http://www.childwelfare.gov/pubs/factsheets/about.cfm for a brief legislative history of CAPTA and succeeding amendments.

3. This example is based on a real case. Identifying information is omitted to protect confidentiality.

4. See, for example, Skiba et al. (2000); Sheppard and Benjamin-Coleman (2001); and Pope, Lovell, and Hsia (2002).

5. In addition to chapter 5, see Bernstein (2005).

6. School safety officers may exercise the same option in school discipline cases. In New York City and many other jurisdictions, school safety officers are now part of the police department.

7. Institutional review boards, or IRBs, review research to ensure that it complies with federal regulations regarding the ethical treatment of human research subjects. Wards of the state, which include children in foster care, and incarcerated populations have special protections in these regulations—see 45 CFR 46 subparts C and D, respectively.

8. See City of New York (1996).

9. All Vera research is reviewed by the Institute's institutional review board to ensure that protocols comply with the ethical treatment of human research participants as codified in federal regulations (45 CFR 46).

10. Brooklyn and Queens are home to more than 2 million people each. Manhattan and the Bronx each house more than 1 million people, while Staten Island has a population of over 400,000.

Chapter 2. Coordinating Law Enforcement and Child Protection in Cases of Severe Child Maltreatment

This chapter is based on original research conducted by Timothy Ross, Francesca Levy, and Robert Hope at the Vera Institute of Justice.

1. See Martin and Besharov (1991).

2. See Finkelhor and Ormrod (2001). This trend is also apparent in Britain: see Moran-Ellis and Fielding (1996).

3. Arrest statistics are from Division of Criminal Justice Services, "Criminal Justice Indicators" last revised September 4, 2002, http://criminaljustice.state.ny.us/crimnet/ojsa/areastat/areast.htm. The number of child abuse and neglect reports between 1990 and 1998 hit 89,940 in 1992 and 76,188 in 1995. See New York Administration for Children's Services (2001), 20.

4. For a classic discussion of the problems of interagency coordination, see Pressman and Wildavsky (1984). For an example related to law enforcement and child welfare, see Moran-Ellis and Fielding (1996).

5. *Instant Response Team Resource Manual* (New York: City of New York, July 2002), p. 64.

6. Detectives are not assigned to every case. Patrol officers may phone in a case to the IRT coordinator or may be assigned in some cases.

7. Child advocacy centers are specialized facilities staffed by doctors and social workers trained in working with victims of child abuse. CACs are designed to offer the child a comfortable and unthreatening environment.

8. This is an actual case, but the names and other identifying information have been changed to maintain confidentiality.

9. Calls made to the IRT hotline on the weekend and between 4 p.m. and 8 a.m. on weekdays are routed to the IRT coordinators at Emergency Children's Services, the ACS office that handles after-hours cases.

10. Without knowing the content of these calls, Vera researchers could not determine how many were part of a series of calls on the same case or how many resulted in an instant response. To adjust for this possibility, they assumed that calls made from the same number within three hours referred to the same case. Eliminating these calls reduces the total number of calls to 260.

11. In 2000, the IRT eligibility criteria were widened to include severe neglect of children age 11–17 and lesser degrees of sexual abuse of children age 11–17.

12. The sources for these statistics are "ACS Update Annual Report 2001" and the author's analysis of program data.

13. Based on 1999 reports from the states to the National Child Abuse and Neglect Data System. For further information, see http://www.acf.dhhs.gov/programs/

cb/publications/cm99/index.htm. Each case may have multiple allegations. For a case to be indicated, at least one allegation has been substantiated.

14. For a discussion of issues related to reporting child maltreatment, see Zelman and Fair (2002).

15. This statistic is based on analysis of State Central Registry data by New York City's child welfare agency, the Administration for Children's Services. See also Kenny (2001). Though the laws and regulations surrounding mandated reporting vary by state, occupations covered typically include medical personnel, social workers, and, in some cases, educators.

16. As part of this project, program staff and researchers worked together to redesign the IRT data collection log. The new log, launched in January 2003, records more precise information on response time and other variables.

17. Because type I cases are less than 3 percent of all IRT cases, comparisons on this variable are inappropriate.

18. Astute readers will notice that there are no results on prosecution and conviction. Data on prosecutions and sentencing proved hard to collect. The decision to prosecute may not occur until days or weeks after the initial investigation, and collecting this information is labor intensive. Sentencing occurs later still.

19. For a discussion of CompStat, see Henry and Bratton (2002). In 2006, ACS initiated "ChildStat," a new program based on CompStat used to review child protective cases.

Chapter 3. Does the Criminal Justice System Force Children into Foster Care?

This chapter is based on original research conducted by Miriam Ehrensaft, Ajay Khashu, Timothy Ross, and Mark Wamsley at the Vera Institute of Justice.

1. George L. Kelling and James Q. Wilson, "Broken Windows: The Police and Neighborhood Safety," *Atlantic Monthly,* March 1982.

2. As explained below, the researchers restricted their analysis to mothers because of the lack of information on fathers in the available child welfare data. They acknowledge this restriction as a weakness, albeit an unavoidable one, and hope that future studies are able to incorporate more information on fathers.

3. Tanya Krupat, "Still a Mother to Her Children: A Preliminary Look at Maternal Arrest in New York City," unpublished paper funded by Mathematica Policy Research, Inc., 1999.

4. PL 105-98 (codified at 42 USC §§ 670–679a).

5. The study group consists of children who entered care during the year, whether they were entering for a first time or reentering.

6. The researchers did not exclude from their sample mothers for whom they were unable to obtain Social Security numbers. They produced Social Security information, where they had it, to DCJS. The Social Security number assisted in the matching process, but matches were also obtained for mothers where the researchers could not provide it, using various combinations of name and date of birth.

7. The researchers analyzed data on the children only for the time between their entry in 1991 or 1996 and the date of discharge. They did not analyze whether any children reentered care after the discharge.

8. See appendix A.1. in chapter 1 for a more detailed description of the datasets referred to in this section.

9. Jails hold people who are arrested and awaiting trial as well as those who have received relative short sentences—typically under a year. Prison is usually reserved for sentences lasting more than a year.

10. The researchers omit two common variables in this type of study, race and ethnicity, because of limits in the data. The administrative data do not distinguish between race and ethnicity and are likely imputed by staff rather than self-identified. The variables also include an "other/unknown" category.

11. Detention without conviction data for the 1991 cohort were not available, so the jail time for this cohort may be underrepresented for this group.

12. In this analysis, the unit of analysis shifts from mothers to children. This is because the arrest and foster care placement sequence may differ for children of the same mother. Accordingly, the timing of these two events was calculated for each child, rather than each mother.

13. Figures 3.12 and 3.13 track arrest events over different periods. The analysis of the 1991 cohort (figure 3.12) used 10 years of retrospective data. The analysis of the 1996 cohort (figure 3.13) used three years of retrospective data.

14. Readers should pay more attention to percentages than raw numbers. The number of children entering foster care can change dramatically. The foster care census in New York City, for example, declined by more than 50 percent from 1996 to 2005 and has started to rise as of this writing. The percentages on maternal incarceration overlapping with child placement imply that 1,376 children in the 1991 cohort and 1,532 children in 1996 had biological mothers who were incarcerated for any period at some point during their foster care stay. The next chapter addresses some of the issues related to the length of these overlaps.

15. See McClanahan et al. (1999); Miller et al. (2006); and Potterat et al. (1998).

16. See National Committee to Prevent Child Abuse (1998); Newmark (1995); and Smith et al. (2007).

Chapter 4. Hard Data on Hard Times: An Empirical Analysis of Maternal Incarceration, Foster Care, and Visitation

This chapter is based on original research conducted by Timothy Ross, Ajay Khashu, and Mark Wamsley at the Vera Institute of Justice.

1. See, for example, San Francisco Children of Incarcerated Parents Partnership (2005); Margolies and Kraft-Stolar (2006); Mumola (2000); and Susan George and Robert J. LaLonde, "Research on Incarcerated Women and Their Children," The University of Chicago, February 2006 (http://www.igpa.uiuc.edu/publicengagement/fis/ppt/SusanGeorge_Incarc-Women.ppt, accessed August 11, 2008).

2. Social Service Law 384-b(7). See also "Implementation of the Adoption and Safe Families Act, Part III: ACS Best Practice Guidelines for Family Visiting Arrangements for Children in Foster Care," a memorandum from ACS Commissioner Nicholas Scoppetta to the executive directors of foster care agencies dated December 19, 2000.

3. See, for example, Hess (2003); Leathers and Addams (2002); and White, Albers, and Bitonti (1996).

4. See Bernstein (2005).

5. Agencies that provided the data Vera researchers used in this study did so with the understanding that no individual information would be released. No individually identifiable data are included in this chapter, nor has any such information been released to child welfare officials or any other agency.

6. The entry cohort numbers can be found at http://www.nyc.gov/html/acs/html/statistics/statistics_links.shtml (last accessed July 9, 2007).

7. Being approved to be freed for adoption means the contract agency providing case planning services has the child welfare agency's permission to petition the court to terminate parental rights. It does not mean the agency has exercised that option.

8. In some instances, a mother had more than one overlap lasting for more than 30 days. This statistic describes only the longest overlap.

9. Felonies are more serious crimes than misdemeanors. Felonies are ranked in seriousness from A to E, with A felonies including the most serious offenses and E felonies the least serious crimes. The felonies referred to here were in the D and E class.

Chapter 5. A Cohort Analysis of Early Adolescents in Foster Care

This chapter is based on original research conducted by Timothy Ross, Mark Wamsley, and Ajay Khashu at the Vera Institute of Justice.

1. See, for example, New York State Social Service Law §384-a.

2. See Molly Armstrong and Dylan Conger, "Adolescent Pathways," unpublished document, Vera Institute of Justice, 1997.

3. Use of the term in this chapter refers to the legal mechanism for entry into care. Many researchers and advocates assert that voluntary placement agreements are often obtained through coercion (see, for example, Pelton 1989, 1997).

4. For a more detailed discussion of status offenders, see chapter 8 of this volume.

5. New York State raised the age for PINS eligibility to include all children under the age of 18 as of November 1, 2001.

6. Child Care Review System [SAS]. Fred Wulczyn. May 1999 ed. Chicago: Chapin Hall Center for Children; 1999 CD-ROM.

7. These youth were in the child welfare data because the child welfare agency paid for the juvenile delinquency placements.

8. Child welfare data on race and ethnicity do not conform to the more nuanced understanding of these concepts that has developed over the past few decades. The

researchers are limited to reporting the data that is recorded in the data examined—and acknowledge that these data are usually recorded by a caseworker as opposed to self-identified as is the usual practice today. Thus, the data should be interpreted cautiously.

9. By definition, half of all children stay for a period shorter than the median, and half longer. Because well over half the children in each group have been discharged, increasing the length of stay for the remaining children has no effect on the median.

10. The federal standard for acceptable placement stability is a maximum of two placements.

11. The 19 percent figure for never discharged is likely an overestimate. The figure includes some children with no record of a discharge but whose last recorded event is an AWOL; presumably, some of these children in fact should have been discharged to AWOL. Under this assumption, the never discharged percentage is 13 percent.

12. Administrative discharge is a procedure rather than a discharge destination. The researchers combined AWOLs and administrative discharges because a high percentage of children with administrative discharges had an AWOL as their last recorded event, with no record of a return to placement.

13. These costs estimates were provided by New York City's child welfare agency. The single figures for each type of placement smooth over variation in the costs of specific placements and do not adjust for inflation over the period. Still, as a heuristic, the numbers estimate comparative costs for different populations well.

14. See, for example, Bruns and Burchard (2000).

15. For this analysis, the researchers eliminated youth whose last activity was either an AWOL or a trial discharge. Although the data extract did not contain a record of discharge in these cases, the children may well have left care permanently and would not meet the definition of longtermer. See also footnote 8.

Chapter 6. Youth Who Chronically Leave Foster Care without Permission: Why They Run, Where They Go, and What Can Be Done

This chapter is based on original research conducted at the Vera Institute of Justice by Marni Finkelstein, Mark Wamsley, Dan Currie, and Doreen Miranda.

1. The names of the people quoted in this chapter have been changed to ensure their anonymity.

2. Some readers may object to the term "AWOL," as it is more generally thought of as applying to soldiers in the military, not foster children. While the author acknowledges the drawbacks of using the term, it has the advantage of being commonly understood in the field.

3. *Doe v. New York City Department of Social Services, 649 F. 2nd 134, 141 (2nd Cir, 1981); In the Matter of Darren H., A Person in Need of Supervision, 684 N.Y.S. 2d 126 (1998); Bartels v. County of Westchester, 76 A.D.2d 517 (New York, 1980).*

4. The length of time a congregate care facility holds a bed for an AWOL youth varies by jurisdiction and where care is contracted out, by the agency responsible for the

youth. In New York, the child welfare agency pays for the bed of an AWOL youth for three days.

5. See Conger and Ross (2001) and Ross and Conger (2002).

6. Also see Ross and colleagues (2001).

7. Administrative databases do not capture all AWOL events. However, this methodology let researchers identify a sample of youth who had *at least* two AWOL events.

8. The AWOL history of one child—whose name was selected with the help of an ACS employee—is not reported in the CCRS because she was placed after the database was last updated.

9. See Wade and Biehal (1998).

10. "Relationship between Staff Turnover, Child Welfare System Functions and Recurrent Child Abuse," National Center for Crime and Delinquency, Cornerstone for Kids, 2006 (http://www.cornerstones4kids.org/images/nccd_relationships_306.pdf).

11. For example, a study of foster youth in Baltimore found rates of sexual activity much higher than that of other young people, with 69 percent of the teenagers saying that they had sex before the age of 15 (Ensign and Santelli 1997). Another study conducted with a nationally representative sample of young women in foster care found that youth in foster care became pregnant at a younger age and had more sexual partners than their nonfoster peers (Carpenter et al. 2001).

12. Organizations working in this field include GEMS (http://www.gems-girls.org), ECPAT USA, Sisters Offering Support Hawaii, and The Sage Project (http://www.sageprojectinc.org).

13. See New York City Administration for Children's Services Press Release # 0203, February 3, 2005.

14. See New York City Administration for Children's Services (1992).

Chapter 7. Betwixt and Between:
Status Offenders and Foster Care

This chapter draws on original research conducted at the Vera Institute of Justice, including Chiu and Mogulescu (2004); Shubik and Khashu (2005); Souweine and Khashu (2001); Weingartner and Weitz (2002); and Weingartner and colleagues (2002).

1. The federal Office of Juvenile Justice and Delinquency Prevention publication *Juvenile Court Statistics 1996* estimates that 162,000 youth were involved in petitioned status offender cases—status offender cases that were heard by a judge (Stahl et al. 1999). Most status offense cases, however, are diverted from court—80 percent, according to Steinhart (1996). Using this figure suggests that over half a million youth are involved in status offense cases.

2. N.Y. Family Court Act Section 712.

3. See *Matter of Patricia A.*, 31 N.Y.2d 83 (1972).

4. N.Y. Family Court Act Section 735.

5. In 1986, 3,351 cases were filed; in 1987, just 1,830 were filed—a 45 percent reduction. In the years before diversion, PINS cases made up 3 percent of the total court caseload. After diversion, they declined to less than 1.4 percent (Office of the Deputy Mayor 1992).

6. In 1999, girls made up just over a quarter (27 percent) of all arrested juveniles (Snyder 2000).

7. These figures come from an interview with the director of PINS diversion and court-related services for the Children's Aid Society.

8. See Sheldon, Horvath, and Tracy (1989).

9. These figures were supplied by New York City child welfare authorities.

10. See Roberts (2003).

11. These data are consistent with interviews with parents.

12. N.Y. Family Court Act Section 718 provides police officers with the authority to either return a runaway to his or her parents or take a runaway to "a facility certified for such purpose." Neither a PINS petition nor a warrant is needed for the police to take this action, though a police officer must have probable cause to believe the youth is a runaway.

13. This figure only counts AWOL events recorded in the primary child welfare database. Many believe that these data underestimate actual instances of running away from care. For more information on AWOLs, see chapter 6.

14. See Ross et al. (2001).

Chapter 8. Bridging Child Welfare and Juvenile Justice: Preventing the Unnecessary Detention of Foster Children

The authors gratefully acknowledge the funding support provided by the New York State Office of Children and Family Services (grant number JB98521040) and the cooperation of the many New York City agencies that participated in this research. The opinions, results, findings, and interpretations of the data contained herein do not necessarily represent the opinions, interpretations, or policy of the Office or the State of New York, or of any New York City government agency.

1. *Schall v. Martin,* 1984.

2. For less serious delinquent acts, the police may exercise their discretion and release the juvenile to the custody of a guardian with a ticket requiring appearance in court.

3. *Martarella v. Kelley,* 1972. More recently, federal authorities have sued the justice departments of Louisiana, Georgia, Kentucky, and Puerto Rico for failure to protect juveniles from abuse by staff and other juveniles.

4. Lisa Rein and Kevin Flynn, "Spofford Shutting Down," *New York Daily News,* December 13, 1997 (http://www.nydailynews.com/archives/news/1997/12/13/1997-12-13_spofford_shutting_down____tw.html). See also Glenn Thrus, "Spofford Shutdown a Hard Cell," *City Limits,* December 1997.

5. The study also finds, however, that among those whose cases resulted in formal dispositions, there was no evidence that pretrial detention affected the severity of the dispositions (Frazier and Bishop 1985).

6. Vera planners conducted informal interviews with 9 Family Court judges, more than 75 foster children, approximately 60 child welfare staff, 15 staff at juvenile probation, and 20 staff from juvenile justice (the agency that operates detention facilities), among others. Those interviewed were selected based on their position, knowledge, and willingness to participate; they included commissioners, middle managers, and frontline workers.

7. In addition to the issues that led to placement in the first place, a biological parent may fear that responding to such a call may jeopardize her child welfare case if she takes custody of her child without authorization from child welfare authorities.

8. For descriptions of the dysfunction of the Family Court in New York City, see Andrew White (ed.), *Child Welfare Watch,* volumes 12 (2006) and 4 (1999). For a more general discussion of Family Court problems, see Amy Neustein and Michael Lesher, *From Madness to Mutiny* (Hanover, NH: University Press of New England, 2005).

9. This number is higher than the one mentioned previously (1,804) because it includes all calls made by juvenile justice staff, probation officers, police, prosecution attorneys, or child welfare workers. More than 4,000 youth entered detention, but only 1,850 entered as overnight admissions—the program's target population during the first year.

10. In New York, status offenders are defined as children who are truant, runaway, disobedient, or considered beyond the lawful control of a parent. See chapter 7 for a discussion of status offenders.

11. Voluntary admissions occur when child welfare accepts a child into care at the request of the biological parent or legal guardian.

12. Over 90 percent of both groups were black or Latino, and the average age for both groups was 14.

13. As mentioned earlier, chapter 9 of this volume examines how well Project Confirm met its goal of preventing the unnecessary detention of foster children.

14. Project Confirm could not always determine the presence or absence of a child welfare representative in cases before court conferencing was instituted. Their presence was unknown in 25 cases.

Chapter 9. An Outcome Evaluation of Project Confirm

1. See 45 CFR 46 Subpart D.

2. See Eric Kodish, ed., *Ethics and Research with Children: A Case-Based Approach* (New York: Oxford University Press, 2005); and Allen Hornblum, *Acres of Skin: Human Experiments inside Holmesburg Prison* (New York: Routledge Press, 1999).

3. Police admits constituted over 40 percent of all admissions to detention (excluding teens on warrants from juvenile prisons and juvenile offender cases, neither of whom are releasable from court).

4. Project Confirm's coverage rates following its July 18, 1998, launch were exceptionally high (95 percent for the year). However, standard implementation obstacles in the first few months of the program limited the program's reach both in the number of eligible juveniles who received services and the amount and quality of services they received. To fairly assess the impact of the program model, the chapter authors counted the first two months of operations as "pre-program" cases. The authors estimated alternative sensitivity analysis omitting these two months of data and found that the results were qualitatively similar (see appendix A.10).

5. This excludes the following three groups of juvenile detainees that the program did not serve: those brought to court the same day as their arrest (court admits), juvenile offenders, and juveniles on warrants from prison.

6. As is true in other administrative databases used in this volume, racial and ethnic data do not conform to modern understandings of racial and ethnic identity. One limit of this work is not having more refined demographic data.

7. Subgroup analyses could not be conducted for whites and by age intervals because too few juveniles were within the categories.

8. Variations in pre-adjudication detention and other justice procedures and outcomes have been found in several studies. For instance, Feld (1999) finds that rural courts in Minnesota are less likely to use secure detention before disposition. These differences can be partially attributed to differences in the demographic makeup of their respective populations, the severity of the charges, and the resources available. Though New York City is one urban jurisdiction, there is some variation across boroughs in these characteristics as well. And though there is little empirical work demonstrating variations in the use of pre-adjudication detention across boroughs within New York City, Project Confirm staff frequently reported differences in individual judges and other justice personnel's orientations toward pretrial detention.

10. Solving Cross-Agency Challenges

1. For a classic discussion of this issue, see Michael Lipsky, *Street-Level Bureaucracy.*

2. Niccolò Machiavelli, *The Prince and The Discourses* (New York: Random House, Inc., 1950), page 21.

References

Abrahams, Caroline, and Roddy Mungall. 1992. *Runaways: Exploding the Myths*. London: National Children's Home.

Ackland, John W. 1981. "Institutional Reactions to Absconding." *British Journal of Social Work* 11(1): 171–87.

Adams, Patricia F., Charlotte A. Schoenborn, Abigail J. Moss, Charles W. Warren, and Laura Kann. 1995. "Health Risk Behaviors among Our Nation's Youth: United States, 1992." Vital and Health Statistics 10(192), Pub. No. 95-1520. Hyattsville, MD: National Center for Health Statistics.

Allison, Graham T. 1971. *Essence of Decision: Explaining the Cuban Missile Crisis*. Boston: Little, Brown.

Anderson, David C. 1998. "When Should Kids Go to Jail?" *The American Prospect* Issue 38: 72–78.

Armstrong, Molly, and Janet Mandelstam. 2003. *Foster Children and Education: How You Can Create a Positive Educational Experience for the Foster Child*. New York: Vera Institute of Justice.

Bailey, William C. 1981. "Preadjudicatory Detention in a Large Metropolitan Juvenile Court." *Law and Human Behavior* 5(1): 19–43.

Beatty, Cynthia. 1997. *Parents in Prison: Children in Crisis*. Washington, DC: Child Welfare League of America Press.

Becker, Marla G., and Richard P. Barth. 2000. "Power through Choices: The Development of Sexuality Education Curriculum for Youth in Out-of-Home Care." *Child Welfare* 79(3): 269–83.

Beckerman, Adele. 1994. "Mothers in Prison: Meeting the Prerequisite Conditions for Permanency Planning." *Social Work* 39(1): 9–14.

Bernard, H. Russell. 1994. *Research Methods in Anthropology: Qualitative and Quantitative Approaches*. Thousand Oaks, CA: SAGE Publications.

Bernstein, Nell. 2005. *All Alone in the World: Children of the Incarcerated.* New York: The New Press.

Biehal, Nina, and Jim Wade. 1999. "Taking a Chance? The Risks Associated with Going Missing from Substitute Care." *Child Abuse Review* 8(6): 366–76.

———. 2000. "Going Missing from Residential and Foster Care: Linking Biographies and Contexts." *British Journal of Social Work* 30:211–25.

Bilchik, Shay. 1995. "Bridging the Child Welfare and Juvenile Justice Systems." Juvenile Justice Bulletin. Washington, DC: U.S. Department of Justice, Office of Justice Programs, Office of Juvenile Justice and Delinquency Prevention.

Bortner, M. A. 1982. *Inside a Juvenile Court: The Tarnished Ideal of Individualized Justice.* New York: NYU Press.

Broering, Jeanette, and Charles Irwin. 1987. "Juvenile Status Offenders' Perceptions of Life Change Events." *Psychiatric Annals* 17(12): 818–21.

Bruns, Eric J., and John D. Burchard. 2000. "Impact of Respite Care Services for Families with Children Experiencing Emotional and Behavioral Problems." *Children's Services* 3(1): 39–61.

Bureau of Justice Statistics. 2003. *Sourcebook of Criminal Justice Statistics.* Washington, DC: U.S. Department of Justice, Bureau of Justice Statistics.

Carpenter, Sara C., Robert B. Clyman, Arthur J. Davidson, and John F. Steiner. 2001. "The Association of Foster Care or Kinship Care with Adolescent Sexual Behavior and First Pregnancy." *Pediatrics* 108(3): 753.

Chiu, Tina, and Sara Mogulescu. 2004. *Changing the Status Quo for Status Offenders: New York State's Efforts to Support Troubled Teens.* New York: Vera Institute of Justice.

City of New York. 1996. *Protecting the Children of New York: A Plan of Action for the Administration for Children's Services.* New York: City of New York.

Cohen, Lawrence E., and James R. Kluegel. 1979. "The Detention Decision: A Study of the Impact of Social Characteristics and Legal Factors in Two Metropolitan Juvenile Courts." *Social Forces* 58(1): 146–61.

Conger, Dylan, and Alison Rebeck. 2001. *How Children's Foster Care Experiences Affect Their Education.* New York: Vera Institute of Justice.

Conger, Dylan, and Timothy Ross. 2001. *Reducing the Foster Care Bias in Juvenile Detention Decisions: The Impact of Project Confirm.* New York: Vera Institute of Justice.

Courtney, Mark, and Yin-Ling Irene Wong. 1996. "Comparing the Timing of Exits from Substitute Care." *Children and Youth Services Review* 18(4/5): 307–34.

Derezotes, Dennette M., John Poertner, and Mark F. Testa, eds. 2004. *Race Matters in Child Welfare: The Overrepresentation of African American Children in the System.* Washington, DC: Child Welfare League of America Press.

Doss, C. Bradley, and Lynda S. Idleman. 1994. "The County Child Abuse Protocol System in Georgia: An Interagency Cooperation Approach to a Complex Issue." *Child Welfare* 73(6): 675–88.

Elikann, Peter. 1999. *Superpredators: The Demonization of Our Children by the Law.* Reading, MA: Perseus Books.

Elliott, Delbert S. 1997. *Blueprints for Violence Prevention.* Vols. 1 and 2. Boulder: Center for the Study and Prevention of Violence, University of Colorado.

Ensign, Jo, and John Santelli. 1997. "Shelter-Based Homeless Youth: Health and Access to Care." *Archives of Pediatrics and Adolescent Medicine* 151(8): 817–23.

Fagan, Jeffrey, and Martin Guggenheim. 1996. "Preventive Detention and the Judicial Prediction of Dangerousness for Juveniles: A Natural Experiment." *Journal of Criminal Law and Criminology* 86(2): 415–48.

Faruqee, Mishi. 2002. *Rethinking Juvenile Detention in New York City.* New York: The Correctional Association of New York.

Feld, Barry C. 1999. "Justice by Geography: Urban, Suburban, and Rural Variations in Juvenile Justice Administration." In *Readings in Juvenile Justice Administration,* edited by Barry C. Feld (52–66). New York: Oxford University Press.

Fine, Michele. 1991. *Framing Dropouts: Notes on the Politics of an Urban High School.* Albany, NY: SUNY Press.

Fine, Paul. 1985. "Clinical Aspects of Foster Care." In *Foster Care: Current Issue, Policies, and Practices,* edited by Martha J. Cox and Roger D. Cox. New York: Ablex Publishing.

Finkelhor, David, and Richard Ormrod. 2001. "Child Abuse Reported to the Police." Juvenile Justice Bulletin. NCJ 187238. Washington, DC: U.S. Department of Justice, Office of Justice Programs, Office of Juvenile Justice and Delinquency Prevention.

Finkelstein, Marni, Mark Wamsley, and Doreen Miranda. 2002. *Educational Obstacles for Children in Foster Care.* New York: Vera Institute of Justice.

Finkelstein, Marni, Mark Wamsley, Dan Currie, and Doreen Miranda. 2004. *Youth Who Chronically AWOL from Foster Care: Why They Run, Where They Go, and What Can Be Done.* New York: Vera Institute of Justice.

Frazier, Charles E., and Donna M. Bishop. 1985. "The Pretrial Detention of Juveniles and Its Impact on Case Dispositions." *Journal of Criminal Law and Criminology* 76(4): 1132–52.

GAO. See U.S. General Accounting Office.

Gendell, Stephanie Jill. 2001. "In Search of Permanency: A Reflection on the First 3 Years of the Adoption and Safe Families Act Implementation." *Family Court Review* 39(1): 25–42.

Genty, Philip M. 1995. "Termination of Parental Rights among Prisoners: A National Perspective." In *Children of Incarcerated Parents,* edited by Katherine Gabel and Denise Johnston. New York: Lexington Books.

Goerge, Robert, Fred Wulczyn, and David Fanshel. 1994. "A Foster Care Research Agenda for the 1990s." *Child Welfare* 73(5): 525–49.

Hagan, John, and Ronit Dinovitzer. 1999. "Collateral Consequences of Imprisonment for Children, Communities, and Prisoners." *Crime & Justice* 26:121–62.

Hagedorn, John M. 1995. *Forsaking Our Children: Bureaucracy and Reform in the Child Welfare System.* Chicago: Lake View Press.

Hairston, Creasie Finney. 1991. "Family Ties during Imprisonment: Important to Whom and for What?" *Journal of Sociology & Social Welfare* 18:87–104.

Hawkins, J. David, and Richard F. Catalano. 1993. *Risk-Focused Prevention Using the Social Development Strategy.* Seattle, WA: Developmental Resources and Programs.

Hemmens, Craig. 1998. "Kids in Trouble." Review of *Juvenile Justice and Youth Violence* by James C. Howell. *Federal Probation* 62(1): 83.

Henry, Vincent E., and William J. Bratton. 2002. *The CompStat Paradigm: Management Accountability in Policing, Business, and the Public Sector.* New York: Looseleaf Law Publications, Incorporated.

Hess, Peg. 2003. "Visiting between Children in Care and Their Families: A Look at Current Policy." New York: National Resource Center for Foster Care and Permanency Planning, Hunter College School of Social Work.

HHS. See U.S. Department of Health and Human Services.

Hochstadt, Neil, Paula Jaudes, Deborah Zimo, and Jayne Schacter. 1987. "The Medical and Psychosocial Needs of Children Entering Foster Care." *Child Abuse and Neglect* 11(1): 53–62.

Hubner, John, and Jill Wolfson. 1999. *Ain't No Place Anybody Would Want to Be: Conditions of Confinement for Youth.* Washington, DC: Coalition for Juvenile Justice.

Huizinga, David, Rolf Loeber, Terence P. Thornberry, and Lynn Cothern. 2000. "Co-occurrence of Delinquency and Other Problem Behaviors." Juvenile Justice Bulletin. Washington, DC: U.S. Department of Justice, Office of Justice Programs, Office of Juvenile Justice and Delinquency Prevention.

Jacobson, Michael. 2005. *Downsizing Prisons.* New York: NYU Press.

Johnston, Denise. 1995. "Child Custody Issues of Incarcerated Mothers." *The Prison Journal* 75(2): 222–39.

Kelly, Malikah J. 2004. *Broken Promises, Broken System: 10 Reasons New York City Should Close the Spofford Youth Jail.* New York: The Correctional Association of New York.

Kenny, M. C. 2001. "Compliance with Mandated Child Abuse Reporting: Comparing Physicians and Teachers." *Journal of Offender Rehabilitation* 34(1): 11.

Klee, Linnea, and Neal Halfon. 1987. "Mental Health Care for Foster Children in California." *Child Abuse and Neglect* 11(1): 63–74.

Lawry, Marcia, and Julia Farber. 2007. *At the Crossroads; Better Infrastructure, Too Few Results: A Decade of Child Welfare Reform in New York City.* New York: Children's Right, Inc.

Leathers, Sonya J., and Jane Addams. 2002. "Parental Visiting and Family Reunification: Could Inclusive Practice Make a Difference?" *Child Welfare* 81(4): 595–616.

Levy, Kenneth. 2001. "The Relationship between Adolescent Attitudes towards Authority, Self-Concept, and Delinquency." *Adolescence* 36(142): 333–47.

Margolies, Julie Kowitz, and Tamar Kraft-Stolar. 2006. *When Free Means Losing Your Mother.* New York: The Correctional Association of New York.

Marshall, Chris E., Ineke Haen Marshall, and Charles W. Thomas. 1983. "The Implementation of Formal Procedures in Juvenile Court Processing of Status Offenders." *Journal of Criminal Justice* 11:195.

Martin, Susan E., and Douglas J. Besharov. 1991. *Police and Child Abuse: New Policies for Expanded Responsibilities.* Washington, DC: U.S. Department of Justice, Office of Justice Programs, National Institute of Justice.

Maxson, Cheryl L., and Malcolm W. Klein. 1997. *Responding to Troubled Youth.* New York: Oxford University Press.

McClanahan, Susan F., Gary M. McClelland, Karen M. Abram, and Linda A. Teplin. 1999. "Pathways into Prostitution among Female Jail Detainees and Their Implications for Mental Health Services." *Psychiatric Services* 50:1606–13.

Mechanic, David. 1983. "Adolescent Health and Illness Behavior: Review of the Literature and a New Hypothesis for the Study of Stress." *Journal of Human Stress* 9:4–13.

Milham, Spencer, Roger Bullock, and Kenneth Hosie. 1978. *Locking Up Children: Secure Provision within the Childcare System.* London: Saxon House.

Miller, Dorothy, Donald Miller, Fred Hoffman, and Robert Duggan. 1980. *Runaways–Illegal Aliens in Their Own Land: Implications for Service.* New York: Praeger Publishers.

Miller, Ted R., David T. Levy, Mark A. Cohen, and Kenya L. C. Cox. 2006. "Costs of Alcohol- and Drug-Involved Crime." *Prevention Science* 7(4): 333–42.

Miller, Theresa A., Colleen Eggertson-Tacon, and Brian Quigg. 1990. "Patterns of Runaway Behavior within a Larger Systems Context: The Road to Empowerment." *Adolescence* 26(98): 271–89.

Moffitt, Terrie E. 1993. "Adolescence-Limited and Life Course Persistent Antisocial Behavior: A Developmental Taxonomy." *Psychological Review* 100:674–701.

Moos, Rudolf H. 2005. "Iatrogenic Effects of Psychosocial Interventions for Substance Use Disorders: Prevalence, Predictors, Prevention." *Addiction* 100(5): 595–604.

Moran-Ellis, Jo, and Nigel Fielding. 1996. "A National Survey of the Investigation of Child Sexual Abuse." *British Journal of Social Work* 6(2): 337–56.

Morgan, Gwen. 1995. "Collaborative Models of Service Integration." *Child Welfare* 74(6): 1329–42.

Mumola, Christopher J. 2000. "Incarcerated Parents and Their Children." NCJ 182335. Washington, DC: U.S. Department of Justice, Bureau of Justice Statistics.

National Committee to Prevent Child Abuse. 1998. *Current Trends in Child Abuse Reporting and Fatalities: NCPCA's 1997 Annual Fifty-State Survey.* Washington, DC: National Committee to Prevent Child Abuse.

Nelson, Douglas W. 1998. "Building Neighborhood Partnerships." Speech to the National Child Welfare Leadership Conference, New York, October 5.

Newman, Cathy. 1989. *Young Runaways.* London: The Children's Society.

Newmark, Lisa C. 1995. "Parental Drug Testing in Child Abuse and Neglect Cases: Major Findings." Paper presented at the 46th Annual Meeting of the American Society of Criminology, November 15.

New York City Administration for Children's Services. 1992. *Children Absent without Leave from Foster Care.* Procedure No. 90. New York: Administration for Children's Services.

———. Office of Management, Development, and Research. 2001. *Progress on ACS Reform Initiatives; Status Report 3.* New York: Administration for Children's Services.

New York State Division of Probation and Correctional Alternatives. n.d. *PINS Adjustment Services Program Quarterly Report, 1/30/01–9/30/01.* Albany: New York Division of Probation and Correctional Alternatives.

Norval, Glenn D. 1977. *Cohort Analysis*. Thousand Oaks, CA: SAGE Publications.

Office of the Deputy Mayor of Public Safety. 1992. *The Voices of PINS Diversion*. New York: Office of the Deputy Mayor of Public Safety.

Orlando, Frank. 1999. *Controlling the Front Gates: Effective Admissions Policies and Practices*. Baltimore, MD: Annie E. Casey Foundation.

Parent, Dale G., and Abt Associates, Inc. 1994. *Conditions of Confinement: Juvenile Detention and Corrections Facilities*. Washington, DC: U.S. Department of Justice, Office of Justice Programs, Office of Juvenile Justice and Delinquency Prevention.

Parker, Roy, Harriet Ward, Sonia Jackson, Jane Aldgate, and Peter Wedge. 1991. *Looking after Children: Assessing Outcomes in Child Care*. London: Her Majesty's Stationery Office.

Pawlak, Edward J. 1977. "Differential Selection of Juveniles for Detention." *Journal of Research in Crime and Delinquency* 14(2): 152–65.

Payne, Malcolm. 1995. "Understanding 'Going Missing': Issues for Social Work and Social Services." *British Journal of Social Work* 25(3): 333–48.

Pelton, Leroy H. 1989. *For Reasons of Poverty: A Critical Analysis of the Public Child Welfare System in the United States*. New York: Praeger Publishers.

———. 1997. "Child Welfare Policy and Practice: The Myth of Family Preservation." *American Journal of Orthopsychiatry* 67:545–53.

Pope, Carl E., Rick Lovell, and Heidi M. Hsia. 2002. "Disproportionate Minority Confinement: A Review of the Research Literature from 1989 through 2001." Juvenile Justice Bulletin. Washington, DC: U.S. Department of Justice, Office of Justice Programs, Office of Juvenile Justice and Delinquency Prevention.

Potterat, John J., Richard B. Rothenberg, Stephen Q. Muth, William W. Darrow, and Lynanne Phillips-Plummer. 1998. "Pathways to Prostitution: The Chronology of Sexual and Drug Abuse Milestones." *The Journal of Sex Research* 35(4): 333–40.

Pressman, Jeffrey L., and Aaron Wildavsky. 1984. *Implementation: How Great Expectations in Washington Are Dashed in Oakland*. 3rd ed. Berkeley: University of California Press.

Puzzanchera, Charles, Anne L. Stahl, Terrence A. Finnegan, Howard N. Snyder, Rowen S. Poole, and Nancy Tierney. 2000. *Juvenile Court Statistics 1998*. NCJ 180864. Washington, DC: U.S. Department of Justice, Office of Justice Programs, Office of Juvenile Justice and Delinquency Prevention.

Reed, David, Harris Meyer, Kim Zalent, and Janice Linn. 1981. *Promises, Promises...Does the Juvenile Court Deliver for Status Offenders? The Record in Cook County, Illinois*. Chicago: Chicago Law Enforcement Group.

Rees, Gwyther. 1993. *Hidden Truths: Young People's Experiences of Running Away*. London: The Children's Society.

Rhule, Dana M. 2005. "Take Care to Do No Harm: Harmful Interventions for Youth Problem Behavior." *Professional Psychology Research and Practice* 36(6): 618–25.

Roberts, Dorothy. 2003. *Shattered Bonds: The Color of Child Welfare*. New York: Basic Books.

Ross, Timothy. 2001. *A System in Transition: An Analysis of New York City's Foster Care System at the Year 2000*. New York: Vera Institute of Justice.

Ross, Timothy, and Dylan Conger, with Molly Armstrong. 2002. "Bridging the Gap between Child Welfare and Juvenile Justice." *Child Welfare* 81(3): 471–94.

Ross, Timothy, Mark Wamsley, and Ajay Khashu. 2001. *The Experiences of Early Adolescents in Foster Care in New York City: Analysis of the 1994 Cohort.* New York: Vera Institute of Justice.

Rossi, Peter H., and Howard E. Freeman. 1993. *Evaluation: A Systematic Approach.* 5th ed. Newbury Park, CA: SAGE Publications.

Runyan, Desmund S., and Carolyn L. Gould. 1985. "Foster Care for Child Maltreatment: Impact on Delinquent Behavior." *Pediatrics* 75(3): 562–68.

Ryan, Kevin M. 1993. "Stemming the Tide of Foster Care Runaways: A Due Process Perspective." *Catholic University Law Review* 42:271–311.

Sabol, William J., Todd D. Minton, and Paige M. Harrison. 2007. "Prison and Jail Inmates at Midyear 2006." NCJ 217675. Washington, DC: U.S. Department of Justice, Bureau of Justice Statistics.

Salahu-Din, Sakinah N., and Stephan R. Bollman. 1994. "Identity Development and Self-Esteem of Young Adolescents in Foster Care." *Child and Adolescent Social Work Journal* 11(2): 123–32.

Sampson, Robert J., and John H. Laub. 1993. *Crime in the Making: Pathways and Turning Points through Life.* Cambridge, MA: Harvard University Press.

San Francisco Children of Incarcerated Parents Partnership (SFCIPP). 2005. *Children of Incarcerated Parents: A Bill of Rights.* San Francisco, CA: SFCIPP.

Schwartz, Ira M., William H. Barton, and Frank Orlando. 1991. "Keeping Kids Out of Secure Detention." *Public Welfare* 49(2): 20–36.

Sheldon, Randall G., John A. Horvath, and Sharon Tracy. 1989. "Do Status Offenders Get Worse? Some Clarifications on the Question of Escalation." *Crime and Delinquency* 35(2): 202–16.

Sheppard, Vanessa B., and Richardean Benjamin-Coleman. 2001. "Determinants of Service Placements for Youth with Serious Emotional and Behavioral Disturbances." *Community Mental Health Journal* 37(1): 53–65.

Shubik, Claire, and Ajay Khashu. 2005. *A Study of New York City's Family Assessment Program.* New York: Vera Institute of Justice.

Silverman, Eli. 1999. *The NYPD Battles Crime.* Boston, MA: Northeastern Press.

Skiba, Russell, Robert S. Michael, Abra C. Nardo, and Reece L. Peterson. 2000. *The Color of Discipline: Sources of Racial and Gender Disproportionality in School Punishment.* Bloomington: Indiana Education Policy Center.

Smetana, Judith G. 1988. "Adolescents' and Parents' Conceptions of Parental Authority." *Journal of Child Development* 59:821–35.

Smith, Barbara E. 1995a. *Prosecuting Child Physical Abuse Cases: A Case Study in San Diego.* NCJ 152978. Washington, DC: U.S. Department of Justice, Office of Justice Programs, National Institute of Justice.

———. 1995b. "Prosecuting Child Abuse Cases: Lessons Learned from the San Diego Experience." NCJ 184386. Washington, DC: U.S. Department of Justice, Office of Justice Programs, National Institute of Justice.

Smith, Barbara E., Sharon G. Elstein, and the ABA Center on Children and the Law. 1994. *Children on Hold: Improving the Response to Children Whose Parents Are Arrested and Incarcerated.* Washington, DC: ABA Center on Children and the Law.

Smith, Dana K., Amber B. Johnson, Katherine C. Pears, Philip A. Fisher, and David S. DeGarmo. 2007. "Child Maltreatment and Foster Care: Unpacking the Effects of Prenatal and Postnatal Parental Substance Use." *Child Maltreatment* 12(2): 150–60.

Snell, Tracy L. 1994. "Women in Prison: Survey of State Prison Inmates, 2001." NCJ 145321. Washington, DC: U.S. Department of Justice, Bureau of Justice Statistics.

Snyder, Howard N. 2000. "Juvenile Arrests 1999." NCJ 185236. Washington, DC: U.S. Department of Justice, Office of Justice Programs, Office of Juvenile Justice and Delinquency Prevention.

Souweine, Jesse, and Ajay Khashu. 2001. *Changing the PINS System in New York: A Study of the Implications of Raising the Age Limit for Persons in Need of Supervision (PINS).* New York: Vera Institute of Justice.

Special Child Welfare Advisory Panel. 2000. *Advisory Report on Frontline Practice.* New York City: Administration for Children's Services.

Stahl, Anne L., Charles Puzzanchera, Anthony Sladky, Terrence A. Finnegan, Nancy Tierney, and Howard N. Snyder. 2005. *Juvenile Court Statistics 2001–2002.* NCJ 216251. Washington, DC: U.S. Department of Justice, Office of Justice Programs, Office of Juvenile Justice and Delinquency Prevention.

Stahl, Anne L., Melissa Sickmund, Terrence A. Finnegan, Howard N. Snyder, Rowen S. Poole, and Nancy Tierney. 1999. *Juvenile Court Statistics 1996.* NCJ 168963. Washington, DC: U.S. Department of Justice, Office of Justice Programs, Office of Juvenile Justice and Delinquency Prevention.

Stein, Mike, Gwyther Rees, and Nick Frost. 1994. *Running–the Risk: Young People on the Streets of Britain Today.* London: The Children's Society.

Steinberg, Laurence, and Amanda Sheffield Morris. 2001. "Adolescent Development." *Annual Review of Psychology* 52(1): 83–110.

Steinhart, David J. 1996. "Status Offenses." *The Future of Children* 6(3): 86–99.

Sumner, Helen. 1970. *Locking Them Up: A Study of Initial Juvenile Detention Decisions in Selected California Counties.* Oakland, CA: National Council on Crime and Delinquency Western Region.

Tjaden, P. G., and J. Anhalt. 1994. *The Impact of Joint Law Enforcement–Child Protective Services Investigations in Child Abuse Cases.* Denver, CO: Center for Policy Research.

Tolor, Alexander. 1989. "Boredom as Related to Alienation, Assertiveness, Internal-External Expectancy, and Sleep Patterns." *Journal of Clinical Psychology* 45(2): 260–66.

U.S. Department of Health and Human Services. 2000. *Child Welfare Outcomes Report.* Washington, DC: U.S. Department of Health and Human Services.

U.S. General Accounting Office. 1995. *Child Welfare: Complex Needs Strain Capacity to Provide Services.* GAO/HEHS-95-208. Washington, DC: U.S. General Accounting Office.

Vreeland, A. B. 2000. "The Criminalization of Child Welfare in New York City: Sparing the Child or Spoiling the Family?" *Fordham Urban Law Journal* 27(3): 1053–1103.

Wade, Jim, and Nina Biehal, with Jasmine Clayden and Mike Stein. 1998. *Going Missing: Young People Absent from Care.* West Sussex: John Wiley & Sons.

Ward, Harriet. 1995. *Looking after Children: Research into Practice.* London: Her Majesty's Stationery Office.

Wasserman, Gail A., and Laurie S. Miller. 1998. "The Prevention of Serious and Violent Juvenile Offending." In *Serious and Violent Juvenile Offenders: Risk Factors and Successful Interventions,* edited by Rolf Loeber and David P. Farrington (197–247). Thousand Oaks, CA: SAGE Publications.

Wasserman, Gail A., Laurie S. Miller, E. Pinner, and B. S. Jaramillo. 1996. "Parenting Predictors of the Development of Conduct Problems in High-Risk Boys." *Journal of the American Academy of Child and Adolescent Psychiatry* 35:1227–36.

Weingartner, Eric, and Andrea Weitz. 2002. *Respite Care: An Alternative to Foster Care for Status Offenders in New York City.* New York: Vera Institute of Justice.

Weingartner, Eric, Andrea Weitz, Ajay Khashu, Robert Hope, and Megan Golden. 2002. *A Study of the PINS System in New York City: Results and Implications.* New York: Vera Institute of Justice.

White, Mary Ellen, Erick Albers, and Christine Bitonti. 1996. "Factors in Length of Foster Care: Worker Activities and Parent-Child Visitation." *Journal of Sociology and Social Welfare* 23(2): 75–84.

Widom, Catherine S. 1994. "The Role of Placement Experiences in Mediating the Criminal Consequences of Early Childhood Victimization." In *Child Welfare Research Review, Volume 1,* edited by Jill D. Berrick, Richard P. Barth, and Neil Gilbert. New York: Columbia University Press.

Wolff, Nancy. 1998. "Interactions between Mental Health and Law Enforcement Systems: Problems and Prospects for Cooperation." *Journal of Health Politics, Policy and Law* 23(1): 133–74.

Wordes, Madeline, and Sharon M. Jones. 1998. "Trends in Juvenile Detention and Steps toward Reform." *Crime and Delinquency* 44(4): 544–61.

Wulczyn, Fred, Kristen Brunner, and Robert Goerge. 1999. *Foster Care Dynamics 1983–97.* Chicago: Chapin Hall Center for Children.

Zelman, Gail L., and C. Christine Fair. 2002. "Preventing and Reporting Abuse." In *The APSAC Handbook on Child Maltreatment,* 2nd ed., edited by John E. B. Myers, Lucy Berliner, John Briere, C. Terry Hendrix, Carole Jenny, and Theresa A. Reid (449–78). Thousand Oaks, CA: SAGE Publications.

About the Authors

Timothy Ross directs the Child Welfare, Health, and Justice Program at the Vera Institute of Justice. Since coming to Vera in 1999, Tim has led Vera's child welfare research projects. From 2002 to 2006, he was Vera's director of research. He has also served on the New York City Administration for Children's Services Commissioner's Advisory Board. The author of numerous reports and articles, Dr. Ross's current research examines issues related to the participation of foster children in clinical trials, youth aging out of foster care, and the training of child protection managers. He has undergraduate degrees from Williams College and the University of Kent at Canterbury and a master's degree and Ph.D. from the University of Maryland.

Dylan Conger is an assistant professor at the Trachtenberg School of Public Policy and Public Administration at the George Washington University. She also worked at the Vera Institute of Justice and at New York University's Urban Education Project. Her research and teaching interests focus on social and education policy, with an emphasis on race/ethnicity, poverty, and nativity. She has an undergraduate degree from the University of California at Berkeley, a master's degree from the University of Michigan, and a Ph.D. from New York University.

Index